In the Mother's House

MERCER UNIVERSITY

MERCER UNIVERSITY PRESS

Endowed by

TOM WATSON BROWN

and

THE WATSON-BROWN FOUNDATION, INC.

In the Mother's House

The Hebrew Bible's Lost Teachings on

Love, Wisdom, and Sacred Marriage

ABI DOUKHAN

MERCER UNIVERSITY PRESS
Macon, Georgia

MUP/ P731

Published by Mercer University Press
1501 Mercer University Drive
Macon, Georgia 31207

29 28 27 26 25   5 4 3 2 1

Books published by Mercer University Press are printed on acid-free paper that meets the requirements of the American National Standard for Information Sciences—Permanence of Paper for Printed Library Materials.

Printed and bound in the United States.

This book is set in Adobe Garamond.

Cover/jacket design by Burt&Burt.

ISBN 979-8-89736-001-7 (Print)
979-8-89736-002-4 (eBook)

Cataloging-in-Publication Data is available from the Library of Congress

To my daughters, born and unborn

Contents

Acknowledgments

I first want to recognize my mother and my father and their extraordinary sacred marriage journey. I want to honor their love, their tenacity, and their humility in making it together for more than fifty years. I want to thank my Queens College "Plato and the Bible" students for exploring and excavating these sacred texts with me, unearthing many a hidden treasure of wisdom and of love in the course of our discussions. A big heartfelt thank you to the sisterhood of the "Moonlights" Rosh Hodesh circle at the Hillcrest Jewish Center in Queens who helped me crystallize my flailing material into the present book. Finally, I want to honor two precious twenty-first century "wise women," Laura Doyle and Mama Gena, whose revolutionary teachings I stumbled upon in my darkest night, and which became the bedrock of this work.

Introduction

In the Mother's House

Twilight. The sun has set on the sixth day of Creation and the first three stars have appeared in the sky. The first man and woman have just received their royal calling to reign over the world and are now being ushered together into a garden of rivers and trees, an oasis of rest, a sabbath of delights. To rest from what, one may ask? What have they of yet accomplished, these two newly fashioned balls of clay? Upon creating Adam and Eve and bestowing upon them both to "cultivate" and "protect" the world (Gen. 2:15),[1] God, interestingly, does not immediately send them on their destiny. Rather, he first invites them into a sabbath rest. I have always wondered why God chose to first open up this interlude of Sabbath, this liminal space where their enthusiastic and restless impulse to master and possess the world[2] sees itself interrupted, this rift, this space between the couple and their destiny. Perhaps God meant to teach them that, before the world can be protected and cultivated, the human couple first needed to craft a space of restfulness; that the condition of possibility for the viability of the world lies in the human couple first entering a rest together, in the human couple finding rest in each other, cultivating rest between each other. As though restfulness between the man and the woman was needed before anything could be done to protect and safeguard the world, as though cosmic harmony depended on the harmony between male and female.[3]

Five thousand years later, according to the biblical timeline, our aging world seems to have somehow lost this sense of rest, this original cosmic harmony. It is a world where the sabbath oasis of rest has gone dry, and where the forces of chaos are slowly seeping in. The man and the woman are at war and, consequently, everyone and everything is at war. Much passion has been poured into the crafting of peace, with little sustainable progress. But what if, as the biblical text seems to hint at, our lost cosmic harmony originated in one single separation, the deepest and most ancient conflict of all, from which all other conflicts have emerged: the conflict between man and woman. And what if the reconciliation of the man and the woman was the key to recovering our lost harmony, and of ushering in a reign of peace? What if the mending of the world had everything to do with the lost and forgotten connection between man and woman, the two facets of the divine essence, once commanded to rule the world *together*?[4]

The ancient cooperation between the two royal genders has been all too forgotten and abandoned. As a civilization we have somehow lost the knowledge, the art of cultivating this relationship. We have become extremely sophisticated in all other domains, yet the relationship between the man and the woman remains primitive, uncultivated, uncouth, instinctual, random, and brutal. The enduring reign of patriarchy has done little to refine the relationship between genders, rather seeking to merge the woman's agency into the man's leadership, giving them "one head," man. But where there is only "one head," there can be no genuine partnership, and the original command of Genesis 1 remains unheeded. The backlash by the feminist voices of the pre-modern and modern eras has not done much better. Neither does the "liberation" of the woman from the man, her "exodus" from the man, and her coming into her own, often in opposition to the man, promote partnership. Feminism has given women a voice, but has not taught her how to modulate it in a way that can be heard by the man, in a way that promotes reconciliation, peace, and rest with their male partners.

And so, the war continues, with the man and woman progressively carving out spaces in the world where the other is excluded, spaces of self-sufficiency, of indifference, fortresses of solitude, of unacknowledged rage, pain, and helplessness. And where partnership still dredges on, we witness—in spite of the advances of feminism—the silencing of women's voices, of their agency, the violence against women's bodies and spirits. And as women and men drift further apart, the world becomes progressively undone, torn apart by unspeakable violence, toxic political spaces, and apocalyptic end-time scenarios. Has not the time come to re-learn the ancient peace, to unearth the forgotten pillars of cosmic harmony, that of the lost partnership between man and woman?

In this re-learning or remembering of relationship, women have a special gift, or *charis,* a special calling. The creation of woman hints at this. Whereas the man is created from the earth and remains burdened and obsessed by it, woman is created from man and as such, her ontology is explicitly relational. She carries in her very flesh an intentionality and an impulse to transcend herself towards another, to live for the other. She is the helpmate, the *ezer kenegdo.* A helper for and against *him*. As such, in addition to ruling alongside of the man, woman has also been given a unique and particular vocation or calling—that of relationship weaver.[5] Her protective and cultivating task lies therefore not only in protecting and cultivating the earth, but in protecting and cultivating her relationships. There is thus a whole labor of love[6] which the woman has also been called to. A labor of love which is much more than a side gig. For upon it rests the entirety of the cosmos. Inasmuch as cosmic harmony depends on the harmony between the man and the woman, it is *precisely* in protecting her marriage that the woman is protecting the world. For as long as the partnership between man and woman is not strong and not balanced, the world risks sliding back into chaos. But for this, woman needs to be recognized by the man as his *ezer,* as the one with whom he must partner.

Sadly, this recognition has been long in coming. History has shown, far to the contrary, the systematic marginalization, incapacitation, and erasure of women by the men in their lives. Called inferior and made to submit to the man in the context of patriarchy, the woman as a relational partner finds herself erased. In patriarchy, the man is the only one called to lead, and alone he must do so. The woman is there to execute his orders, certainly not to contribute to the discussion. Things are no better on the other side of patriarchy where feminism, although giving back to the woman her voice, has not taught her to modulate it for the purposes of reconciliation and peace. Women have a voice, but it is still too strident, too aggressive, too angry to have any effect on the men of their lives. If anything, it has widened the chasm between men and women, rendered men often confused, helpless, harboring deep-seated anger and resentment.

Must we however submit to these two fatalities? Where patriarchy has muted women, and feminism made them too loud, women can strive to remember the forgotten and ancient song of peace, and compose from it a "new song," one still unsung, a song of reconciliation, and a song of love. Has not the time come for women to reclaim the lost art of relationship, the ability to courageously take up the task of redeeming their partnerships, the secret art of elevating their men to their highest destiny, and in turn receiving from them new life and new fecundities? Have we completely forgotten how to activate our men's inherent goodness, their courage and their nobility? And have we forgotten the dormant gifts within them that we so deeply desire from them and have the power to awaken? The redemption of the planet rests on the courage of women to learn to weave anew. Women need this, men need this, our world needs this. Women need to reclaim their unique destiny, their power, their lost calling: that of being relationship weavers. The destiny of the world rests on this women's work and labor.

But where are women to find direction and mentorship in this ancient art? Who will teach us? Where are the wise women of old capable of mentoring us younger women in the difficult and courageous weave-form of womanhood? I have found these wise women in a most peculiar place, at the heart of the very bastion of patriarchy, the Bible. And yes, the Bible is a patriarchal book. Written for men and by men, women are often sidelined. Many of them are unnamed, remain invisible, and few play major political roles like prophet, king, or priest. Their voices are often muted, and the violence against them goes unquestioned.[7] Their bodies are deemed the ward of men, and their sexuality remains contained first in the father's house, then the husband's.

Yet, at the heart of this patriarchal book, matriarchy endures, birthing powerfully subversive feminine characters and voices: from the wise and cunning woman Eve, to the beautiful daughters of Job; from the striking woman Ruth, to the powerful Queen Esther; and finally, at the very heart of the Bible, the Solomonic writings on Woman Wisdom in the book of Proverbs, Ecclesiastes, and Song of Songs.[8] These voices, often ignored by a predominantly male readership, are only beginning to rise. And with them, a radically different teaching arises also, one that often is at odds with patriarchy, countercultural, subversive, yet striking a deep chord in the human psyche, giving us a radically different vision of God, of femininity, of masculinity, and a powerful vision of the profound significance of the partnership between man and woman.

These feminine voices, although often subversive and countercultural, are not spoken, however, with the intent of overpowering or overshadowing masculine voices and teachings. Rather, they mean to be heard in counterpoint with them. Both voices are meant to be heard *together* in the Hebrew Bible. Neither voice is meant to replace or erase the other. They are held together in a canon which, although shaped by male interpreters, has faithfully held a space for the uniqueness and otherness of women's voices and experiences. Two seemingly opposite and conflictual teachings which, however, both lead to God: The teachings of the father's house and the teachings of the mother's house.[9] Both are needed and should be heard together. It is in their delicate equilibrium that God might be found as the book of Proverbs intimates: "Listen, my son to your father's instruction and do not forsake your mother's teaching" (Prov. 1:8–9).[10]

These two houses constitute in fact two schools of thought: One which is religious, law-based, and vertical, privileging temple ritual; the other more secular, wisdom-based and horizontal, privileging ethics. As such, they will inevitably appeal to widely different and contrasting audiences—and this is precisely the point. To those who prefer a strong frame of reference, with clear rules, rigorous discipline, and charismatic authority figures, the father's house will provide exactly this. But to those who just cannot seem to "walk the line," who continuously find themselves veering off the path, the black sheep of the family, who just can't seem to be able to submit to authority, the mother's house offers a welcoming haven. The Biblical canon seems to have been constituted with these two contrasting audiences in mind and caters to both.

The question remains, however, of where, in the Hebrew Bible, the mother's house has made its secret abode. Secret, because the mother's house, although a part of the Biblical canon, does remain in many ways an underground, subcultural teaching, concentrated in what the rabbis have called the *ketuvim*. The *ketuvim* (literally the "writings") constitute the wisdom literature of the Hebrew Bible. They complete the other two sections of the Hebrew Bible—the *torah* (the five books of Moses) and the *nevi'im* (the prophets). Unlike the other two sections, the focus of the *ketuvim* is neither narrative, law, nor even prophetic admonishment, but the philosophical and existential reflection on life, love, suffering, death, and pleasure. As such, the *ketuvim* constitute the philosophical books of the Hebrew Bible, featuring a number of connections with Ancient Near Eastern and Egyptian wisdom literature, both thematically and stylistically, and therefore clearly targeting a wider audience beyond the walls of Jerusalem: the nations (or *goyim)* and, by extension, anyone who does not hold allegiances to a religious community, anyone having fallen out of grace with their church, synagogue, temple, or mosque. As such, these books are more secular, more existential, with a focus on ethics rather than on worship.

These books, moreover, have the added quality to all have a strong feminine flavor: They include the book of Job, the book of Ruth, the book of Proverbs, the book of Ecclesiastes, the Song of Songs, and the book of Esther. The book of Job with its pivotal female characters, the wife and the daughters of Job; the book of Ruth with its central protagonist played by the strong and gritty woman Ruth; the books of Proverbs, Ecclesiastes, and Song of Songs, all three of which featuring the elusive Woman Wisdom; the book of Esther with its powerful and sensual queen. To these books, I have added the book of Genesis with its foundational narrative about man and woman. But more needs to be said about the significant shift in worldview that we find in the mother's house in contrast to the father's house. The mother's house differs from the father's house in five fundamental ways: 1)its emphasis is on feminine voices and experiences vs. masculine ones; 2) its interest in exploring horizontal relationships *between* human beings, or ethics vs. the vertical, ritual-based movement that we find in the father's house; 3) its privileging wisdom vs. law; 4) its promotion of hospitality to the other, the stranger, the misfit, vs. a holiness code commanding separation; 5) and, finally, its attitude of receptivity, of *receiving*, vs. father's house's emphasis on keeping the law and *doing* or performing commandments. Let us examine each of these five paths in greater detail.

Feminine vs. Masculine

The first obvious distinction between the father's house and the mother's house is the centrality of women protagonists and experiences in the latter. In the father's house, it is the men who take center stage: they are the patriarchs, the judges, the priests, the kings, and the prophets who lead the community and protect it. Abraham, the first patriarch, leads his whole family from Ur (the land of the Sumerians) into Canaan. The judges are the ones responsible for saving and redeeming the people from their enemies. The kings, such as King David and King Solomon, build the foundations of the civilization of the Hebrews, through intricate works of literature and of architecture, writing profound texts, and building magnificent temples, palaces, and gardens. Finally, the prophets are the ones responsible for protecting the moral compass of the community, ensuring that justice endures. In such a context, some women do emerge at times as wise matriarchs, powerful judges, influential queens and prophets, but only a small minority do so, and their appearance is rare.

Not so in the mother's house. Women, in the mother's house, are no more relegated to the margins of history as they are in the father's house. Rather, they often *make* history, shift the destiny of entire communities through their wisdom and courage. Women such as Eve, the wife of Job, Ruth, Esther, the Shulamite, and Woman Wisdom are seen intervening at pivotal moments, and often end up shifting entire destinies, their own and those of the ones connected to them. These women do not wait for a man to dictate to them their destiny. Rather, they are often seen as the ones inspiring, orienting men into their highest calling. As such, these women embody leadership roles unheard of in patriarchy. These women *lead,* they do not follow, nor submit.

The women of the mother's house thus resemble the Ancient Near Eastern goddesses of old, such as Inanna, Ishtar, Asherah, Maat, Isis, powerful feminine figures who do submit to patriarchal norms, but rather subvert them by stepping into strong leadership roles. These goddesses, moreover, are seen as the forces behind the man's power and authority. They are the ones who inaugurate, protect, and guide the Ancient Near Eastern kings of old. The powerful women in the mother's house, although not goddesses, share many traits with them. Like the ancient goddesses, they do not fit into gender norms, neither do they submit to the men in their lives; rather, they hold the keys to the man's highest calling, and often are the ones that awaken the man from his slumber and propel him into his destiny—one that is profoundly life-giving, redemptive, and restorative, not only to the world around them, but to the very women who inaugurated it.

Vertical vs. Horizontal

The second main difference between the father's house and the mother's house lies in its spiritual orientation. In the father's house, the spiritual orientation is vertical, aimed at serving God and drawing near to him through temple rituals. In the father's house, the priesthood is the highest calling—one which facilitates the sacrificial system necessary for accessing the realm of the divine. In the father's house, sacrifice becomes the means of proximity with God. And the priest, as the one facilitating the sacrifice, becomes the locus of the presence of God in the world. Drawing near to God thus involves traveling to the centralized temple of Jerusalem and offering up an animal sacrifice, mediated by the priest. God is only approached in a definite sacred space and through certain prescribed rituals and actions, and in the presence of a male officiant. This priestly verticality would eventually morph, after the destruction of the temple, into the male-centered traditions of study and prayer becoming the new holy spaces where encountering God became possible.

Not so in the mother's house. In the mother's house, God is found at the kitchen table, in the marketplace, in the solitude of mountains and plains, and in the bedroom. In the mother's house, God is especially found in conversation. It is a conversation which provokes the expulsion from Eden into the harsh yet beautiful reality of the world; it is a conversation which provokes Job's outburst and assault on God; it is a conversation between Ruth and Boaz which saves the Davidic line; a conversation between Esther and Ahasuerus which saves the Hebrews from extinction; and finally, conversations between the Shulamite and her lover which sets their course towards a love as strong as death. God is thus found "between" us,[11] and his power and wisdom is manifested through human conversation.

But there is one powerful feature that unites all these pivotal conversations: They are all intimate conversations between a man and a woman. They are all "bedroom" conversations. It is as though the bedroom has replaced the temple as the new locus for the connection between God and humanity. As though the bedroom has become the new point of connection between the human and the divine. Commenting on the Song of Songs, featuring a man and a woman in intimate conversation, Rabbi Akivah calls it the Holy of Holies—alluding to the sacred space in the Jerusalem temple where only God could enter, where the presence of God rested. In the Song of Songs, the lovers' verdant and fragrant bedroom has become, for Rabbi Akivah, the new Holy of Holies. In the mother's house, likewise, God might be found in the bedrooms of our female protagonists, in those intimate and often courageous conversations, and in the way that those conversations usher in redemption, restoration, and new beginnings. Thus, in the mother's house, intimate "bedroom" conversations—often necessitating incredible grit and courage on the part of the woman—offer an alternative to the temple sacrifices as mediators of divine providence.

Law vs. Wisdom

The third main difference between the father's house and the mother's house lies in the latter's emphasis on wisdom versus law. In the father's house, it is the law, the oral and written word of God, which ought to orient one's life. The law was given to Moses at Sinai, and later developed by Moses into oral law, and further expounded throughout the centuries in the Jewish masterpieces of the Mishnah, the Midrash, and the Talmud. These laws, rooted in the arid and wilderness sands of Sinai, are seen as a "tree of life" to those who observe them. They are the words that offer guidance, light, and protection in our precarious lives. They hold the keys to happiness, to prosperity, to health, and to redemption. No human life can truly thrive without some alignment—conscious or unconscious—with these precepts.

In the mother's house, however, the law is never mentioned. Rather, it is wisdom which is taught and sought in order to achieve life, prosperity, and abundance. The female protagonists in the mother's house thus open their mouths in wisdom rather than in commentary. This is not surprising inasmuch as, in most Ancient Near Eastern cultures, wisdom is seen as the prerogative and inheritance of women. Wisdom is embodied by powerful feminine figures, or goddesses. The Sumerian goddess Inanna is described as stealing wisdom from the male God of wisdom, Enki. Ma'at, the Egyptian goddess of justice, is also the goddess of wisdom.[12] This Ancient Near Eastern tradition of associating women with wisdom is explicitly developed in the book of Proverbs where Woman Wisdom is depicted with traits closely resembling the Ancient Near Eastern goddesses aforementioned. By extension, the woman, as the embodiment of wisdom, often holds center stage in wisdom literature. Wisdom is taught and learned by woman.

The teachings of wisdom also can be contrasted with the teachings of the law. Whereas the law warns against forbidden behavior, relationships, and places, wisdom, on the other hand, encourages exploration, experience, and curiosity. For it is precisely from these explorations, experiences, and curiosity that wisdom is accumulated. Whereas the law discourages transgressive behavior, wisdom seems to partner with it. The goddess Inanna "transgresses" when she steals wisdom from the god Enki, Eve "transgresses" when she takes from the tree of wisdom and gives of its fruit to her husband. King Solomon, in the book of Ecclesiastes, pushes the limits of what is allowed in his quest for wisdom, falling also into transgressive behavior from which he emerges with an uncanny combination of deep cynicism and hedonistic enjoyment. The "foreign woman" whom one is forbidden to approach in the book of Proverbs, becomes the central character in the Song of Songs.

It is as though wisdom, spiritual maturity, can only be found at the price of transgression. Why? Because only by tasting the darkness, chaos, and pain that arise out of transgression, can one experience or re-experience the creative power of God, which takes darkness and forms it into light, chaos and shapes it into a fully ordered *cosmos,* or world. In the father's house, God's essential nature is that of a Judge of transgression. In the mother's house, God is Creator, or creative. God is an artist! And like all artists, his art thrives in chaos, in the *ex nihilo* of primordial matter. To the artist-God, our transgressions can be seen as a pure source of joy and excitement, in as much as they provide the very material for his creative power. To the artist-God, what was meant for evil becomes transformed into good.[13] Our transgressions, far from being a source of disappointment for the God of the mother's house, become golden opportunities for his creative work.

Holiness vs. Hospitality

One of the most distinctive contrasts between the father's house and the mother's house is the one between holiness and hospitality. In the father's house, the emphasis is on separation from the world and keeping oneself "holy" or separate (*qadosh*) in order to best represent a God who is also "holy" and separate from the mundanity of the world. Holiness in turn means to think, eat, act, even pray differently from those around us, it encourages separation, distinction from the ways of the world. The goal becomes then to keep oneself pure from the corruption of the surrounding world, to keep oneself pure from certain foods, images, sounds, places, even people. In the context of holiness, eating with a non-believer, intermarrying with a non-Jew, entering a pagan place of worship, reading certain books, having certain conversations, are all forbidden. All this in the name of holiness, with the purpose of keeping one's light pure and strong, thus safeguarding the perennial divine presence in the world.

Not so in the mother's house. In the mother's house all are welcome: Seducers, instigators, foreign women, sinners, transgressors, and pagans are all invited to the table. And so, we have the seductive Eve placed at the head of the table. The cynical wife of Job, who exhorts him to "curse God and die." We have a woman born and raised in the abhorred nation of Moab marrying a Jew and becoming the great-grandmother of King David. We have a Canaanite sage composing poetry and seeing his work appendixed to that of the most prolific king of Israel, Solomon. We have an African shepherdess seducing a Jewish prince and awakening him to the subtle arts of love. And finally, we have a Jewish beauty queen sleeping with the king of the Persian empire.

Why so many strangers and troublemakers at the table? Because wisdom, unlike law, does not flow from a single source. Wisdom is tapestry that is woven from different voices, from a broad spectrum of experiences and teachings. As such, wisdom is found in dialogue rather than in revelation, through conversation rather than contemplation. The sages of the *ketuvim,* writing along the lines of the mother's house, knew this: That to be wise, one must learn to listen to other voices beyond oneself, that the organ of wisdom is the ears, ever sensitive to what is going on outside of oneself. This is reminiscent of the Egyptian concept of wisdom as the ability to "hear."[14] In Egypt the sign of wisdom did not lie in the person's powers of deduction (as would later be the case in Greece). Rather it lay in the person's ability and capacity to listen to others. The book of Proverbs follows this line of reasoning with its emphasis on listening: "My son, listen to my speech…" (Proverbs 4:20). The more dialogue partners one has, the wiser one becomes: the mother's house principal virtue is hospitality.

Doing vs. Receiving

The final contrast between the father's house and the mother's house lies in the importance of doing vs. receiving. In the father's house, the emphasis is overwhelmingly placed on what one ought to *do,* how one ought to *act.* The commandments for the most part are there to guide human *action,* orienting it towards life rather than death. Spirituality in the father's house is not separated from life and its mundane tasks, all of which ought to be permeated, saturated with Spirit. From the waking to laying down to sleep, human daily tasks are oriented, sanctified by the divine commands. Moreover, spirituality is a *doing* because it is precisely in doing that the body, mind, and spirit are shaped and molded according to the life of the spirit. For the father's house existence does not only precede essence, it inaugurates it, it fashions and molds it.

The mother's house, although not downplaying the need for action at times (many of the women in the mother's house are women of action), is especially oriented towards receptivity, towards the practice of, the positioning to *receive.* One of the most fundamental teachings of the mother's house is the relinquishing of an attitude of grasping, and the cultivation of an attitude of receiving. To grasp for what is not yet ours, or what is not meant to be ours, is to miss the gift, the graces of God. This is what the ambitious Eve had to learn the hard way in the garden. This is what the perfectionist Job had to understand before he could "see" God, and truly experience the fullness and abundance of a life well lived. This is the attitude that Ruth would embody, and which would prove to be a source of fruitfulness. This is what King Solomon would grapple with, and eventually surrender to, in the books of Ecclesiastes and Song of Songs. And finally, this is what Queen Esther must realize in order to find the courage to confront the king. As such, the mother's house moves us out of "temple spirituality," where certain prescribed and precise actions are what manifests the divine presence, to "garden spirituality" where it is not us, but *God* who is doing. In the temple, we serve God. In the garden, God serves *us*! He sets a table before us and gives us our hearts' desires.

Such are the five characteristics of the mother's house that will saturate the stories that we are about to explore, eight of them total, each featuring powerful feminine characters. Our first story (chapter 1) will be taken from the ancient Sumerian story "The Courtship of Inanna and Dumuzi" and will feature the ancient Sumerian goddess Inanna. This story will serve as the foundational story for all the others that will follow inasmuch as it sets the stage magnificently for a powerful dynamic between man and woman—celebrated through the "sacred marriage" ceremony—which will prove foundational to the gender dynamics being constructed and explored in the Biblical stories. The "Courtship of Inanna and Dumuzi" was a story well known to the Biblical writers and was generously drawn from in the construction of their male and especially female characters, and in the elaboration of the gender dynamics between the two.[15] I will argue that the theme of the "sacred marriage," although birthed in ancient Sumer, constitutes a guiding thread and a key to understanding the Biblical stories recounted in the mother's house.

Our next story (chapter 2) will be the story of Eve and of Adam. In this story we will continue to explore the theme of the "sacred marriage" as it is elaborated between the first human couple. We will first notice a number of similarities between Eve and the goddess Inanna and between Adam and Dumuzi. Like Inanna, Eve finds herself powerfully attracted to the divine prerogative of wisdom, only to fail tragically in her quest for divinity. Ensues the breakdown of cosmic order, the seeping through of chaos and of death, and a widening and painful rift between the man and the woman. It will take divine intervention for light to begin to dawn again for the human couple and the now fallen world. Far from being a punishment or a curse as it has been traditionally read, however, the divine word spoken onto the snake, the woman, and the man, can be interpreted as a redemptive moment of restoration not only for the human couple, but for the whole world, drawing extensively from the Sumerian "sacred marriage" literary context.

Our third story (chapter 3) will focus on the female characters in the book of Job. Although the focus of that story seems to be on the main character Job, the women in the book are behind every pivotal moment of the story. The wife of Job, harshly criticized by traditional commentators, is in fact the motivating force behind Job's eventual conversion. She is the one, after all, who awakens Job out of his dogmatic slumber and forces him to turn to God with authenticity and vulnerability. And it is out of that authenticity that a genuine vision and experience of God can finally arise in Job's life. The daughters of Job arise in the second pivotal moment—when Job finds his fortunes "restored." Their presence takes the reader by surprise and hints at a very different ending than the "obvious" one, where God seems to simply reward Job for his faithfulness. The presence of the daughters thus orients the reader's hermeneutical stance towards a more subtle and profound understanding of the ultimate meaning of suffering.

Our next story (chapter 4) takes us to the book of Ruth. The story takes place on the backdrop of famine, exile, and death. Yet the main character, Ruth, a Moabite woman, in choosing to follow her heart's imperatives, ends up shifting not only her own destiny, but that of an entire community. This chapter follows in her footsteps as she moves from precarity, drought, and death into abundance, saturation, and life, exploring what steps she takes (and what steps we might also take), how she adroitly positions herself for the renewed life and grace that encounter her along the way, and the beautiful union that develops with the rich landowner Boaz. Again the "sacred marriage" motif appears in this story, especially in the portrait it makes of the woman Ruth and the man Boaz, of their eventually union, and of the cosmic renewal that ensues.

The book of Proverbs is the story that we explore next (chapter 5). Although primordially a teaching of a father to a son, this book contains traces of a powerful feminine figure: Woman Wisdom. Interestingly, Woman Wisdom will be portrayed by King Solomon with traits reminiscent of the Sumerian goddess Inanna, and the Egyptian goddess Ma'at. The intent of the writer is clear: Woman Wisdom functions in this book as an Ancient Near Eastern goddess inaugurating and legitimizing the king's reign. The king is commanded to "embrace her" (Prov. 3:18), to unite himself with her, as the Ancient Near Eastern kings of old did, in order to receive the legitimacy, wisdom, and authority to reign. This book is the Hebraic version of the "Courtship of Inanna and Dumuzi," following the same motif of the marriage between the king and the goddess of wisdom as the foundation, the basis of the king's authority and political power.

Expanding on the book of Proverb's "sacred marriage" motif, the book of Ecclesiastes (chapter 6) shows in vivid detail what happens when the king loses his connection with the goddess of wisdom, or Woman Wisdom. The connections with the Egyptian goddess of justice, Ma'at, are here even more obvious, and show a kingdom thrown into chaos because the king has clearly lost his Ma'at. Reconnecting with wisdom will entail that the king change his orientation radically, from an attitude of limitless grasping, to one of recognizing his limits and his dependence on grace. Only by recognizing his limits—and thereby reconnecting to his Ma'at who, as the goddess of justice, places limits on all—will the king find himself, paradoxically, fit again to rule. And only by recognizing that he has no control over his own life, that he cannot "strive" his way to success, will the king find himself again capable of receiving the abundance of life.

The Song of Songs (chapter 7) closes this trilogy on Woman Wisdom, and this time brings us into her secret garden, to sit at her feet and learn from her. Woman Wisdom is now embodied by the young and restless Shulamite, who is in love with Solomon. The Shulamite in our text does not immediately seem wise, but in time, as she begins to taste the bittersweetness of love, she gains wisdom. This wisdom she "drops" along the way, addressing her friends, the "daughters of Jerusalem" and, by extension, all of us women interested in learning the ways of love. And like her, we learn that true love does not grasp, it does not possess. Rather, it must learn to release, to let go, to surrender. For only then will love draw near and bestow on us the sacred gift of its presence. Again, the "sacred marriage" motif emerges in this story, in the ways that the woman and the man of the Song awaken and challenge each other and the cosmic fecundity that ensues.

Continuing the theme of love and sacred marriage, we enter the book of Esther (chapter 8). In this book we first encounter a failed "sacred marriage" in the story of Vashti and Ahasuerus. Failed because there is really no partnership here, no mutual awakening and the result is cosmic stagnation and death. Arrives on the scene young Esther, still inexperienced in the arts of love, yet nevertheless winning the heart of the king. Her crowning as queen will however happen later in the story, when she finally rises out of her passivity and courageously confronts the king. The way that she does so is particularly illuminating: preparation, the choice of words and timing, all reveal Queen Esther's striking emotional intelligence and tact and set an example for the rest of us. Again, the theme of "sacred marriage" permeates the story, with

Queen Esther playing a powerful role in awakening the king to his higher self and his true power and the cosmic redemption that ensues.

Chapter 1

The Sacred Marriage of Inanna and Dumuzi

Introduction

Why speak on Inanna in a work dedicated to the Hebrew Bible? Isn't Inanna a pagan goddess, the forebearer of the forbidden goddess Asherah that the prophets in the Hebrew Bible loved to hate? Why then turn to her story, and to the cultic texts surrounding her worship? The first reason lies in the strong matriarchal flavor of her story, and the profound lessons one can learn, as women, from the evolution of this goddess from a young Inanna dreaming of her "bed and throne," to the mature, sensual Inanna who ends up wedding the shepherd Dumuzi and inaugurating his destiny as king. The stories of the goddess Inanna in many ways resonate with our stories as women, with our experiences, and open a breach onto our most hidden dreams and desires. And as the goddess journeys to self-individuation as a woman and as a goddess, we journey with her, hoping to glean along the way some wisdom for our own individuation as women.

The other reason lies in the fact that the Biblical stories we are about to explore, plunge their roots in Sumerian and Egyptian literature. It must be reminded that Biblical stories do not happen in a vacuum. They emerge against the backdrop of Ancient Near Eastern literature, borrowing from it themes, motives and even phraseology.[1] The stories of the goddess Inanna constitute an important part of this literary corpus, and one of the central themes borrowed from these stories—albeit in a profoundly modified way[2]—and woven throughout the Hebrew Bible, is the trope of the "sacred marriage." The theme of "sacred marriage" can be glimpsed already during the reign of the kings of Jerusalem,[3] emerging again in the discourse of the prophets,[4] and finally (and this will be the main argument of the present work), finding its way into the wisdom literature of the Bible, notably in the books of Genesis, Ruth, Esther, Proverbs, and Song of Songs.[5] But before we can begin to make this final connection, more must be said on the ritual itself and its significance for Ancient Near Eastern religious life.

The earliest versions of the "sacred marriage" date back to 2000 B.C. in ancient Sumer and were narrated on clay tablets, which, although discovered in the mid-twentieth century, have only recently begun to be deciphered and translated. Ancient Sumer was located in Southern Iraq, in the valley of the Tigris and Euphrates, and was the civilization that gave rise to the Babylonian Empire. The Sumerians, unlike the Hebrews who tended to be herders, were masters of agriculture and built the great cities of Ur, Eridu, Nippur, Kish, and Babylon. They worshipped a pantheon of gods (again unlike the Hebrews who were monotheistic), as is evident from the sprinkling of ziggurats[6] across the territory honoring different deities. But very quickly, one of these, a goddess, began to emerge as supreme: the goddess Inanna, goddess of love and wisdom.

But who is this spectacular goddess? Inanna was primordially the goddess of the Sumerian city-state Uruk but her influence eventually spread all over the Ancient Near East. Stories depict her youth as an ambitious young maiden dreaming of marriage and power. Inanna is described as tending a tree, stealing wisdom from the god Enki, and falling in love with the hero Gilgamesh.[7] The most important story surrounding Inanna will however be that of her courtship with the shepherd Dumuzi. The "sacred marriage" that ensues will be transformative for both Dumuzi and Inanna, inaugurating the reign of the former and awakening the fecundity of the latter, ensuring that year's fruitful harvest. This "sacred marriage" would then be celebrated every year, and eventually re-enacted by future kings and Inanna's high priestesses. The king would be brought to the temple of Inanna, lay with the priestess embodying the goddess, and emerge with the authority to rule over a land brimming over with rains and fruitfulness. In time, this "sacred marriage" ceremony was passed on to the Babylonians and would spread throughout the Ancient Near East to Canaan, and eventually to the nation of Israel. Inanna and Dumuzi would morph into the Babylonian Ishtar and Tammuz (also worshipped in the land of Israel) and into the Canaanite and the idolatrous Israelite worship of Asherah and Baal.

The story of the sacred marriage between Inanna and Dumuzi thus permeates the Ancient Near East, eventually surfacing in the Hebrew Bible, notably in the poetry of the Hebrew prophets, and in the wisdom literature of the Bible, in the stories of Adam and Eve, Ruth and Boaz, Woman Wisdom and the king's son, The Shulamite and the king, and Esther and Ahasuerus. The Inanna stories thus constitute the founding stories of the mother's house, with the Hebrew stories borrowing their character, their flavor, and their worldview from these Sumerian stories, while profoundly reworking them to fit the Hebrew monotheistic and monogamous contexts. But before we go into the actual stories, an analysis of the mother's house character of the Inanna stories must be elaborated.

Feminine vs. Masculine

The ancient empire of Sumer enjoyed a culture that had a strong matriarchal character. There, the divine realm was not limited to the masculine, and powerful female goddesses dominated the religious landscape. It was not until the Babylonian conquest (1700 BCE) that patriarchy destroyed the powerful matriarchal golden age of Sumer, with the defeat of the feminine goddess Tiamat at the bloodthirsty hands of the male god Marduk. The latter then established himself king of the gods (without the help of a goddess!) and the reign of the powerful Sumerian goddesses came to an end. Only Inanna survived, morphing into Ishtar—goddess of love and war. Until then, however, the goddess Inanna would flourish in ways deeply subversive to patriarchy: she is not interested in motherhood, refuses to stay home, is seen "wandering about" in the streets in a way reminiscent of Woman Folly in the book of Proverbs, she does not do women's work such as the spinning and weaving of flax, and she eventually becomes the patron saint of prostitutes and unattached women.[8] Moreover, not content with rejecting traditional women's work, she comes to embody the traditionally masculine roles of warrior and protector of the king. Clearly, when it comes to Inanna, we are witnessing one of the most ancient subversions of patriarchy, perhaps even a glimpse into a pre-patriarchal era, that of the golden age of matriarchy, a time when "God was a woman"[9] during one of humanity's most ancient civilizations.

Vertical vs. Horizontal/Holiness vs. Hospitality

Although the worship of Inanna involved temples and rituals, the heart of her cult was the "sacred marriage" ceremony during which the king would lay with the high priestess of Inanna and emerge with renewed power and with the assurance of the land's rebirth. Thus, it is sexual intimacy rather than sacrifice that becomes the way to approach the divine or to connect to God. The movement is one of shocking proximity and intimacy with the divine, unheard of in ancient Israel where God remains entrenched in his holiness, striking down any inappropriate touch or unwanted proximity. In ancient Israel, God could neither be seen nor touched, on the penalty of death. Here, however, the feminine goddess Inanna not only allows herself to be seen, she lends herself to the loving caresses of her worshipper, welcoming him to herself in a striking act of hospitality. The temple thus becomes a place of unparalleled proximity with the divine, unmediated by animal sacrifices, and leading to the blossoming of plant life rather than the shedding of animal blood. It is very likely that it is these ancient visions of intimacy with the divine that inspired the Hebrew prophets to speak of God as the bridegroom or husband of Israel, in terms saturated with sexual imagery, culminating in the works of King Solomon, notably the Song of Songs. And it is these visions of intimacy that will saturate the stories of the mother's house. There too, we will see traces of the Sumerian "sacred marriage" where the divine presence is accessed, awakened, activated, through the relationship between the man and the woman.

Law vs. Wisdom

Unlike their Babylonian conquerors, the Sumerians were not so preoccupied with legal matters. Their task was a civilizing one, rather than a legal one. While the Babylonians sought to build a just society and ended up composing the code of Hammurabi—which became the blueprint for all later legal documents including those found in the Hebrew Bible—the Sumerians were more interested in the principles of civilization (such as architecture, craftsmanship, worship, wisdom, lovemaking, and war), or the *me,* for the cultivation of an oasis of wealth, beauty, and harmony worthy of the gods that dwelt among them. The *me* can thus be assimilated to the wisdom associated with cultivating a civilized world: A world where freshly harvested grain was kneaded and baked into bread, where raw flax was woven into tapestries, rugs and garments, where clay was fashioned into bowls and cups, and where love was cultivated as an art, most of which was women's work. As such, wisdom came to be associated with women in the Ancient Near East, including Egypt. The woman, as the civilizing agent—in her kneading, baking, weaving—came to represent wisdom. It is then not surprising to see Inanna, in one of her stories, boarding a boat and traveling to the abode of Enki, the god of wisdom, to steal from him the *me* and share it with the citizens of Uruk.[10]

Doing vs. Receiving

One of the most interesting ideas of Ancient Sumer had to do with the acquisition of power. For the Sumerians, and in contrast to their Babylonian conquerors, power could not be grabbed, nor taken by force through violent conquest or by the masculine-dominated arts of war—

as would be the case with the god Marduk and, subsequently, every Babylonian king in history. Rather, power was bestowed by a female goddess upon a man endowed with qualities of leadership whose criteria differed radically from the Babylonian ones. Whereas in Babylon, the king was characterized by his conquering ability and his architectural prowesses[11], the shepherd-kings of Sumer were to resemble their forefather Dumuzi, himself a shepherd of humble origins. The story of the courtship of Dumuzi and Inanna recounts that Dumuzi was not chosen on the basis of what he had built and achieved. On the contrary, compared to his rival, the farmer, he had nothing of his own. It is rather his humility and poverty that made him the ideal candidate for marriage to the goddess. Why? Because only a poor and humble shepherd boy can truly *receive* that which can only be *bestowed*. Thus, in Sumer, the precondition of power was, paradoxically, powerlessness. For only then would the monarch be open to receiving his power from another, and to protecting a space for his divine consort to rule with him, or through him. Thus, only a man capable of making room for an Other, of receiving and sharing power, a man not full of himself, of his own achievements and power, could be a legitimate candidate for the throne and become a true shepherd-king. The Inanna stories thus clearly belong to the "mother's house" and serve as the foundational texts for this Biblical genre. We now turn to two of the most famous stories in the Inanna repertoire: "Inanna and the Huluppu tree", featuring young Inanna on the journey to womanhood, and "The Courtship of Inanna and Dumuzi" where Inanna weds her first love thereby inaugurating the "sacred marriage" rite.

Inanna and the Huluppu Tree

Our first story features young Inanna and a tree. This narrative shares a number of parallels with Eve and the tree and might have served as a source text for the Biblical story.[12] Understanding this text thus gives us an Ancient Near Eastern lens through which to view the story of Eve and the tree, serving to illuminate meanings and significations not hereto discovered. And so, we turn to the Sumerian story:

> At that time a tree, a single tree, a Huluppu tree
> A woman who walked in fear of the word of the Sky God, An
> Who walked in fear of the word of the Air God, Enlil
> Plucked the tree from the river and spoke
> I shall bring this tree to Uruk
> I shall plant this tree in my holy garden
> Inanna cared for the tree with her hand
> She settled the earth around the tree with her foot

Inanna tends to her tree for ten years, expecting that from it would arise her "shining throne and bed," but instead the tree starts to grow thick (rendering it difficult to make anything out of it!) and to attract unwanted creatures:

> The tree grew thick
> But its bark didn't split
> Then a serpent who could not be charmed
> Made its nest in the roots of the huluppu tree
> The Anzu bird set his young in the branches of the tree
> And the dark maid Lillith built her home in the trunk
> The young woman who loved to laugh wept
> How Inanna wept

Thankfully, to her rescue comes the hero Gilgamesh, who, dressed in heavy armor, proceeds to "enter Inanna's garden," strikes the serpent, causes the Anzu bird to take flight, and smashes Lilith's home. Then, from the tree he carves a throne and a bed for Inanna, and she a *pukku* and a *mikku*[13] for Gilgamesh, the hero of Uruk.

So goes the story. Its symbolism is dense, and it is up to us now to begin to interpret it and draw lessons from it. The tree in the Ancient

Near East is often associated with fertility. As such, it represents Inanna's budding womanhood. From it, she intends to build her "throne," that is, her reign as the goddess of fertility, and a "bed," that is, her calling to become the beloved of the king. Thus, it is Inanna's womanhood (or the tree) which, when in full bloom, will inaugurate her destiny as a goddess of fertility and protector of the king of Uruk. Womanhood in ancient Sumer was thus considered a source of power. The woman's ability to bring children into the world affiliated her with the Creator God, with divinity. It was believed that sexual contact with a woman connected the man directly with the very source of life and empowered *him.* It is probably from this awe-inspiring ability of women to bring life into the world that their affiliation with divinity began, inaugurating the reign of the goddesses.[14]

Tragically, however, the tree is not developing as it should. It begins to attract some unsavory inhabitants that serve only to jeopardize Inanna's destiny. Among those unwanted visitors we have the snake, who will also visit Eve's tree, the Anzu bird, and Lilith. But what do these three creatures symbolize? The snake is clearly a fertility symbol. But it is also a creature of chaos.[15] Thus, the serpent could symbolize a woman's unbridled fertility or life-force, which, when not properly channeled, can open the door to the forces of chaos rather than of order and harmony. The Anzu bird, in other stories, represents the transgressive taking of what is not meant for it. In one story, the Anzu bird is seen attempting to steal the *me* for itself. Thus, the Anzu bird could represent a woman's selfish and grasping attitude towards life, the taking of what is not meant for her, of what has not (yet) been given to her.[16] It thus represents a woman's unbridled desire, which, if serving mere selfish purposes, can lead to transgression and as a result, chaos. Finally, Lilith represents the dark feminine, the feminine that finds no rest, no purpose and that, as a result, becomes toxic and destructive.[17]

These three unwanted guests thus give us a wonderful picture of a woman's precarious and dangerous journey to maturity. They show us the dangers of a woman's erotic power when not properly channeled, and the chaos, darkness, and toxicity that can ensue from this. Toxic femininity (and not just toxic masculinity) is a reality, and occurs, according to our story, when a woman's erotic power becomes self-serving and turned inwards. As such, she is not able to find a suitable partner capable of giving direction, orientation to this erotic power, carving from it a "throne" and a "bed." For, in the Huluppu Tree story, the journey of maturation of a woman necessarily entails a relationship with a partner. It is the latter who in a way "makes" the woman a full-fledged woman.[18] There is no sense here of a woman reaching full individuation by herself (and the same goes for the man as we will see in the story of The Courtship of Inanna and Dumuzi). She needs to enter into partnership for her erotic power to be life-giving, nourishing, and fecund. Outside of this relationship, she risks the ever-lurking danger of attracting the creatures of chaos, and of seeing her erotic power become a source of darkness rather than of light.

But more needs to be said on the nature of this partnership. In our story, Gilgamesh brutally fells the tree and makes out of it Inanna's bed and throne. There is here an element of violence, a "cutting" that nevertheless constitutes in our story the means by which the woman blossoms into full-fledged womanhood. Gilgamesh "strikes" the serpent, he "smashes" Lilith's home and then he "cuts off" the branches and "carves" a bed and throne. But why this violence? Perhaps because the process of maturation necessarily entails pain. Perhaps because a woman can never become a full-fledged woman until she has known the searing pain of heartbreak and of loss. Thus, until her strong will to power has been broken, a woman cannot rise to full-fledged individuation as a woman. Until a woman has released her grasp on life, her selfish impulse to take rather than to give or receive, she has not fully blossomed as a woman. And while Gilgamesh behaves like a brute, he nevertheless succeeds in opening her up and releasing her womanhood. He effectively breaks her heart and cruelly crushes her egotism, yet, in doing so, he births the woman in her. Relational pain thus serves as a rite of passage for the woman Inanna. For only through being "cut open" by this pain, does Inanna awaken a woman.[19] Only pain can effectively combat and break through narcissism and egocentrism, and awaken the dormant feminine to her relational destiny.

It is quite a powerful lesson in this story that, in spite of the violence of her first relationship, Inanna still ends up with her "throne" and "bed." There is no shame here from her mistreatment, no shame of having endured this form of violence. This story shows us that even the worst, most painful relationships, rather than destroy a woman's psyche, have the potential to open, awaken, and empower her. From the devastation of such a relationship, a woman can still emerge with an even stronger sense of who she is and what she wants, and with an even deeper capacity to love and to pour new life into the world.

The Courtship of Inanna and Dumuzi

This narrative is one of the most important in the repertoire of the Inanna cultic texts and will resurface in many of the mother's house stories of the Hebrew Bible. This story also has a historical background: the goddess Inanna had many lovers (including Gilgamesh), but she was only married once, to a lowly shepherd called Dumuzi. And although he was not her first choice, she eventually falls in love with him and gives him the scepter to the city-state of Uruk of which she is already the patron deity. This union was henceforth celebrated year after year in Uruk, with the king of the city acting as a proxy for Dumuzi and uniting with the priestess of Inanna, thereby announcing the revival of nature and of the fall harvest. So, in this story, both partners awaken each other: The king sees himself empowered by the goddess to rule and the goddess becomes fruitful, and by extension the land. Our story begins with the introduction of Dumuzi to Inanna as a potential husband. Inanna does not hide her disappointment:

> Brother, after you've brought my bridal sheet to me
> Who will go to bed with me?
> Dumuzi the shepherd! He will go to bed with you.

Inanna spoke:
No, brother!
The man of my heart works the hoe
The farmer! He is the man of my heart!
He gathers the grain into great heaps.
He brings the grain regularly into my storehouses.
The shepherd! I will not marry the shepherd!
His clothes are coarse, his wool is rough
I will marry the farmer

This segment of the story is very interesting. We can see here one of the foundational stories of the Biblical story of Cain and Abel, a farmer and a shepherd. Initially, of course, Inanna is drawn to the farmer, the one who, like his later version Cain, owns and possesses the land. The farmer, unlike the shepherd who merely rents out the land for his flocks, owns it. There is a stability to the farmer that the shepherd, because of his nomadic lifestyle, will never achieve. The farmer thus represents sedentary urban life that characterizes the Sumerian city-states, and the shepherd the nomadism of the invading ancient Semites who later would build Babylon. Given this historical backdrop, it is striking that Inanna's brother advises her to marry the shepherd. Perhaps, though, there is some wisdom here: the shepherd, because of his poverty and humility is better suited for the goddess inasmuch as he will be more receptive, more open to her influence and gifts, than the farmer who is already powerful and confident of his own endeavors. The true king is thus one capable of receiving, capable of listening to the voice of the goddess, and therein will lie his wisdom and his ability to rule justly. This story has a strong reverberation in the story of Cain and Abel where, there too, it is the shepherd who ends up the favorite of God. Perhaps for the same reason. But back to our story where Inanna eventually allows herself to be convinced by her mother to marry the shepherd and proceeds to prepare herself for him.

Inanna ran to Ningal, the mother who bore her
Ningal counseled her daughter saying:
My child, the young man will be your father
My daughter, the young man will be your mother
Open the house, my Lady, open the house
Inanna at her mother's command
Bathed and anointed herself with scented oil
She covered her body with the royal white robe
She readied her dowry
She arranged her precious lapis beads around her neck
She took her seal in her hand

Here we witness a scene that will resurface a number of times in the mother's house stories and so merits our attention. We first have the notion of the mother and of her house, where Inanna shelters in order to sort things out. The mother's house will reappear in the Song of Songs as well as in the book of Ruth, also as a haven or resting place for the female characters to mend broken relationships. We can infer from this that the mother's house, unlike the father's house, which tends to focus on the political and the legal, constitutes a space dedicated to more private, intimate matters, such as love, relationships, and marriage. The notions of bathing and anointing can be found in the stories of both Ruth and Esther and indicate a transition or turning point in the lives of the heroines: hereto defined as maidens, this ritual bathing and anointing signifies their entry into the powerful relational destiny of womanhood. The bathing and anointing symbolize the birth of this new relational self, the emergence of their full-fledged womanhood. The "royal white robe" that we will see again in the story of Esther, symbolizes the woman's evolution from maiden to queen, her ascension into her highest destiny as a relational being, with all the pain and ecstasy that this new role will entail. Having thus prepared herself for this pivotal moment, Inanna is ready for her wedding night.

Dumuzi spoke:

My sister, I would go with you to my garden
Inanna, I would go with you to my orchard
He brought her into his garden.
My brother Dumuzi brought me into his garden
Before my Lord Dumuzi
I poured out plants from my womb
I placed plants before him
I poured out plants before him
I placed grain before him

This scene also is striking in its similarity with some passages in the Song of Songs. There we also have the notion of entering the beloved's garden and the partaking of the beloved's fruits, in Inanna's case, plants and grain. The only difference is that here, it is Dumuzi's garden that is entered rather than the Shulamite's garden, as narrated in the Song of Songs. Here, the man invites the woman into deeper intimacy whereas in the Song of Songs, it is the woman who invites the man into deeper intimacy: "Let my beloved come into his garden. … I have come into my garden, my sister, my bride. I have gathered my myrrh with my spice. I have eaten my honeycomb and my honey. I have drunk my wine and my milk" (Song 4:16–5:1). There is thus an interesting reversal. In the Sumerian text, it is the man who awakens the woman to love, whereas in the Song of Songs, it is the woman who arouses the man. Both, however, make the same point: the awakening to full-fledged womanhood or manhood can only happen through intimate contact with the other. It is the man who awakens the woman, and the woman who awakens the man. Both need the other in order to come into their full blossoming. But our story continues with the sexual exploration and awakening of the garden leading to a proper wedding ceremony:

I bathed for the wild bull
I bathed for the shepherd Dumuzi
The shepherd Dumuzi filled my lap with cream
He watered my womb
He caressed me on the bed
Now I will caress my high priest on the bed
I will caress the faithful shepherd Dumuzi
I will decree a sweet fate for him
The Queen of Heaven
Inanna the First Daughter of the Moon
Decreed the fate of Dumuzi:

In battle I am your leader
In combat I am your armor bearer
In the assembly I am your advocate
On the campaign I am your inspiration
You the chosen shepherd of the holy shrine
You, the king, the faithful provider of Uruk
You, the light of An's great shrine
In all ways you are fit:

To hold your head high on the lofty dais,
To sit on the lapis lazuli throne
To cover your head with the holy crown
To wear long clothes on your body
To bind yourself with the garments of kingship
To carry the mace and sword
To guide straight the long bow and arrow
To fasten the throw-stick and sling at your side
To race on the road with the holy scepter in your hand
And the holy sandals on your feet
To prance on the holy breast like a lapis lazuli calf
You the sprinter, the chosen shepherd

In all ways you are fit
May your heart enjoy long days.

This passage is, of course, the most important one of our story. In it, we find ourselves at the heart of the "sacred marriage" relational dynamic. The first thing we notice is the self-definition of the goddess as a leader in battle, an armor bearer in combat, and an inspiration on the campaign. This military portraiture of the woman will resurface in the stories of Eve, Esther, and in the Song of Songs. The bestowing on Eve of the title of *ezer* (helper)[20] at the moment of her creation, is laden with military connotations as we will clarify later. The Shulamite in the Song of Songs is also described with a number of uncanny military metaphors: she is likened to "pharaoh's chariot horses;" her neck to the "tower of David" made from "a thousand shields," "shields of warriors;" she is compared to a "wall" and her breasts to "towers."[21] Finally, in the book of Esther, we see the young maiden rise to unparalleled equality and power with the king of Persia, and decreeing war on the enemies of the Jews. This idea of the woman as the bodyguard of man sheds a powerful new light on woman's destiny, going beyond her being a mere "helper."[22]

But it is the day after the wedding night that interests us most. There we find a happy and satiated Inanna, who having been loved well, rises to declare the fate of Dumuzi as king of the land, as evidenced by her bestowing upon him the "dais," "throne," "crown," and "scepter". The goddess Inanna thus becomes the one who inaugurates the reign of this earthly king—setting the gold standard for all future enthronizations in the Ancient Near East. From then on, the king or the pharaoh will receive his authority from a goddess, the latter taking many faces, from that of Ishtar in Babylon,[23] to that of Ma'at in Egypt.[24] Even the kings of Israel, as I will show later, will receive their authority from a powerful feminine figure reminiscent of the goddess, i.e., Woman Wisdom.[25] From then on, the king becomes responsible for preserving cosmic order and keeping the forces of chaos out of the kingdom. In Sumer, the king does so by receiving and preserving the *me* (or set of laws) generously given to him by Inanna who is also the goddess of wisdom.[26] In Egypt, the king's most precious offering to the gods is a representation of the goddess Ma'at herself, embodying the laws governing order and justice.[27] And in Ancient Israel, the first thing a newly enthroned king is given, is the book of the law that he is then commanded to copy and set upon his heart.[28]

Thus, it is through an intimate rapport with the goddess of wisdom that the king receives his authority to rule wisely and justly. But special attention needs to be given here to this dyad love/rulership that emerges from this story. Sexual intimacy with the woman and the inauguration of the man's destiny as king, are intertwined and exist in reciprocal connection: as the man receives the goddess's love, he becomes empowered, as a result, to rule the land. As a result of this sexual encounter, she becomes fecund, and the land finds itself rejuvenated and productive. Thus, the love they have just shared serves to awaken both of them to their respective destinies: he as king of the land, and she as protector of the natural order of things, as the guardian of life and fruitfulness. The king thus does not conquer his kingship through war or cunning, rather, he *receives* it from the divine feminine. And it is inasmuch as he remains receptive to this divine feminine that he will continue to rule justly and in a life-giving way.[29]

Conclusion

Our journey with the goddess Inanna has come to an end. But not for long inasmuch as her wildness and subversiveness will be reborn in the powerful feminine figures of the mother's house in the Hebrew Bible. There too, we will meet powerful women who, through their wisdom, courage and love, will awaken their men to their highest selves. These too will become figures of the ancient goddess of wisdom in their ability to speak life into the lives of their partners. But the Hebrew stories will also feature men who can be likened to Dumuzi, in their humility and capacity to remain open to the voices of the women who love them.

And there too, like Dumuzi, these men will not only reach their highest calling, but also powerfully redeem, restore, and pour new life into the women that love them, and into the world around them. There too, will these men rise up to their royal destinies, through their openness to the figures of wisdom around them, and pour their powerful life-force into the cosmos, thereby making it come alive again and redeeming it from certain death, deterioration, and corruption. Thus, male and female redeem, empower *each other.* And through this interaction, God emerges in his restorative and creative power. Unlike the Sumerian stories, the divine is not, in the Hebrew Bible, the prerogative of only one of the partners, but moves *between* the man and the woman when their love merits it.[30] The love between the man and the woman, when characterized by openness and mutuality, becomes a resting place, a channel, a temple for the divine presence in the world.[31] With this in mind, we now turn to the Hebrew stories.

Chapter 2

Eve and Adam and the Lost Kingdom

Introduction

Tradition[1] ascribes to Moses (twelfth-century BCE) the monumental task of compiling and redacting the stories of the book of Genesis.[2] Moses would have had access to these stories as oral traditions, and then proceeded to edit them together in a single book. The stories narrated in the first eleven chapters of the book of Genesis, however, date back millennia before the arrival of the patriarchs on the Biblical scene, and entertain some interesting thematic connections with Ancient Near Eastern stories, notably the Sumerian stories.[3] Some common themes are: the garden as an abode of the gods, the woman and the tree/snake, the flood, the tree of life, the sexual intimacy between god-like beings and human beings.[4] Our story thus seems to belong to an ancient oral narrative tradition with narrow ties to Sumerian stories dating as far back as 3000 BCE.[5] The original storyteller of the story of Adam and Eve was familiar with the Sumerian stories and borrowed motifs and themes from them in his/her storytelling, albeit re-arranging them at will, sometimes even in a polemic way.[6] Read in this light, our story pre-dates the patriarchal developments arising later in the region and, like many Sumerian stories, exhibits a strong matriarchal feel. As such, far from being a story about the superiority of man, or on the domination of woman by man, the story of Adam and Eve tells a very different tale. One that, in line with its Sumerian literary context, will give a powerful, pivotal role to the feminine character, and see in her the uplifting of man rather than his downfall. But more must be said as to how our story, and the book of Genesis as a whole, might be shelved among the mother's house books of the Hebrew Bible.

Masculine vs. Feminine

We have just commented on the strong matriarchal flavor of Genesis 1–11 and argued that the Sumerian matriarchal context of these stories must come to light if we are to understand them properly. But the matriarchal character of Genesis 1–11 is also found in Genesis 12–50. Let us not forget that Abraham came from Ur, one of the city-states of the Sumerian empire and that, given his wealth, he might also have been well-educated and well-versed in Sumerian cultic practices and literature. The Abrahamic tribe will therefore, inevitably, carry on some of the matriarchal culture of its Sumerian origins. We see this in the strong matriarchs that birth the lineage of Abraham. These are strong women, who show wisdom and cunning, and whose voices are listened to. These are women who also find themselves addressed by God, sometimes on equal footing with their husbands. The Lord speaks directly to Sarah and promises her a son. Hagar rises to unprecedented equality with Abraham when she too finds herself the ancestor of twelve tribes.[7] Rebekah consults God about her painful pregnancy and is given a direct and clear message about her two sons. Clearly, the book of Genesis as a whole, because of its Sumerian origins, contains powerful matriarchal elements that coexist with the often more ostensible patriarchal ones.

Vertical vs. Horizontal

The God of the book of Genesis is portrayed in stark contrast to the Mosaic God encountered in the last four remaining books of the Pentateuch. In the rest of the Pentateuch, God is doing most of the speaking, he is laying down the law and giving his ordinances through Moses. The movement in the four remaining books is vertical, with God emerging as an authority, law-giving and judging figure. We are clearly in the father's house. The book of Genesis, on the other hand, gives us a very different portrait of God. God, there, is much more of a facilitator of human development. He is no more center stage but working behind the scenes to help human beings in their journey to becoming human. There are three main roles that God can be seen stepping into, none of them authoritarian: the instigator, the interlocutor, and the responder.

First of all, God plays the role of the instigator. In many of the stories, God, rather than doing anything, is seen *provoking* human action, and *instigating* human reaction. He places a forbidden tree *in the middle* of the garden, thereby drawing powerful attention to it. He accepts Abel's offering and not Cain's, with the intended result of triggering Cain and getting his attention. He confuses the languages of Babel thereby breaking the Babelians' powerful bond and precipitating their exile. God calls Abraham out of Ur, thereby giving him the opportunity to awaken to the life of faith. He gives an unwanted prophetic gift to Joseph, thereby intensifying his brothers' jealousy and precipitating Joseph's expulsion to Egypt. In all of these, and many more, God is seen as the instigator of human actions.

God also plays the role of mirror, or interlocutor, in order to awaken human conscience and awareness. Rather than laying down the law explicitly, he seeks to awaken the human's still dormant moral sense through open conversation. He does this by asking questions and initiating conversation: To Eve, he asks "what have you done?" To Cain, he asks "where is your brother?" To Abraham, "where is your wife?" These questions are less about obtaining an answer, as they are to get the human being to open up and express what they are bottling in. These questions are meant to foster difficult and thought-provoking conversations. But God is not the only one conversing in the book of Genesis: Husband converses with wife, parent converses with child, brother converses with brother. It is the conversation between Abraham and Sarah that precipitates the birth of Ishmael, the conversation between Rebekah and Isaac that enables her pregnancy, a conversation between Rebekah and her son Jacob that precipitates his exile from

Canaan, and a conversation between Joseph's brothers that brings about his expulsion to Egypt. Through all of these conversations, seismic shifts in destinies occur. At these moments, God lurks in the shadows of humans making and provoking their own destinies.

Finally, God is often seen serenely responding to human action rather than austerely commanding it. When Adam and Eve eat the fruit, God is seen "strolling" in the garden and then breaking into a poetic tirade addressing serpent, woman, and man. When Cain kills his brother, God expulses him into a wilderness from which would rise the first civilized urban areas of mankind. When the Babelians begin to build the tower, and forge a problematic unity, God simply confuses their languages and then steps back to witness what happens next. When Hagar gives birth to Ishmael, God, without missing a beat, broadens Abraham's blessing to include many nations, rather than just one nation.[8] When the brothers sell Joseph, the hand of God begins the steady work of moving Joseph up into his destiny as the second most powerful man of the Egyptian empire. In each of these three roles—instigator, interlocutor, responder—we see a God engaging with humans horizontally rather than vertically, bending down to the level of humanity, rather than addressing it from the heights of his holiness. We are clearly here in a mother's house horizontal dimension.

Law vs. Wisdom

The book of Genesis also has an interesting approach to transgression. Unlike the remaining four books of Moses, where transgression finds itself swiftly followed up by punishment and where breaking the divine law leads to death, the book of Genesis offers a much more flexible, compassionate view on transgression.[9] Usually, the transgressor is profiled in the story as the most interesting character—not only to us, but to God—as well as the one who actually gets things done. Eve, for example, is clearly the star of the story in Genesis 1–3. And while she is the one who falters first, she ends up being the one that God addresses the most gently.[10] She also ends up being the one who propulses humanity out of the garden into the world. Cain is also the more substantial and interesting character in the story. He is the one that God seems interested in, and the one whom God addresses. He is also the one who will build the first civilization. Hagar, although profiled as the villain by Sarah, ends up receiving a powerful revelation of God in the very wilderness that she finds herself expulsed into.[11] She is also the one that God takes notice of and speaks to first, before her mistress Sarah. Hagar is also the only woman in the Hebrew Bible to rise to a level of matriarchal power equal to Abraham's patriarchal prowess. Like him, she births twelve nations.

But not only transgressors make the hall of fame, but transgressions. Human transgression, far from leading to death, very often breathes new life into the story. Thus, Eve's eating of the fruit shakes the couple out of its indolence and ushers them into the real world. Cain's crime and exile drive him into creative and civilizing action. Hagar's insolence leads her straight into the wilderness of revelation and of an encounter with God. Rebekah's deceit expulses Jacob into his own destiny away from Esau's overpowering presence. Joseph's brothers' sin against Joseph leads to his extraordinary position in Egypt and the eventual redemption of his tribe from famine. It is as though sin and error were mere steppingstones or milestones in the divine plan. It is as though each transgression had become the canvas for God's creative response and action, as though each transgression was the raw material, the clay, for the artist's hands to make of it something beautiful. God is never seen condemning and punishing iniquity in these stories, rather he eagerly works with it. Human mistakes, far from disappointing God, become opportunities for creative action. In the book of Genesis, God is first and foremost Creator, not Judge. He is an artist who rejoices and gets excited at the sight of the chaos, disarray, and muddiness that human transgression leaves in its wake—eager and excited to see what good, what beauty, he might shape out of it.

Holiness vs. Hospitality

Contrary to the rest of the Pentateuch, which remains deeply distrustful of the surrounding nations and commanding a separation from those nations, the characters of the book of Genesis seem to constantly move beyond themselves towards unknown and unfamiliar regions of the world. In fact, the book of Genesis, rather than narrating a history of civilizing, technological, architectural, and cultural achievements as would be the case in the narratives of Sumer, reveals rather an unbroken string of expulsions and exiles.[12] Adam and Eve find themselves expulsed beyond the comforts of the garden into a world of toil and pain. Cain is exiled even further from the garden into a foreign land where (mercifully?) no one knows him. The builders of the tower of Babel are forced into exile to the four corners of the world by a God wary of their isolationism. All of the patriarchs' journeys are marked by exile into a foreign land where they are seen, almost without exception, engaging in positive and fecund relationships with foreigners. Abraham and Isaac cultivate excellent relationships with the Canaanites, a far cry from the violent and genocidal tendencies of the returning Hebrews from Egypt portrayed in the rest of the Pentateuch. Joseph becomes the right-hand man of first Potiphar and eventually pharaoh, rising to unprecedented power and influence in the land of Egypt. Again, a very different experience than that of the Israelites five generations later.

The book of Genesis is also a book marked by hospitality rather than holiness, as we will see in the rest of the Pentateuch. Hospitality is first and foremost the one offered by the surrounding nations *to* the Hebrews. Abraham thus finds himself welcomed and honored in the territory of Canaan, and the Canaanites are often portrayed as more righteous than the Hebrews.[13] His sons, too, enjoy the same hospitality, until the massacre of Shechem by the sons of Jacob which ends up destroying decades of peaceful coexistence. Egypt offers a haven for Joseph, and eventually for his father and brothers in times of drought. In all of these stories, the Hebrews are seen as thriving in the midst of the very nations that they would be called to separate themselves from in the later Pentateuch stories. But hospitality goes both ways in the book of Genesis. Abraham is praised for *his* hospitality to strangers and does not hesitate to share a meal with them.[14] Lot, too, is known for his hospitality and is the one who protects the angels from the violence of the citizens of Sodom and Gomorrah.[15] And the latter are destroyed by God precisely *because* of their lack of hospitality to the stranger.[16] Finally, Abraham's blessings are bestowed on him with the explicit intent that these would overflow into the nations among whom he had been called to dwell by God himself.[17]

Doing vs. Receiving

The book of Genesis, unlike the rest of the Pentateuch is also about receiving rather than doing. In the rest of the Pentateuch, the emphasis is on teaching the newly freed Hebrews how to *act* in their new reality. The Hebrews are given laws as well as cultic responsibilities that are to inform all their actions. The emphasis is there on their walk with God, their responsibilities towards God and towards each other. The book of Genesis, with its first story set in a garden, offers a very different theology. In the book of Genesis, the emphasis is on *receiving* from God, rather than *doing* for God. In the garden, the human couple *receive* from God the gift of nourishment. This is, incidentally, strikingly different from the Sumerian creation narrative which, far to the contrary, narrates that the gods created the humans for the purpose of feeding *the gods.*[18] In the Hebrew narrative, it is God who feeds human beings. In Sumer, humans are created in order to slave away and make bread and beer for the gods. This in turn sheds a powerful light on the story of the tower of Babel, or the first *ziggurat. Ziggurats* in the Ancient Near East were temples where the gods were served by human beings, offered their beer and their bread. Thus, the tower of Babel constitutes the very antithesis of the garden. There, humans give to the gods, whereas in the garden, God is seen giving to humans. Later, in the book of Genesis, we witness Abraham being again *given* what most humans toil for or achieve in their own power: land and children. These are incidentally the two things that, according to the divine decree in Genesis 3, would be marked by pain and toil! In a powerful reversal of this decree, Abraham finds himself now *receiving* these blessings without toiling for them, or even having to suffer for it (although we know that he nevertheless did).

Thus, the book of Genesis belongs on all five counts to the mother's house. Its culture, reflecting its Sumerian origins, is matriarchal. Its theology shows a non-authoritarian, creative God who seems to love our transgressions. And its emphasis is on integration versus separation, receiving versus doing. The story that we are about to explore must then be read against this matriarchal, mother's house backdrop if we are to truly make sense of it. In this story, we will focus primordially on the woman's central role. We will first explore the creation of woman as the *ezer kenegdo* (helpmeet) of man, and then we will explore the moment of her individuation at the serpent's contact, her pivotal actions, as well as to whether God's response to her actions must be read as a curse or a blessing.

The Creation of Woman

The creation of the world is written like a symphony moving steadily into a crescendo and climaxing with the creation of man (*adam)*. The astute reader will notice right away, however, the identification in our text, of man (*adam)* with the human couple: "Let us make man in our image, after our likeness. *They* shall rule the fish of the sea, the birds of the sky, the cattle, the whole earth and all the creeping things that creep on earth.... And God created *man* in His image in the image of God he created him: *male and female* he created *them*" (Gen. 1:26–27). *Adam* then is not a mere man; he englobes both man and woman. A better translation of *adam* would then be the "human," or the "earthling" as the semantic connection with *adama* (humus, or earth) indicates. And this human is two. What makes it human is precisely this duality, this relationality between two. To be human is to be two, is to be relational. Unlike Descartes who defined man as a "rational animal," the Biblical text defines man, or the human, as a "relational animal," one that is defined primordially by his/her capacity to relate to his/her gendered other. More importantly, the image of God is reflected in this duality. It is inasmuch as a man or a woman shows him/herself capable of relating to the gendered other, that the image of God is fully revealed or fulfilled in them. Moreover, both are called to rule and master the earth. Unlike Greek thought who gave to the man the sole responsibility to rule and to wield authority,[19] the Biblical narrative gives the scepter to both man and woman.

In the second story of Creation,[20] a few more pieces are added to the mosaic of the creation of the human couple. There, the *adam* (i.e. the human) is made from both clay and spirit. God shapes (*yazar*) the clay and breathes his spirit into it. At this point, the human being is still asexual, it does not yet have a gender. It is only with the creation of woman, the building (*banah)* of the woman, that the original *adam* finds himself split into "man" (*ish*) and "woman" (*isha*). Thus, the man does not precede the woman, but rather emerges simultaneously with the woman.[21] It is as though the man can only emerge as such in the presence of a woman, and vice versa, a woman can only awaken to her womanhood at the contact of a man. The man and the woman thus are created at the same time, from the same materials, and with the same spirit. This is again very much against traditional Greek thought which distinguishes the man and woman ontologically: the man's body, with its upward rising V-shape, is closer to the heavenly realm, and therefore the man is more rational; the woman's body and downward pulling hips, on the other hand, draws her closer to the earth, and therefore she is more emotional and material, as well as more vain and fickle and therefore needs the man's rule to be kept in line.[22] Not so in our story. Both the man and the woman are of clay and of spirit, and neither is made to rule over the other.

Upon emerging from the creation process, the human couple is blessed and gifted with the calling to "be fertile and increase, fill the earth and master it. Rule the fish of the sea and the birds of the sky and all the living things that creep on earth" (Gen. 1:28). They are thus given two tasks: that of procreation, of building and raising up a family, and that of ruling and subduing the world. Together. Here, there are no gender roles.[23] The woman is not relegated to the private sphere and held solely responsible for childbearing, as Greek, and later Western thought, would have it. And the man is not relegated, by the same Greek worldview, to the public sphere of ruling the world.[24] Rather, they are *both* called to *both* tasks. Both the man and the woman are called to the private realm and held responsible for childbearing and child-rearing, and both are called to the public sphere to rule the world *together.* In the second creation story, it is the *adam*, that is to say, the human being, who is placed in the garden and given the task to "work it (*avad*) and to protect it (*shamar*)" (Gen. 2:15),[25] and commanded not to eat of the tree of knowledge. Thus, it is to the human being, which implies both male and female, that these tasks and commands are given, and not merely to the man. The implication is that they are to work/serve/worship (*avad*) and to protect (*shamar*) the earth *together,* as a couple. We will see, as we progress into the narrative, however, that the woman will see her destiny crystallized into a powerful and specific calling: that of becoming the *ezer kenegdo* of the man. This unique calling needs further elaboration. Let us first go to the context preceding her creation.

In Genesis 2, right after their creation, the human is placed into the garden to begin the momentous task of tilling and tending to it. There is only one problem, one shadow cast upon this idyllic scene: the human being is alone and therefore, based on Genesis 1, is still lacking the fullness of its being. The image of God and all the creative power that comes with it, is not yet fully activated in its being. Although the whole world around the human being is deemed perfect and good (*tov*), this solitude is judged "not good" (*lo tov*) by the Creator himself. And so God does something very strange: he puts the man to sleep. The first question that arises here is why is this detail in the text? Why must man be put to sleep before God can create a partner for it? The first lesson one can distill from this interesting detail is that love comes to us by grace, when we are sleeping, without any effort on our part.[26] We cannot strive to make love come to us, or to force someone's love. Love is a gift that comes to us precisely when we have stopped all strivings, all attempts to control or master the process. All attempts to force, coerce, manipulate, and seduce others into loving us.

But there is a second lesson: In being forcefully put to sleep, the man ends up having no say in how this partner will look, how she will think or act. In other words, she is created without his input. As such, she escapes becoming a mere projection of his own ideals and fantasies. She is her own woman. But also as such, she will inevitably fail to look like his "ideal woman" and as such run the risk of being overlooked by her mate. For as long as he is still wrapped up in his narcissistic fantasies of the "perfect mate," he will not be able to recognize the woman that God made for him. He will remain in a state of confusion as to how this woman could possibly be the one for him. He will feel himself being both attracted to and repulsed by her. Only once he has opened up to a realm of possibles beyond the persona he has built for himself and the life he has projected for himself, will he be able to recognize her. Only once his false self has been broken open by pain and heartbreak, will he be able to recognize the one that comes from him. And only by surrendering himself fully to the potter's hands and resting in the knowledge that the Creator knows what he is doing, will he be able to receive the gift of the Creator with tears of joy upon awakening.

But the woman was created for far more than offering a mere solace to man. The text describes her as the *ezer kenegdo.* This is a very rare expression which merits attentive analysis. Let us turn to the first words of the description: *ezer.* Translated as "helpmeet" by most Bibles, it would seem that woman was created to somehow "help" man with his work, with his career, with his destiny. She is in a way the supporting cast in a scenario where man is the main protagonist. This translation, however, is far removed from the original and native meaning of the word *ezer* in the Hebrew Bible.[27] In the Hebrew Bible, the word *ezer* is primordially used to describe God's saving action in battle. The psalmist uses it often to describe God saving him from his enemies.[28] The word *ezer* thus has military connotations, it indicates the notion of reinforcements, or of offering cover during man's spiritual or existential battles. The woman thus is given the powerful military role of being the protector, the reinforcement in battle to the man. It is hard not to see the connection with the Sumerian goddess Inanna, who defines herself as the bodyguard of man, the "king's protector."[29]

> In battle I am your leader
> In combat I am your armor bearer
> In the assembly I am your advocate
> On the campaign I am your inspiration.[30]

But there is more, she is the ezer *kenegdo.* The word *kenegdo* is a very rare word which is composed of two words: *ke* which means "like, with" and *neged* which means "against." The woman is thus called to help the man in battle by being both "with" and "against" him. What does this mean? Let us start with *neged* (against). The idea that the woman has been called to be "against" the man, and this for *his* sake, in a redemptive way, is stunning. Especially when one is aware of the later Greek/Pauline understanding of the woman as having to submit to the man,[31] which has marked the Western world for millennia. In the Hebrew Bible, woman was, however, never called to submit to the man. She was called, on the contrary, to oppose him, to stand up to him, to stand her ground before him, to stand face to face with him—all ways of translating *neged.* The woman's redemptive power thus depends on her ability to stand up to her man when it is needed, to face him off. She was never called to be a subaltern but an equal. And it is as an equal that at times, she knows to stand her ground before him. When it is needed. When lives are at stake, including her own life and dignity. When danger is lurking. When she is in danger, when her man is in danger, when the relationship is in danger. Conflict is thus built into the dynamic of the human couple by the Creator himself. And it is only through this conflict, that the redemptive work of the *ezer* can take place. The redemption, restoration, renewal of the relationship passes through conflict. Without it, the couple is condemned to stagnation, and eventually death.

And yet, there is a way that she is to engage in conflict with her man. She is also called to be *ke* (like, with) him. The Biblical text thus qualifies the *neged* with the *ke*. The woman is called to stand her ground before the man *for* him (*ke)*, for *his* sake. She is not to fight him, but to fight *for* him and for their love. The woman is never called to fight for herself, in a self-protective stance. That is not the role of the *ezer*. The *ezer* always fights *for*. And yes, fighting for her man also means that her dignity and her life matter. But not for her sake, for *his*. She fights first and foremost for him, for who she knows that he is, deep down, for the love that she knows he could give her, for all that he could be as a man. She fights for the relationship, for their love, for the capacity to love him freely without fear of violence, without resentment for the pain he has inflicted and continues to inflict upon her. *Kenegdo* thus implies confrontation, but it is a confrontation which remains "with" the other. "I love you; I am for you and I will never leave you, but this is untenable, something has to change!" And it is the ability to hold *both* the "with" and the "against" which constitutes a woman's redeeming power. Were she to just be "with," she would remain a mere victim, a prey to his violence and his abuse. Were she to just be "against," she would opt for complete antagonism or, worse, indifference to the man whom she used to love. The key, however, is to hold both at the same time, "with" and "against." It is to stand one's ground, to oppose, sometimes even separate, while at the same time holding on to the hope that things can change. The *ezer kenegdo* is thus woman's essential work and the unique and particular way that she is to serve and protect the world around her, her *charis*. Sadly, the beautiful Eve would fail lamentably at this task, thereby engendering the ruin of not only her man, but of the whole world. We now turn to this painful moment in her history.

Eve and the Forbidden Tree

The history of interpretation of the story of the temptation and fall of woman and man has been disastrous for woman, the consensus being that woman is inherently morally weak and deficient and, therefore, predictably, she succumbs easily to the temptation. But not satisfied to fall by herself, she then uses her powers of seduction to bring the man down with her.[32] Therefore, and this interpretation is based on God's words to her later in the passage, she must be mastered and her seductive powers must fall under the control of men, to prevent her from causing their downfall again.[33] This interpretation, however, does not do justice to the Hebrew context of our passage which describes woman as the *ezer* of the man, that is, the one who is to bring his uplifting. Woman, in the Hebrew context of the preceding passages, is therefore not seen as morally weak and deficient, far to the contrary, she is the reinforcement, the strong tower that the man needs in times of trouble. Moreover, the Hebrew context of the creation of the human couple describes them as equal, meant to rule over the world together. Never is it said that one partner ought to rule over the other. Their rule is always applied to the natural world, *never* to one another.

How does one explain, then, these traditional interpretations. How did they all come to the same erroneous consensus? Simply in this: most of the early interpreters of this passage, both Jewish and Christian, emerged during the Hellenistic era and were deeply influenced by Greek thought, notably that of Aristotle. For Aristotle, women were inherently weak both physically and morally, because of their overall low energy. The man, with his higher physical energy is therefore more apt to resist temptation and therefore the stronger physical and moral partner. As such, he is more capable of leading, he has more energy to do so and will make better decisions. And the woman, because of her overall lower energy, is more naturally submissive and susceptible to be led. It is hard not to notice the parallels between traditional interpretations of this text and the philosophy of Aristotle. Clearly, these interpreters are looking at the text through a Greek lens, not a Hebrew lens. And as such, they tragically miss what is truly going on.[34]

This work offers a different lens on the passage of the "fall" of woman: a Hebrew and an Ancient Near Eastern lens. To be sure, our passage must be read in light of its Hebrew context—that is obvious. But our text needs also to be read with an attention to its broader Ancient Near Eastern context. We have already mentioned the parallels that exist between the Hebrew Bible and Sumerian literature. In this chapter we will take a closer look at some of the parallels between the story of Eve and the stories surrounding the Sumerian goddess Inanna. There are a number of interesting connections between the story of Inanna and the Huluppu tree, and our story of Eve and the tree, which we already pointed out in the preceding chapter. But there are also parallels between the "sacred marriage" thematic in Inanna's literature, and the content of the divine judgment of the snake, woman, and man in Genesis 3:14–19. It is these parallels that this section will attempt to highlight. The story of Eve, to be rightfully understood, must be approached from within its immediate Hebrew context, as well as within the larger cultural and literary context of Sumerian literature. This new lens will reveal woman to us as a splendid character rather than as a fallen creature, as well as open up a redemptive interpretation of this passage, one that highlights God's grace and redemptive power even in the most dire of circumstances. Let us then proceed to study the first part of this story: Eve's encounter with the snake.

> Now the serpent was the shrewdest
> of all the wild beasts that the Lord God had made
> He said to the woman. . .
> You are not going to die
> But God knows that as soon as you eat of it your eyes will be opened
> And you will be like divine beings
> When the woman saw that the tree was good for eating

And a delight to the eyes
And that the tree was desirable as a source of wisdom
She took of its fruit and ate
She also gave some to her husband and he ate.
(Genesis 3:1, 4–6)

The first step we need to take, before we can attempt to understand the nature of Eve's transgression and the divine judgement that ensues, is to situate this passage in its Ancient Near Eastern context, notably the story of Inanna and the Huluppu tree. In this story we learned that the tree represents fertility, and by extension, the womanhood of the goddess. As such, the tree represents the life-giving goddess who gives the king his power and wisdom. This idea is present in many ancient engravings, where the king is always depicted standing next to a tree representing the life-giving power of the goddess.[35] Thus, the tree in the earlier Sumerian context represents the fully mature goddess, her wisdom, and her life-giving powers.

In light of this, the tree in the garden of Eden represents a projection of Eve's deepest feminine desires: she desires the power, beauty, and wisdom that are contained within the tree and that she senses were always meant to be hers. And just like Inanna, her attitude towards those attributes is a grasping and controlling one: She "takes" (*laqah*) the fruit. She does not receive the fruit, but rather aggressively takes (*laqah* being a very strong word, implying forcefulness and sometimes violence).[36] We remember that Inanna's three unwanted visitors—the Anzu bird, the snake, and Lilith—also represented the powers of unbridled desire, chaos, and selfish grasping. Only by overcoming this selfish urge to take and possess what has not yet been given her, would Inanna attain true womanhood. The same might be said of Eve and it is God's command which here is meant to curb the woman's unbridled and selfish desire: "You must not eat of it" (Gen. 2:16).

This reading reveals to us a whole new meaning behind the command to not eat of the tree. Far from simply testing the obedience of the human couple, this command has a positive teaching—that of limitation. In a garden where everything is offered and available without limit, God chooses to insert limitation. But why? Perhaps because without limitation of one's powers and urges, there can be no room for another. If everything is mine, can there ever be a "yours"? A shared world implies that we limit ourselves for the sake of the other, that we curb our own desire to have it all and offer it up to the other by our side. There is thus an ethical signification to limitation. But there is more. This opening up onto the other constitutes the very definition of wisdom. Let us remember that in the Ancient Near East (and this includes Egypt), wisdom can only be acquired when one is ready to listen to an Other, when one is capable of opening up to the transcendence of another and learn from them, grow from them.[37] The limitation that marks the forbidden tree thus constitutes the very path, the very teaching and key to wisdom. What Eve sought to gain by trespassing on the tree, was at her fingertips as long as she respected the limitation imposed on her.

Tragically, Eve misses this. She misses the breach onto transcendence allowed by limitation, and falls back upon her solipsistic, solitary, and selfish self. For this is precisely Eve's problem. From the start, Eve is depicted in our text as solitary and as having no concept of the other. When she is created, she seems oblivious to the man who has just broken into song upon encountering her. As the story progresses, we never hear her talk to anyone, neither to man nor to God. Neither is she addressed. Eve, in many ways, seems to be in a solitary bubble until the serpent gets her attention, initiating the very first genuine conversation in the garden of Eden. Seeing the tree, Eve notices the power and wisdom it could give her, but she wants them for *herself,* to become a goddess,[38] to rule the world alone. Even though the man is standing right there with her,[39] she never asks for his advice or opinion but rather acts *alone,* and then, in a profoundly usurping gesture, she gives (*natan*) some of the fruit to the man. This is not about sharing, but about taking the place of God. *God* was the one who first gave *(natan)* the human couple its sustenance in the preceding chapter. Now, it is she, queen of heaven and earth, who bestows upon Adam his sustenance. She is not behaving like a good care-taking wife here, but like a goddess.

Her newly found divine powers and prerogatives, however, leave her in a profoundly solitary position. In fact, in striving for divinity and sole reign, she has lost everything. She has first and foremost lost her faithful companion whom she was meant to rule with. He is now out of the picture as an equal partner and has become one with the natural world that she is now ruling over. She has lost God, by usurping his power and taking over his prerogative as the sustainer of the world. And, even more tragically, she has lost herself, her destiny as the *ezer kenegdo* of man, her calling to love and protect her man and the world around her, and her unique gift of relational wisdom. For only by acknowledging her limits and opening up to an other (as *ezer kenegdo*) can her womanhood and wisdom awaken. Only in her ability to make room for another can her wisdom begin to surface. Not able to recognize or accept her inherent relationality, Eve chooses to individuate by herself, apart from her man, apart from relationship. She chooses self-reliance and independence from those that surround her. But self-individuation will only reveal a stunted version of herself, one that has forfeited her noble calling of protecting her man and the world around her. The deeper roots of Eve's transgression lie in her self-interested desire to rule alone, without the man, as goddess of Heaven and Earth. We are now in a position to fully understand God's judgment of her actions.

> To the woman he said
> I will make most severe your pangs in childbearing
> In pain shall you bear children
> Yet
> Your desire[40] shall be for your husband
> And he shall rule over you.
> (Genesis 3:16)

The first question that arises is: Why the reference to pain and why the reference to desire? What does that have to do with the nature of her transgression, the solipsistic desire to rule alone? Well, everything. Here, we see God doing to her exactly what Gilgamesh had to do to Inanna: he cuts her open. Just like Gilgamesh had to cut down Inanna's tree in order to carve from it her bed and her throne, God here cuts down Eve's solipsistic urge for divinity and throws her back upon her humanity. And the way he does so is to cut her open through pain and desire. The experience of pain is thus given to Eve not as a punishment, but as a means to throw her back on her humanity, her fragility, her limitedness. Pain is that which we cannot control, over which we have no power. Pain serves thus to remind Eve that she is clay, that she is limited and that she does not have power over her own body and survival. But pain is also that which will force from her lips the cry for help, thereby opening her up forcefully onto the dimension of the other who can come to her assistance. And as such, pain cracks her open onto a dimension beyond herself, onto transcendence.[41]

But she is given much more than the gift of pain, she is also given desire (*teshuqah*) for her man. It is as though God here is turning her back to her man, re-orienting her desire towards the man.[42] Unlike the woman, man, wounded as he was by the taking out of woman from him, will always naturally desire his "missing rib." Man, thus, always carries in his very flesh the memory of the woman that was once lodged there. He is thus always naturally drawn and powerfully attracted to the woman.[43] Not so the woman Eve, who, unlike the man, has no original wounding and therefore no natural desire for the man. Thus, unlike the man, the woman at this point of her evolution, still knows nothing of longing, of desire, or of love. And so God gifts her, he graces her with this powerful desire and single-minded love and devotion for the man. Little does she know at this point of her story that this loving desire (*teshuqah*) will become the very source of her power and influence on the man. For it is her loving desire which will activate her very destiny as the *ezer kenegdo* of the man. It is out of her love and desire for him that she will rise up to protect and defend him. It is this fire, which God has put within her, which will propel her to stand up for her man and fight for him. And so, what God is giving her back, in turning her back to the man, is her lost destiny as the *ezer kenegdo,* as the bodyguard and protector of the man and by extension of the world.

But what of the man's "ruling" (*mashal*) over her? What can this possibly mean? Is God here backtracking on his creation blueprint that the human couple ought to rule *together* by making one rule over the other? Or is he simply stating the inevitable that will now be woman's fate as a result of her transgression, thereby predicting the abuses of patriarchy as they would unfold in history? A deeper look at this is needed. We must now turn to the man's story.

Adam and the Lost Scepter

Traditional interpretations of the story of the fall of the human couple tend to make the man into some sort of helpless victim who was seduced by the woman to transgress the divine command. These interpretations deviate the blame onto Eve and make *her* the one responsible for the downfall of the man and the ensuing destruction of the cosmos. Eve thus has become the one who ushered death into the world and is henceforth associated with death and corruption.[44] These interpretations do a profound disservice, not only to the woman, but to the man. By depicting him as a weak, easily seduced victim of circumstance, they miss his power, his royalty, and his nobility. For the man, in our text, is anything but a gutless victim of the woman. The man, in our story, is given the features of a king. In Ancient Sumer, one of the symbolic roles given to the king of the land was that of gardener of the sacred abode of the gods, which often were cultivated as gardens meant to attract the gods into the world and offer them the comfort needed for them to want to remain and dwell among men. Adam, then, is much more than a mere tiller of the ground; he is the royal gardener of the abode of the gods, a priestly role that ensured that God would continue to dwell on the earth.[45]

But man is also given a royal role in the responsibility bestowed on him to protect the cosmic order from chaos. This responsibility is given to him, of course, at the moment of the divine command to "not eat" the fruit (Gen. 2:16). Notable is the fact that this command is given right after God's calling of the man to "work" and to "protect" the garden (Gen. 2:15).[46] The command to not eat is thus directly connected, in our text, to the calling of the man to protect and safeguard the cosmic order. This command is not a mere whim on the part of God, meant to test the man's loyalty. Such a command, in its limiting intention, mirrors the Ancient Near Eastern cosmic law: the Sumerian *me,* the Egyptian *ma'at,* the Greek *nomos,* and eventually the Hebrew *torah,* given by the gods to protect the world from the forces of chaos.[47] By receiving this command from God, man is thus given the royal task of protecting and safeguarding the cosmic order from chaos. And while it is true that he receives this command in his primal androgynous state, meaning that this command concerns both the man and the woman, it is *man* that God will eventually hold responsible for the transgression of eating the fruit, and the resulting destruction of the cosmic order: "Because *you* did what your wife said and ate of the tree about which I commanded *you* (masculine singular) '*you* (masculine singular) shall not eat of it,' cursed be the ground because of you" (Gen. 3:17).

Tragically, like his wife, the man fails lamentably at his task. For the sake of the woman he loves, he forfeits his throne, his scepter, and his royal calling as guardian of the cosmic order. He gives it all up for her. And he does so in full awareness of what he is doing. Whereas the woman was deceived by the serpent to eat of the fruit, man knew what he was doing. And as he falls, the whole world falls with him: "Cursed is the ground because of you," God informs him a few verses later. Death is thus ushered into the world not by woman, but by man, the only one of the two who transgresses with the full knowledge of what he is doing. Man has effectively given up his reign for the woman he loves. The judgment is severe:

Cursed be the ground because of you
By toil shall you eat of it
All the days of your life
Thorns and thistles shall it sprout for you…
By the sweat of your brow
Shall you get bread to eat
Until you return to the ground
For from it you were taken
For dust you are
And to dust you shall return.
(Gen. 3:17–19)

Death is the decree. But we will see that these are not God's final or only words. A look at the structure of the divine judgment as a whole (Gen. 3:14–19), addressed to the snake, the woman, and the man, reveals a profound moment of hope and redemption: Genesis 3:16b, situated in the exact middle of the text. This position in the text of Genesis 3:16 is deeply significant. In Biblical literature, the center of a given passage typically constitutes the climactic moment of the text, the heart of the text, the key to the text. In the Hebraic context, then, the ending is not the most important moment like in Western literature. The center is. The author of the text, by situating Genesis 3:16b in the center, does so, therefore, with the clear intention of shining a powerful light upon it, of highlighting it, of directing his readers back to it. This passage emerges thus from the rest of the text as qualitatively different. This is further accentuated by the author's use of the preposition *ve*, which means "yet"[48] ("yet your desire shall be for your husband"), thereby further distinguishing Genesis 3:16b from the rest of the divine judgment.

The idea that Genesis 3:16b might constitute a redemptive moment for the human couple has, however, hardly been popular. We have already seen how this passage is redemptive for the woman. The question remains, then: is it redemptive for the man also? When God arrives on the scene, man has just forfeited his throne and broken his crown, all for the sake of the woman he cannot live without. Man, by taking the fruit, has not only destroyed himself, he has destroyed the world. His kingdom lies in shambles, and his scepter is broken. And precisely at this moment when man has lost everything, God gives him a path back to royalty:

> Your desire[49] shall be for your husband
> And he shall rule over you
> (Gen. 3:16b)

The rule (*mashal*) that is mentioned here has nothing, in fact, to do with the woman. *Mashal* is a word that signifies the reign over a vast and cosmic kingdom. For example, the sun and the moon in Genesis 1:16 rule *(mashal)* over the vast expanses of the day and of the night. In later Biblical passages, *mashal* is used to refer to a king's authority over his entire kingdom.[50] Never is *mashal* used for a single individual. Moreover, having understood the meaning of *teshuqah* as signifying the woman's loving intention towards the man (and not her destructive and seductive powers over the man as tradition would have it), what use is there for man to dominate woman? If she comes to him in love, why does man still need to control or master her? In light of our translation of *teshuqah* as love, it becomes much more plausible to understand *mashal* as having to do with cosmic rule, which is precisely what man has just forfeited and lost. God in a way, is giving him back a path into his destiny as king, as protector of the cosmos.

But this time, his reign will not be conditional on him obeying a divine command, but, stunningly, will lie in his ability to engage in a reciprocal relationship with his wife. Our passage puts *teshuqah* and *mashal* in reciprocal connection: "Your desire[51] shall be for your husband *and* (as a result, in consequence) he shall rule over you" (Gen. 3:16). The rule of the man is thus relative to the love of the woman. The two concepts are interrelated. What does this mean? In order to understand what is going on here, a detour through the Ancient Near Eastern "sacred marriage" literature is needed. In "The Courtship of Inanna and Dumuzi" we discovered a powerful reciprocal connection between the goddess' love for the shepherd Dumuzi, and his authority to reign as King of Uruk. It is in his capacity to receive the love of the goddess, that Dumuzi shows himself deserving of the scepter of Uruk. It is to the degree that he embraces the goddess, receives her, loves her, that he is deemed worthy of the throne and is given the authority to reign.

Our passage, Genesis 3:16, contains the same reciprocal language and the same thematic content: We have the woman's powerful love intention (*teshuqah*) and the man's reign (*mashal*) in reciprocal relationships. Based on these parallels, one can argue that what God is doing in Genesis 3:16 is performing a "sacred marriage" ceremony—wherein the woman turns back to the man in love, and, in turn, the man is given back his lost power[52] through the woman's love for him. It is as though God were reconciling, re-marrying the couple whose bond had been shattered by the serpent, thereby giving Eve her destiny back as the *ezer kenegdo* of the man, and bestowing anew on the man his destiny as protector of the cosmic order. Thus, far from signifying the domination of the woman by the man, this passage signifies the receptivity, the opening up, the embracing of the woman by the man and, as a result, the inauguration of his reign as protector of the cosmos. It is as though man cannot reign justly or in a life-giving way until he has encountered and loved a woman.[53] And it is to the degree that he is capable of opening up to her, of receiving her, of listening to her, of *sharing* power with her, that the cosmic order will be redeemed and protected anew from chaos.

With all of this in mind, it becomes possible to offer an alternative translation of Genesis 3:16. Instead of "he shall rule *over* (*b-)* her", we can translate "he shall rule *through* her,"[54] through her love, through her presence by his side. Translating our text in this way not only aligns with its Ancient Near Eastern context but respects the divine decree in

Genesis 1 and 2, of power needing to be shared between the man and the woman. In Genesis 1 and 2, the human couple is created to rule *together*, and it is to the degree that they do so that the world is safeguarded from chaos. Far from backtracking in Genesis 3 from this decree, God in fact is consolidating it: he turns Eve towards her man and away from her solitary and solipsistic dream of ruling the world alone as "goddess," and he opens Adam to his wife, to her voice, to her wisdom, as the very modality by which he is to reign. Far from constituting a command for the man to rule alone over the woman, Genesis 3:16 is in fact reminding both partners that they ought to rule *together* and not alone. Only then can the world recover from the chaos that now permeates it, only then can it be redeemed, and only then can the curse of death be overturned into new life.

And this is precisely the first thing that Adam does with his newly found *mashal.* God has just spoken the final words of death to the broken man, he has just thrown him back onto his humanity and decreed the curse of the earth, when Adam, in a single-handed power move, in one sweep, overturns the divine decree and reverses his wife's destiny:

> The man named his wife Eve
> Because she was the mother of all the living
> (Genesis 3:20)

In doing so, the man effectively overturns the divine curse over the earth, and the death sentence it condemned him to. This is a stunning and achingly beautiful moment in the story. This man whom we had despised and who had appeared weak and cowardly in our eyes, this very man is now seen powerfully rising to his feet and standing up to the Creator of the universe, taking on the divine prerogative of speaking life into darkness. Such is the power of the man's newly found *mashal*, and the way that he finally rises to the level of the divine image that lay dormant in him. And such is the power of a woman. For it is only through her loving intention that he gathers up the courage to do and say what he did. And only through the strengthening effect of her love can the man now be seen facing off with the Creator of the universe and overturning his decree. Crowned by his woman to reign, the man in turn crowns her, empowering her to flow into the world with life-giving power. She who had ushered death into the world, has now become the very gateway for new life. By the man's royal decree, it is not only the world that is renewed, but his woman.

Such is the true meaning of *mashal:* not to exercise power *over,* but to *em*power others, to offer them the space, the support to blossom into the fullness of their being. To rule justly (*mashal)* thus means to make room, open a way for the other to find expression, to exist, to emerge. To rule means to protect, to encourage, to nurture the individuation of the other. The man's words over the woman awakens her to her true destiny, names her, redeems her, opens and awakens her true possibilities. Such is the definition of love. To see the beauty beneath the dust, the purity beneath the dirt. His love lifts her up rather than presses her down. The true king is thus the one that makes sure that all living beings in his kingdom *live,* grow, blossom, bear fruit. This is the true meaning of the title "shepherd-king." Far from using his subjects for his benefit, the shepherd-king is keenly aware that his royal role is rather to *serve* (*avad)* and to *protect* (*shamar*) the world and all that is in it and to ensure that they *live.*[55]

Conclusion

Far from constituting a story of oppression, Genesis 3:16 is in fact a story of redemption. The divine decree, far from being a mere punishment, or prediction, or judgment, offers, at the heart of the pain and darkness, a powerful moment of light: that of the restoration of the human couple. This healing of the human couple in turn holds the key to the redemption of the world. For it is to the degree that they show themselves capable of empowering each other, of loving each other, of making room for each other, in one word, of sharing the world, that the cosmic order will be safe-guarded. This is how they were always meant to rule, *together.* She by turning to him and including him in her dreams and works; he by receiving her, acknowledging her, listening to her as he enters into his own responsibilities. The stage is set for the remaining Biblical stories where we will witness precisely the difficult emergence of this delicate equilibrium and dynamic between man and woman, as well as the redemption of the world that will flow from it.

Chapter 3

Job and the Goddess of the Storm

Introduction

Tradition identifies Moses (twelfth-century BCE) as the author of the book of Job.[1] This identification of Moses with the author of the book of Job is, however, surprising given the contrast that exists between the worldview of the Pentateuch (also authored by Moses) and that of the book of Job. In the Pentateuch, the reward for righteousness is prosperity. Not so much in the book of Job—on the contrary. There, our main character, Job, finds himself the object of cruel adversity, and this, in spite of his righteousness. These differences between the two masterpieces do not pose a problem, however, in as much as Moses might have had two different target audiences in mind. The Pentateuch, whose target audience are the newly freed slaves, would thus offer more structure and moral clarity. The book of Job, on the other hand, might have targeted more spiritually mature and thoughtful audiences, and as such, offers more nuance and moral ambiguity. The apparent contradiction thus resolved, we can now proceed to situate the story in our text around 1300 B.C.E, making it one of the most ancient reflections on suffering. The question now arises as to whether the book of Job belongs to the mother's house. At first glance, the book of Job seems to belong much more adequately in the father's house with its male protagonists, and the authoritarian portrait that emerges of God in the prologue of the book. At the same time, a finer reading of the book of Job will reveal a number of feminine elements, thereby qualifying it as belonging to the mother's house canon. Let us take a closer look.

Masculine vs. Feminine

A superficial look at the book of Job seems to reveal mostly male protagonists, from Job to his friends, to God himself. A closer look, however, uncovers a number of powerful and pivotal female characters. We first have Job's wife who, we will see, is the true impulse behind Job's "conversion" from a two-dimensional, passive, and bland character to a courageous and authentic voice of revolt. A woman thus initiates the whole plot of the book. But women also conclude the book. The daughters of Job are mentioned at the very end of the book, and they are named. This is a significant clue in our text which we will not fail to explore. Women thus frame the book of Job. They are present at the beginning and at the end of Job's journey. One might even read this framing as a merism—a literary device meant to signify the presence of the feminine *throughout* Job's journey. This omnipresence of the feminine is heightened when we finally encounter God, whose traits, we will see, reveal a feminine wildness and fierceness, that we did not suspect in the usual patriarchal renderings of God.

Vertical vs. Horizontal

Interestingly, Job cultivates neither vertical nor horizontal relationships before his tragedy. Although Job shows the traits of the submissive servant, there is really no relationship to speak of between him and God. The Job of the prologue[2] seems to be robotically going through what he believes are the right motions (that will bring about divine favor) and hoping for the best. God is at best a force or energy that needs to be pacified. But there is, at that point, no genuine relationship between the two. There is also no sign of a horizontal relationship in the life of the Job of the prologue. That Job seems to be a profoundly solitary character, bearing a lot, and going through a lot alone. Job is not seen speaking to anyone, whether it is his wife, his children or his friends. The real conversations start after tragedy hits. And once they do, they do not stop: From the pivotal conversation between Job and his wife, to the stormy conversations between him and his friends, and, finally, the ultimate and stunning conversation between Job and this wild God whom he did not expect. And it is at the locus of these conversations that transformation occurs, that Job begins to shift, to change, and to journey into authenticity and deeper spirituality. The tonality is here clearly horizontal, the conversations becoming the very locus of a deeper intimacy with God.

Law vs. Wisdom

The book of Job starts out with Job playing the part of the law-abiding citizen and ends with Job crossing every line and being accused of blasphemous and inappropriate behavior with the divine. The Job of our story, once silently acquiescing to his sufferings, suddenly erupts into insolence and violent discord. Once living under the fearful all-seeing eye of God, Job now turns his own face against God, effectively putting *him* on trial. His words question the justice of God, the motives of God, the very essence of who God is. Job is seen violently pushing back on the perceived actions and decrees of God. In other words, Job becomes progressively *lawless,* to the horror of his friends who can be seen desperately trying to set him straight, back on the narrow path of obedience. Job in our story evolves from piety to rebellion, and yet this is seen as a progressive evolution in as much as it is the rebellious Job (and not the obedient one) who receives a shocking vision of God. It is at the crux of his lawlessness, of his violence, of his doubts and questions, that Job accesses true knowledge of God, and thereby becomes truly wise. Thus, wisdom has a price: That of having the *chutzpah* of questioning God and his designs. Wisdom in our story does not stem from blind obedience, but from the courageous ability to enter into conflict with God, to doubt and to question him, thereby opening up a space for revelation. The story of Job is really a story about moving from blind piety to lucid wisdom, and an invitation for us to follow in Job's footsteps should we also desire an authentic rapport with God and the people around us.

Holiness vs. Hospitality

Holiness seems to be the primary occupation of the Job of the prologue. There we see a Job obsessed with purity, begging his children to sanctify themselves after festivities, and offering up atonement for them after each festival, for fear that they might have sinned "in their thoughts" (Job 1:5). This obsession with holiness wanes as Job becomes more and more wild and angry, ultimately crossing the line of holiness, for hand-to-hand combat with God. In response, God himself erupts out of his holiness, his separateness, and engages Job in conversation. The whole book is really about the trespassing of the boundaries marked by holiness between the human and the divine, with both Job and God engaging in this trespassing behavior. What emerges from this loss of holiness, however, is shocking hospitality. God is the first to make a gesture of hospitality in his invitation to Job to step out of his narrow comfort zone and enter the wide and terrifying expanses of the world, in his beckoning of Job to leave behind his fear of life, and courageously face both the ecstasies and horrors of existence. Job too, however, becomes more hospitable. The unholy Job that emerges from bloody combat with God has a much larger heart and a much more refined sensitivity to the other, beyond his narrow field of interest and beyond his immediate family enclosure. We will see that the Job that emerges, dusty and wounded, from his combat with God, is a Job capable for the first time of hospitality, of receiving a reality, a perception, a wisdom beyond his narrow categories.

Doing vs. Receiving

In our story, Job moves from doing to becoming undone. From his anxious strivings to achieve divine favor and attracting divine providence, Job moves into a state where everything he has diligently worked, prayed, and sacrificed for, is cruelly and suddenly destroyed. All of his achievements become dust; he himself is reduced to dust as he himself acknowledges towards the end of the story (Job 42:6). And it is precisely at this moment, when all strivings for piety and favor have ceased, that Job *receives* a powerful revelation of God. It is as though he needed to come to a realization of the futility of his actions, before he could have a true vision of God and be capable of *receiving* renewed abundance and wisdom. Job first needed to be cracked open before he could receive. He needed to suffer before he could experience the grace of divine providence. The book of Job narrates this journey of Job from the father's house where actions matter, to the mother's house where the ultimate futility of our actions is unmasked, in order to make room for grace. We are now ready to go deeper into the story.

The Blameless Job

Before we begin our exploration of Job's journey, a few words are needed about the structure of the book. The author of the book of Job has chosen to divide the book into three sections: the prologue (Job 1–2), the dialogues between Job and his friends/God (Job 3–42:6), the epilogue (Job 42:7–17). We know this from the stylistic differences between the three sections: the prologue is in prose, the dialogues are in poetry, and the epilogue is in prose again. The attention of the reader is thus automatically drawn to the poetic section, away from the prose sections. The author is clearly wanting to emphasize the dialogues over the prologue/epilogue. The key to the book of Job lies thus in the dialogues section and it is from there that we ought to draw any lesson or wisdom as to who God is, and why humans suffer. The prologue serves only to set the stage, to prepare the canvas for the real action that will take place in the dialogues. As such, it offers no real theology nor wisdom—it only provides the point of departure for Job's journey. And we will see that Job will journey a long, long ways from this starting point.

As for the epilogue, it provides a very cliché and standard ending to the story, and we are barely surprised to see the righteous man reinstated. This is standard procedure in this genre of literature. There will emerge, however, cracks in this "perfect ending" pointing the reader to a possible alternative ending, one that has in fact nothing to do with the reinstatement of the righteous Job. And it is these cracks that we will explore in the epilogue. Suffice to say for now that neither the prologue nor the epilogue will provide any substantial content or wisdom. They serve only as "strawmen" that the author of the book of Job will be consistently attempting to challenge. We must, therefore, take both the prologue and the epilogue with a grain of salt, knowing that whatever is unfolding there does not constitute the real plot or real outcome of the story. Everything must be sought in the middle section of the dialogues. But before we enter the "meat" of our story, we must go back to Job's starting point as narrated in the prologue.

In the prologue, we encounter a Job still very much in the father's house. He is described by the text (Job 1:1) as *tam* (blameless) and *yashar* (upright). The word *tam* has a connotation of naïveté. Job is blameless as a young child is blameless, because he has led a hereto sheltered life, because he has not yet encountered any great temptation or seen any great iniquity. In other words, Job is blameless in a naïve sort of way. Not because he has had to surmount great temptations or fight against great odds. Simply because, in the peaceful, pastoral context that he has evolved, it is difficult not to become a nice and pleasant guy. The word *yashar* has the connotation of "straightness." Job is here depicted as someone who is straight, who is walking the line. In other words, Job is shown as someone who respects certain pre-ordained norms, who respects the law, and obeys the rules. Job is a law-abiding citizen who is keen on following the script he is given.

In the prologue Job is thus still a full-fledged resident of the father's house: A Job that keeps the rules and has respect for authority. A Job who knows to respect procedure, follow the script and walk the line. Job is thus blameless and upright, but he is not yet wise.[3] To be wise, he would have to have lived more, to have experienced more, to have rubbed shoulders with transgressors and allowed himself to be challenged by others. The Job of the prologue is still very much an insular Job, in his cocoon, respectful of authority, and careful to follow all the rules. But as such, he is a man whose true heart has not yet been revealed or tried in the furnace of affliction and difficulty. We see that on the surface he is a nice guy, but maybe he is so nice simply because of his pleasant and comfortable circumstances. Who wouldn't be nice in *those*?

This is precisely the observation of the Adversary: "Does Job not have good reason to fear God?" Shockingly, the author of our text seems to side with the Adversary in the way that he juxtaposes Job's virtue to an exhaustive, almost comical list of his possessions: "The man was blameless and upright; he feared God and shunned evil. Seven sons and three daughters were born to him; his possessions were seven thousand sheep, three thousand camels, five hundred yoke of oxen and five hundred she asses, and a very large household. The man was wealthier than anyone in the East" (Job 1:1–3). The reader of this passage cannot help but associate Job's integrity with his wealth. The author is thus tacitly signaling to his readers that the connection between the two is very much real. The Adversary has hit a nerve. It could well be that Job is virtuous because he knows that in so doing, he will attract divine providence. This in turn is very revealing as to the nature of God as perceived by the Job of the prologue

The God of the prologue is first of all a God who is a stickler for transgression. While the God of the prologue rewards virtue, he also seems to severely punish iniquity. We see this in the way that Job begs his children to sanctify themselves after their festivities, and then, rising *early in the morning*, offers himself a sacrifice of atonement for *each one* in case they might have sinned against God *in their thoughts!* (Job 1:5). We see here how diligent, meticulous, and *fearful* Job is towards this God. We also see how Job resents these festivities and the boundaries that such festivities inevitably cross. The feast always contains the potential for going too far, for crossing lines, and for, God forbid, transgression! It is in its nature to be so, to sew chaos in order, and to shake up social conventions. This liminality of the feast is precisely what Job—accustomed as he is to never crossing a line and remaining carefully entrenched in safe zones—most fears. But in his fear of transgressing and sinning, Job has knit a very narrow space for himself, one that is condemned to always remain fearful of the "big bad world" out there.

The God of the prologue is also a predictable God who responds in a foreseeable way to human actions. Thus, Job knows that if he is virtuous, he will be blessed; if he sins, he will be punished. There is, in Job's mind, a clear cause and effect relationship between his actions and God's rewards, a clear blueprint as to what the rules of the game are and how to play them. Job thus certainly feels as though he might have a grasp on "how God works" and as such, complete control over what comes his way and happens to him in the world. God is thus easily manipulated into releasing his favor as Job continues to "pull the strings" through his righteous behavior. There is thus not much difference between the God of the prologue and the pagan gods who, when properly pacified, benefit humanity.

Finally, the God of the prologue is a punitive God, one who does not hesitate to destroy a man's whole world, should that man cross him. We saw this in Job's fearfulness and anxiety for his children's potential accidental sinful thoughts, and his scurrying to appease God in sacrifice over these. But we see this also carried over in the discourses of his friends who see his demise as sure punishment by God for his iniquities. For the friends of Job, the cruel massacre of his children, the sudden and arbitrary destruction of his animals, and Job's painful and shameful skin disease, all come from the hand of God. Even Job seems to think this is so, in his appeal to God as to why he is inflicting such suffering on him. Although Job is perplexed, he does not hesitate, in the whole first segment of his journey through suffering, to ascribe such cruelty and arbitrariness to God.

Job's universe is thus a well-ordered one, where effects have causes, where one's actions matter, and where one can assert control over one's destiny and life through meticulous virtue. God, in such a universe, is little more than a force that man can come to tame and domesticate by finding the proper stance and positioning. And it is precisely such a stance that Job seeks to adopt when the first wave of suffering hits him: "The Lord has given, and the Lord has taken away; blessed be the name of the Lord" (Job 1:21). Here, Job is exercising magnificent self-control, for he knows the rules of the game. To sin here would only make things worse; to maintain integrity on the other hand, will most certainly turn God's face towards him and bring redemption. The text approves: "For all that, Job did not sin, nor did he cast reproach on God" (Job 1:22). This of course, is all about to change.

The Cursing Wife

For rather than appeasing God and bringing about redemption, Job's submission brings about a *second* wave of suffering, now much more intimate: He becomes afflicted in his very flesh with a painful and humiliating disease. It is at this point that cracks begin to appear in Job's perfect integrity. For it is not so much the nature of the suffering that breaks Job, as the unexpectedness of it. After all, Job did the right thing when hit the first time. He exercised restraint, he kept himself from sinning, and this, in a moment of profound grief and pain. And yet, rather than receiving the expected reward, relief, or even salvation, Job is hit by a second wave of tragedy even worse than the first. It is at this moment that doubt begins to creep into Job's mind as to whether he has truly been living in the "best of all worlds" where the gods bend to human resolve and where an effect always has a cause. We see this weakening of Job's moral courage in the way the text comments on it: "For all that Job *said* nothing sinful" (Job 2: 10). No more is the text saying categorically that Job did not sin, rather it now specifies that Job *said* nothing sinful. Meaning that while his mouth stayed closed, nothing can be said as to the nature of the thoughts and emotions that are starting to well up in him. Job is silent, but inside, he is volcanic. And yet, once more he remains silent.

This silence, however, is different from the first. Beneath this silence, everything is waiting to erupt, and the tension is palpable. And it is at this very moment that Job's wife arrives on the scene. Faced with her own losses, having also cruelly lost her children, her wealth, her status and her home, she looks upon this man who continues to bend in the face of tragedy. She looks upon the ruin that this man has become, her husband, that man who used to walk tall before God and man, that man who used to bear the noble traits of a disciplined and virtuous life, now deeply humiliated and broken in spirit. And she opens her mouth to speak: "Curse (*barech)* God and die!" (Job 2:9)[4] Rise! Rise up and rebel against this God whose traits are unrecognizable. For it is better to die standing than to grovel shamefully before this idol as you are doing! And Job, waiting to erupt as he already was, does so in the face of his wife: "Shameless woman!" he cries out "should we accept only good from God and not accept evil?" (Job 2:10). His words are the same as before, but the tone has changed. The anger, the resentment, the violence in his voice, betray him. She has opened something in him that he will not be able to reseal. She has awakened feelings in him he will not be able to repress again. She has set him off.[5] And so, a couple of verses later, in spite of his resolve, Job erupts.

"Afterwards Job began to speak and cursed (*yeqalel)* the day of his birth" (Job 3:1). Although the word used here for Job's cursing (*qalal*) is different from the word used by his wife exhorting him to curse (*barech)* God, the idea is the same. Job's cursing is a response to his wife's exhorting him to curse God. The intention of the text is clear: It is his wife who has awakened this cursing in him, who has released this rage in him. She is the one who sets Job on a radically different course than the one he was engaged on. She is the one who opens before him a field of new possibles, a door onto a new reality, and a path towards transformation. For the Job that will emerge from this journey will be unrecognizable.

The first thing that we notice about this new Job is his emotionality. Whereas the Job of the prologue is known for his composure—and this in spite of the obvious anxiety and tension that we can sense in all of his actions—the Job of the dialogues cannot seem to be able to suppress his anxiety, his anger, and his despair: "I will give voice to the anguish of my spirit" (Job 7:11), he says. "Let there be no resting place for my outcry" (Job 16:18), he exclaims. Over and over again, Job gives himself the freedom to *express* what he had hereto covered up in his heart. He gives himself the freedom to *feel*, unabashedly and inappropriately. Inappropriately for, in the eyes of his friends, such feelings should not arise in the true believer's heart. The true believer, for the friends of Job, is one who serenely rests in his assurance that he is right with God. And when calamity strikes, he continues to rest in the assurance that God will save him and provide for him. Anguish becomes thus a sign of lack of faith, and therefore a sin. And the expression of this anguish becomes a stumbling block for those already struggling with their own vacillating faith.

But Job does not calm down. Everything he knows about the world lies in ruins. The rules of the game are not respected. God—who prescribed the rules, and the blessings/curses attached to them—seems to be cheating at his own game. God is no more playing by the rules! He is not keeping his side of the bargain, of the covenant. Heartbroken, Job is reeling in confusion: "Why do you not pardon my transgression?" (Job 7:21) he asks, in a desperate last attempt to figure out why this is happening to him, and how to straighten himself up and regain divine favor. His honest, heart-rending questions soon escalate however into raging confusion: "What is Shaddai that we should serve him? What will we gain by praying to him?" (Job 21:15). Job here is beginning to realize that God was not who he thought he was. His representation and conceptualization of God shattered, he begins to wonder who this God is and why he should even serve him. His friends, of course, are appalled. What is man that he might question God as Job is doing? And with what insolence he objects to serving a God who does not serve him anymore!

As Job's pain and rage escalates, he begins to cross a hard line by challenging God's very nature: His justice. "Man cannot win a suit against God" (Job 9:32), in other words, God is an arbitrary judge who does what he wants without any concern for justice. Worse, this God whom everyone thought was benevolent, is beginning to look more and more like his own nemesis, like the Adversary himself: "He destroys the blameless and the guilty" (Job 9:22), "he mocks as the innocent falls" (Job 9:23), and finally, the climax: "The earth is handed over to the wicked one" (Job 9:24). Job is here identifying God with the wicked one. It is as though Job is finally perceiving the true colors of God, his true face, that beneath a veneer of benevolence hides a cruel and arbitrary deity. His transgressive and blasphemous words are strongly refuted by his friends who warn him to turn from this path of no return: "Would you condemn the just and mighty one, would you call a king a scoundrel?" (Job 34:17–18).

As Job enters ever deeper into his pain, it is not only his world that lies in ruin, but the God that he once feared and worshiped. This God whom he once saw as the source of his life, the Creator God, now has become the source of his undoing: "Your hands shaped and fashioned me, then destroyed every part of me" (Job 10:8). This God whom he once saw as the guarantee of justice being wrought on the earth, as the Judge of the world, now has become identified with injustice, arbitrariness, and gratuitous cruelty. This God that had fathered him, protected him, provided for him, gone! The God of the father's house—the protective, just, authoritative God—has been smashed to pieces by Job's unspeakable pain. As Job becomes undone, so does his concept of God. Yet, out of this undoing of his self and of his concept of the Father-God will come a powerful revelation: the wild, untamable, yet life-giving God of the mother's house.

This vision of God, however, could not emerge as long as Job lived his life disconnected from his emotions, as long as the cultivation of his persona took precedence over the expression of his true self. Such a vision could not arise in a man who felt he already knew everything there was to know about God, who felt that his concept of God was adequate and needed no further elucidation. Finally, such a vision could not be understood by a man who had never suffered, never questioned, never doubted, never transgressed the dividing line between humanity and God. Only when Job's false self and persona had been broken open by pain, and his emotions had surfaced, was he ready for an authentic encounter with the divine. Only when his questions had challenged and destroyed his idolatrous conceptualization of God, could new revelation be given. Job had to become empty of his certainties, to be filled anew with truth. Finally, only when Job—propelled by his wife to do so—through sheer rage and despair, had found the guts to stand before God, as an equal partner, challenging him and refuting the status quo, was he worthy of receiving a deeper revelation of God's nature. For it is only by wrestling with God that intimacy with God can be achieved, only by grappling with the divine mystery that an invitation into the sacred inner sanctum of God will be given. And it is to this powerful mother's house revelation of God that we now turn, in what follows.

The Goddess in the Storm

The encounter of God in a storm is significant. We are not here in the ordered house of the father, where the law rules supreme ensuring that the forces of chaos are mastered, and where we have control over the direction that our lives take through choices and actions. Rather, the storm is clearly meant to introduce the element of chaos, of unpredictability and of loss of control in our story.[6] The storm is also cruelly destructive, yet at the same time, it is restorative and life-giving. The author thus warns us that the powerful vision Job is about to have will not line up with the father's house God, the God of order, of mastery, and of discipline. The storm announces a very different vision of God, one that has much more to do with chaos, wildness, and unpredictability. The vision that Job is about to have is also unusual in that it is sourced in the natural world. There is no law here, no temple, no ordinances, no rituals, and no sacrifices. All we have is wild, untamable nature, and the savage creatures that inhabit it. All we have are deep oceans, infinite expanses, and unbreachable mountains. Job in such a world is vulnerable, exposed, lost, used to as he is, to his comfort zone, safe spaces and predictable outcomes. And yet, it is precisely in this wild and savage natural world that he will receive his most profound revelation of the mother's house God—the Mother Goddess.

This Mother Goddess will differ profoundly from the Father God. While the God of the father's house focuses primordially on sin and transgression, and establishes the narrow and rigid boundaries of what a man ought and ought not to do, the Mother Goddess has a whole other agenda: Her invitation to Job is to precisely step over those limits, those "fences around the torah" and enter the vast expanse of creation: "Where were you when I laid the earth's foundations" (Job 38:4), "have you ever commanded the day to break, assigned the dawn its place" (Job 38:12), "have you penetrated to the sources of the sea, or walked in the recesses of the deep, have the gates of death been disclosed to you, have you seen the gates of deep darkness, have you surveyed the expanses of the earth" (Job 38:16–18), "which path leads to where light dwells, and where is the place of darkness" (Job 38:19), "have you penetrated the vaults of snow, seen the vaults of hail" (Job 38: 22), "can you tie cords to Pleiades or undo the reigns of Orion?" (Job 38:31). It is as though the Mother Goddess were calling Job out of the narrow spaces of his piety, of his fear of sinning into the vastness and expansiveness of the created world.

But why do so? Why incite the man away from his virtue? Perhaps because she is sensing that his fear of sinning is really a fear of life itself, of its unpredictability and of its wild, uncontrollable flow. Perhaps because she intuits that Job is much more about control than about virtue. That his virtue has become a tool for him to control life, to keep it on leash to his narrow agendas and expectations. Perhaps because she senses that the self-made prison that Job has constructed for himself with his blamelessness, can only be shattered by transgression, by revolt, and by blasphemy. And because she would rather her creature be alive and transgressive than dead and blameless; she recklessly invites him out of this narrow space into the wild and terrifying expanse of the world. It is as though she were reassuring Job: Stop being so afraid!

Stop being so afraid of life, of living, of feeling, of suffering, of making mistakes, of transgressing, lest you never truly live!

The Mother Goddess also differs from the Father God in her unpredictability. While the God of the father's house has clear expectations and offers clear rewards, the Mother Goddess functions very differently. Faced with the human being's natural desire to control and manipulate the divine, the Mother Goddess refuses any attempt to coerce her into catering to her creatures. Her wildness and untameableness are mirrored in the powerful animals featured in her poetic words: "Would the wild ox agree to serve you? Would he spend the night at your crib? Can you hold the wild ox by ropes to the furrow? Would he plow up the valleys behind you? Would you rely on his great strength and leave your toil to him?" (Job 39:9–11) "Take now behemoth, whom I made as I did you…Can he be taken by his eyes? Can his nose by pierced by hooks? Can you draw out Leviathan by a fishhook? Can you press down his tongue by a rope?...Will he plead with you at length? Will he speak soft words to you? Will he make an agreement with you to be taken as our lifelong slave? Will you play with him like a bird? And tie him down for your girls…lay a hand on him and you will never think of battle again?" (Job 40:15, 24–32). Like her creatures, the Mother Goddess will not allow herself to be taken captive by man's narrow agendas. She is her own Goddess, impossible to manipulate or coerce, refuting all attempts by her creatures to dominate her.

But who can worship such a Goddess? How is she any different from the unpredictable and arbitrary gods of Antiquity worshipped by the Sumerians, Babylonians, Egyptians, and Greeks? She is different because, as Mother, she cares for her creatures. But her love, unlike the Father's *rachamim,* infinite compassionate love, is tough love. Where the Father God is cautious, the Mother Goddess is reckless, inviting her creatures to not fear life, to not fear suffering, to not fear contamination and to not fear death, but rather to engage with it, to penetrate it fearlessly. For it is only at the price of truly entering life that one can boast of a life well lived. Where the Father God is protective, the

Mother Goddess is transgressive. She knows that she must wean her young, expose them to the extremes of existence, the ecstasy and the horror, if they are to grow strong and wise. She does not merely coddle, but also challenges. She does not merely strengthen but also destroys. For she knows that her children sometimes need to be broken in order to be rebuilt. Like the potter, she does not hesitate to break the pot in order to fashion a new one in its stead. She is fierce yet loving. She is wild, yet compassionate. She provokes, she undoes, she expulses, she instigates, she breaks, and she tears open.

Finally, the Mother Goddess differs from the Father God in her ultimate vision for her creatures. Whereas the God of the father's house repeatedly warns of death and of death-inducing behavior, the Mother Goddess's focus is on life. What matters to the Mother Goddess is not so much virtue, blamelessness or integrity, as life. What matters to her is for her children to *live,* and to live full, abundant lives unstunted by the straight jacket of a morality which merely seeks to avoid or control life rather than experience it. While her actions can be fierce, leading to the undoing of her creatures, her goal is always life-giving. She breaks in order to rebuild, she pierces in order to heal, she undoes in order to rebirth. This trait is evident in our text through the overwhelming references to birth and to female animals giving birth:[7] "Do you know the season when the mountain goats give birth? Can you mark the time when the hinds calve? Can you count the months they must complete? Do you know the season they give birth, when they crouch to bring forth their offspring, to deliver their young? Their young are healthy, they grow up in the open. They leave and return no more" (Job 39:1–4), "the wing of the ostrich beats joyously, and her pinions and plumage like the stork's. She leaves her eggs on the ground, letting them warm in the dirt, forgetting they may be crushed underfoot, or trampled by a wild beast" (Job 39:13–15), "does the eagle soar at your command, building his nest high…his young gulp blood, where the slain are there, he is" (Job 39: 27–30).

The Mother Goddess knows, however, that birth passes through excruciating pain that at times feels like death. She knows that, without pain and suffering, her children will never be fully birthed into the wildness and fullness of their lives. Likewise, Job must make this journey through pain and despair if he is to grow into all that he was meant to be. The suffering and pain that Job is going through are really the birth-pangs of the Mother Goddess, struggling to birth him, writhing to expel him into a life of authenticity, of spiritual maturity, and of compassion. Job moves into the moment of his death, as any unborn child does as it nears the birth canal, only to be expulsed into a resurrected life. And it is to this new life that the suffering has graced Job with that we now turn in the epilogue.

The Beautiful Daughters

We are now leaving behind the poetic sections featuring the transformative journey of Job, as well as the numinous revelations that he received, and re-enter the prose of the epilogue. Through this stylistic shift, the author is indicating a shift in the discourse, from the extraordinary, unexpected narrative line of the dialogues back to the conventionality and orthodoxy of the epilogue. The epilogue, to be honest, is somewhat disappointing at best, anti-climactic at worse. Here we fall back into the comfortable thought patterns of the prologue where the righteous are rewarded and wicked punished. We see a Job rewarded for all that he suffered, and his "evil" friends punished. And we see the same comically long list of possessions: "Thus the Lord blessed the latter years of Job's life more than the former. He had fourteen thousand sheep, six thousand camels, one thousand yoke of oxen, and one thousand she-asses. He also had seven sons and three daughters" (Job 42:12–13). In other words, we are back to square one: to the Job whose virtue rewards him and to the God who predictably blesses the righteous. Nothing is said of Job's profound transformation and powerful encounter with the Mother Goddess. Nothing is said of his wife. It is as though nothing happened. Everything is the same, nothing has changed. Except…

The daughters of Job are named, their beauty is noted, and they are given estates along with their brothers. These three little details are the cracks in the system, and the evidence that something *has* changed. And as such, the daughters of Job open up a new horizon of meaning and point the reader to a very different ending than the more overt one where Job receives all his possessions back. They are the clue, implanted by the author into the text, to orient our eyes to an alternative denouement, perhaps more genuine than the one that we are used to hearing about. For the three little details mentioned about the daughters of Job, when explored, are profoundly revelatory of all what Job has been through, his entire journey through the dark night of suffering, and the man that emerged from it. It is as though these last few lines about the daughters of Job contain the whole trajectory of Job. They tell us more about who Job has become than the entire book. Let us then turn to these three little details.

The first thing that we learn about the three daughters of Job is that they have names. Now this is interesting inasmuch as, in the Biblical context, women are rarely named. If one reads through a typical Biblical genealogy, one finds mostly male names, with the occasional exception. Here we have a reversal of this in that the male sons are not named, only the daughters are. This reversal is very interesting and is deeply revelatory of whom Job has become. But first, we must explore the significance of naming in the Biblical tradition. A name is always a destiny, usually bestowed by God, or by a family member. Thus, Adam names Eve, reversing thereby her destiny. God changes people's names in order to operate a shift in their life-journey and fate. To have a name, then, is to have a destiny, a calling beyond merely existing. When Job names his daughters, he is effectively saying: these will have a destiny of their own, a calling beyond their being mere daughters, wives, and mothers. They will have a role to play in this world, they will have a say in the direction of the tribe, they will have an influence on where history flows, they will be, like their mother, pivotal figures in the lives of the people around them, and in their community. In other words, Job is giving his daughters leadership roles in the tribe. They will be more than mere women; they will be matriarchs called to rule *together* with their husbands.

But more than this, they will be beautiful. What does this mean? What does beauty signify in the Hebrew Bible? Three other women are described as beautiful in the immediate context of the book of Job: Sarah, Rebekah, and Rachel. Beauty is thus not about mere attractiveness, but about matriarchal power. The three daughters of Job echo the three matriarchs in their becoming, like them, influential forces in their community or tribe. They are called to become, like Sarah, voices of wisdom and insight;[8] like Rebekah, women of compassion, prophetic insight, and of bold action;[9] like Rachel, women capable of inspiring their men to become the highest versions of themselves.[10] In other words, beauty is a code word for feminine power and wisdom. Beauty is a sign that one is dealing with much more than a mere, insignificant woman. One is dealing with an *ezer kenegdo.*

Finally, the three daughters are given an estate among their brothers. It is hard not to remember here the story of the daughters of Zelophehad—also narrated by Moses in the Pentateuch.[11] These women who found themselves unmarried and therefore without resources, asked Moses to overturn the patriarchal law which only allowed males to inherit their father's estates. These courageous women single-handedly defied patriarchy and challenged divine law. And God approves! The law ends up being re-written in their favor, setting a Biblical precedent for the women's liberation movement that would emerge centuries later. Likewise, the three daughters of Job are to become symbols of this emancipation of women from the straight jacket of patriarchy. By giving them estates among their brothers, their father sets them free upon the path of emancipation from patriarchy and allows them a life of freedom, and independent from male oversight.

But much more than giving a description of Job's daughters, these three details—names, beauty, and estates—reveal what has become of Job. The Job of the epilogue is completely different than the Job of the prologue. The Job of the prologue was the law-abiding citizen, walking the line, and following the script. Now, all of a sudden, with these powerful daughters, we enter uncharted territory. As Job is freed from his own narrow-minded and dogmatic beliefs, he is able to free others from them too, and usher in a new era—unscripted, revolutionary, and liberating. Job has now become a rebel with a cause, capable of breaking free from the limiting beliefs of his time, from the patriarchal system that he was born and raised in. His journey has broken him open, enlarged his heart and mind, so that he is now able to see what history has erased and hear what culture has muted: the women in his life. The Job of the epilogue is a Job that sees and hears. He is no more the self-absorbed Job captive of his fears and anxieties. The Job of the epilogue is open onto the world, sensitive to what is going on, and capable of opening up new breathing spaces of life and freedom for the captives of patriarchy. The Job of the epilogue is redemptive, supportive, and protective of the forgotten of history. No more obsessed with his belongings and with consolidating his place in the world—like the farmer in Inanna's stories—he now turns his face to making the world open and livable *for others.* He has become the shepherd-King.

Conclusion

The book of Job is saturated with women. We first meet Job's wife, the instigator, the one responsible for propelling him onto his journey into the crucible of suffering and transformation. Second, we have the shattering encounter with the Mother Goddess who undoes Job only to birth him anew, wounded, but a new man. Finally, we meet Job's daughters, to whom he has given back their lost and forgotten throne, their destiny as leaders of the tribe and rulers of the world alongside their men. And as Job moves from one feminine encounter to the other, he changes, he morphs into a man that is unrecognizable. From his wife, he receives the permission to be himself, to be authentic with God, even if this means shattering the sacred limits and boundaries. From the Mother Goddess he receives the freedom and courage to enter the circle of life, to make mistakes, and to experience the painful throes of rebirth. And to his daughters he grants a passport into a world hereto ruled by men, thereby freeing them from the rigid and narrow shackles of patriarchy and bestowing upon them a renewed royal destiny to rule *with* the men in their lives.

Chapter 4

Ruth or The Oasis of Love

Introduction

Tradition recognizes the prophet Samuel (tenth-century BCE) as the author of the book of Ruth, along with the books of Judges and the books of Samuel.[1] The book is set during the time of the Judges,[2] an era characterized by violent conflict between Israel and its neighbors, as well as troubling unrest within its own borders.[3] The book of Ruth emerges from these violent and xenophobic times as an oasis in the desert,[4] and this in more ways than one. In contrast to the political climate of the book of Judges, which encourages violence towards, and even the extermination of, the surrounding nations and/or the separation from them, the book of Ruth is thus an ode to peace and hospitality. As such, this book might have been written as a polemic against the pervasive xenophobia and hostility to the surrounding nations that characterized the times of the Judges.[5] It is also, shockingly, a testament to the socio-political renewal and revival that can happen when hospitality towards the other is honored. This attitude towards the other, as well as the centrality of strong female characters throughout the narrative of Ruth, invites us to think of this book as belonging to the canon of the mother's house. Let us take a closer look.

Masculine vs. Feminine

The book of Ruth opens with powerful female protagonists. Next to them, the men fade into insignificance. Noami's husband quickly disappears from the picture through premature death, and her sons,

Mahlon (whose name alludes to "sickness"), and Chillion (whose name alludes to "annihilation),[6] also die quickly in the narrative. We are thus left with three powerful female characters early in the story: Naomi, Ruth and Orpah. And out of these, Ruth quickly immerges as the lead character. This is shocking inasmuch as Ruth (with the exception of Orpah who quickly fades out of the story) is the only character who is not of Hebrew descent. Worse, she is from the nation of Moab, from whom the Hebrews have been commanded to radically separate themselves. Even more stunning is the connection our text intentionally makes between Ruth and the divine attribute of *hesed* (gracious love), otherwise used to describe God in the Hebrew Bible.[7] Yet, in the book of Ruth, it is used to describe Ruth in two out of its four occurrences,[8] the other two occurrences being ascribed to God himself.[9] Our author thus seems to be drawing a clear connection between Ruth and God himself. Ruth, as such, becomes a striking embodiment of the divine love and divine character, a very figure of the divine feminine.

Vertical vs. Horizontal

In the book of Ruth, God is conspicuously absent—until the very end where he suddenly appears at the moment of Ruth's conceiving. Instead, the book of Ruth pivots around the notion of chance, *bemiqreh* (2:3), which literally means "happenstance", or "it so happened that…," or "as luck would have it." The entire story of Ruth thus seems oriented by sheer luck or chance. It will be shown, later, that behind this luck and chance hides the invisible hand of God. The hidden work of God remains relative, however, to the movements of the characters of the story. As they move, God himself moves. In fact, in the book of Ruth, it very much seems like God's attributes are not expressed, except as they are embodied by its characters. Thus, Ruth expresses the divine attribute of *hesed*, or gracious love, while Boaz will express, in response, the divine attribute of *goel*, protective and redemptive power.[10] Thus, God is not somewhere in the heavens determining human destiny, but rather moves "between" the characters of the story. He is revealed and present through them, through their decisions and actions.[11] God's power thus finds itself channeled and expressed through the protagonists' actions.[12] God is implicitly present in our story as embodied by the characters of the story. He only explicitly appears at the end of the story, to help Ruth conceive, at the term of a long chain of human actions and decisions, and as a response to human activity.

Law vs. Wisdom

The book of Ruth breaks one of the most adamant and direct prohibitions of God concerning Israel's relationship with Moab: "No Moabite will be admitted into the congregation of the Lord because they did not meet you with food and water" (Deut. 23:4–7). This command is given on the borders of the promised land, after the despicable incident of the nation of Moab breaking the sacred laws of hospitality, prescribed to inhabitants of the desert from time immemorial. To add to the shame of Moab is the story of its origins: the book of Genesis narrates that the people of Moab were the product of an incestuous relationship between Lot and his daughter. This story thus sheds a deeply pejorative light on Moab, notably its founding mother. The moral depravity of Moabite women is further confirmed in the sending of the women of Moab to the sons of Israel to perversely seduce them during the time of the conquest of Canaan, thereby distracting them from their warmongering. Moabite women thus truly have a sordid reputation. The book of Ruth, however, performs a profound reversal of the Moabite lack of hospitality, first with Naomi's family escaping the famine in Bethlehem and receiving hospitality from Moab, and second, with Boaz offering food and water to Ruth the Moabite. Both Moab and Israel thus are shown being hospitable to the other, with the Moabite hospitality being exacerbated by Ruth's promise to care for her aging and vulnerable mother-in-law. The story of Ruth thus constitutes a powerful annulment of the divine decree against Moab. The book of Ruth also reverses the negative stereotypes given to Moabite women as perverse and seductive, for here we have the woman Ruth, described as a "woman of valor" (*eshet chayil)* throughout our story. We thus find not only the divine law but negative stereotypes being overturned in the book of Ruth, and all for the sake of love. It is as if there were a deeper principle at work in the book of Ruth, deeper than any divine decree: the principle of *hesed*, constituting the very essence of the divine. The book of Ruth thus teaches us that love has precedence over law, and that relationships are more important than the scrupulous keeping of that law.[13] Why? Because love is the very substance of the law,[14] its very heart and *raison d'être.* If there is love, true love, love in the way that it is expressed in the book of Ruth, then there is no more need of the law.[15]

Holiness vs. Hospitality

As mentioned before, the book of Ruth is essentially a book about hospitality. It is interesting, however, to note that Ruth, although welcomed into the land of Israel, continues to be referred to as "Ruth the Moabite" (Ruth 1:22; 2:2; 2:6; 2:21; 4:5; 4:10). The text emphasizes her foreignness, her strangeness, and the fact that she is never fully integrated into the social fiber of Israel until her marriage to Boaz. She remains an outsider until the very end of the story. One wonders why the author chose to highlight Ruth's otherness so starkly. Perhaps to show that it is precisely as other, as an unassimilated foreigner, that Ruth was able to so potently revive not only her mother-in-law's destiny, but that of the whole lineage of King David. Perhaps to emphasize the fact that there can be no true revival, no genuine fecundity or fruitfulness, without a drastic and unforgettable encounter with the other. We thus witness, in our story, the powerful rejuvenating and fecundating effect of the encounter between the self and the other. This is in line with Biblical thought, by the way, inasmuch as the movement, in Biblical stories, is always a movement onto otherness. Abraham, who in many ways is mirrored by Ruth in our story, is also called to transcend his own national and familial identity and embark in a journey towards self-transcendence. And it is to the degree that he is able to transcend himself towards this otherness that he becomes fruitful, and that the nations who welcome him end up becoming blessed. Ruth in many ways is a figure of Abraham[16]—except that it is *she*, the Moabite, who now brings blessings to the Israelite community in the midst of which she finds herself.

Doing vs. Receiving

It is interesting that Ruth's name comes from the verb "to saturate with water" (*ravah*).[17] The name Ruth is in fact the passive form of that verb and means "well-watered" (*rout*). We have an interesting occurrence of *ravah* in the book of Jeremiah where there is an allusion to the restoration of Israel, and their being made by God into a well-watered garden: "They shall come and shout joy on the heights of Zion, radiant over the bounty of the Lord—over new grain and wine and oil, and over sheep and cattle. They shall fare like a well-watered (*raveh)* garden, they shall never languish again" (Jer. 31:12). Thus, the name of Ruth, "well-watered," has the connotation of rains, abundance, fertility, and harvest. Ironically, the book of Ruth does not start on this note of abundance and fertility, but rather speaks of drought, famine, death, and infertility. And Ruth, in the beginning of our story, hardly lives up to her name. She is barren, surrounded by death, and the land is struck by famine. And yet, at the moment where everything seemed to be over, and where our story seemed to have reached a dead end, we have a powerful shift in the story, a shift brought about by Ruth herself. It is she who turns the tide of the story and it is she who brings about a new beginning. The question is, how? What is the secret to her eventually moving from drought to harvest, from barrenness to becoming one of the matriarchs of King David? Does her secret lie in her *doing* or in her *receiving*? This is what we will now turn to discover.

The Courage to Love

We do not know much about Ruth until the time comes for Naomi to go back to Bethlehem, and part with her two daughters in law. It is at that moment that Ruth emerges from the shadows, in an act of courageous and reckless sacrificial love: she chooses to go back with Naomi to Bethlehem. Let us measure the magnitude of this decision. When Naomi decides to leave, Ruth has a choice. She, who has known only death and barrenness, she who has come to a dead end in her life, could go back home to Moab, get re-married, and perhaps even have children. In other words, she could get her life back, she could start over and still fulfill her feminine destiny as a wife and mother. The temptation is powerful, and Orpah ends up succumbing to it. But Ruth knows that if she leaves Naomi, her mother-in-law will die resourceless. In Biblical times, a widow with no children had no dignified chance of survival. Who would take care of her? Ruth knows that, back in Bethlehem, Naomi would end up begging for bread every day, live in shameful and dire poverty and eventually die a miserable death alone. And so, Ruth sacrifices her own chance at a new beginning for the sake of Naomi being granted a dignified ending.[18] She turns from her own happiness and offers it up for the sake of Naomi's survival. Out of her own poverty, she gives the little she has left to Naomi, her companionship, her support. She chooses a life of hard work, of poverty over the life of ease that she might have led back in her father's house in Moab. In other word, she offers up herself.

And it is precisely at this moment, when Ruth seems to have sealed her painful destiny and stoically chosen to make Bethlehem her new home, that something interesting happens. *Vayiqer miqreh*, "It so happened," or "as luck would have it," (2:3) Ruth, in her desperate attempt to glean barley from the fields of Bethlehem to sustain herself and her mother-in-law, finds herself in the fields of Boaz. Ruth does not know yet who Boaz is, but we do. The writer had already informed us, in passing, that Naomi had a kinsman by the name of Boaz (2:1). And so, Ruth, by sheer chance, stumbles upon this kinsman's fields. In the darkest night of these two women, a shy new dawn, a trembling glimmer of hope seems to be emerging. But more needs to be said about the expression *vayiqer miqreh.* We find a similar wording of this expression in the book of Genesis, notably in the story of the encounter between Eliezer and Rebekah, when the former prays to God: "Let it happen (*heqreh*) to me[19] this day and deal graciously with my master Abraham" (Gen. 24:12). In the context of Genesis, God is clearly behind the "happenstance" that Eliezer is praying for. The book of Ruth might also be read as such: that although God remains in the shadows, and that everything seems to occur by "happenstance" or luck, the course of events is in fact the result of the invisible hand of God at work. The subject of *vayiqer miqreh* might thus be understood as God himself.[20]

But the question arises as to what makes God move *now*? For so long, Naomi, Ruth, and Orpah have lived without divine intervention and blessing: from drought, to barrenness, to the premature death of all of the men in their lives. These women have lived for so long without support, protection or love. Why does God arise at *this* particular moment? Perhaps because "deep calls to deep" (Psalm 42:7). Perhaps because, at last, out of the brokenness and dead-end lives of these women, rises, like a rose from the concrete,[21] a gesture worthy of God, a choice profoundly aligned with the divine nature, perfectly in tune with God's own *hesed.* And as such, a gesture and a choice capable of powerfully magnetizing divine providence and divine presence. Thus, Ruth's sacrificial actions have the powerful effect of drawing God near. Her choice has the effect, like a sacrifice (*qorban*), to bring God close (*qarav*).[22] There is no temple here, no altar, no priest. Only a broken life offered up completely to another. Such a sacrifice pierces the heavens and powerfully pulls God down into the humble and wretched lives of the two women. And so, *vayiqer mikreh* Ruth finds herself in the fields of her future husband, unbeknownst to herself.

It is, then, to the degree Ruth chose love, aligned herself with love, that she ended up attracting love. It is inasmuch as she gave herself up for another, that she received all of her life back in overflowing abundance; and it is to the degree that she poured herself out, that she was filled, saturated, well-watered, as her beautiful name, Ruth, indicates. We learn here a profound metaphysical law: that it is in giving that one receives, in pouring that one is filled, in releasing one's grasp that one receives everything back. As Ruth empties herself, she becomes a vessel for divine abundance, a vessel that becomes so full, so saturated, that it overflows into the community that welcomed her in a profoundly life-giving way. As she sacrifices herself, she is reborn and with her everyone around her. The story of Ruth teaches us that the choice to love sacrificially, far from leading to the dead-end of victimhood, contains resurrection power. When we choose to love, even when it is difficult, even when it is painful and seems to spell the end of us, such a love is powerful, and has a powerful impact on our relationships and the world around us. This is why Ruth is called an *eshet chayil*, a "strong woman"[23] (3:11). The expression *eshet chayil* is typically translated as "virtuous woman,"[24] but the word *chayil* actually has nothing to do with virtue but has powerful military connotations. From it is built the word *chayal* which means soldier.[25] Ruth is thus described in military terms as a "strong woman," a woman who has what it takes to battle and to win, who is capable of reckless courage and determination.

Far from being a victim of circumstance, Ruth, by *choosing* to love sacrificially, is in fact a conqueror, a victor. For it takes tremendous courage, grit, and determination to love in this way. The path of sacrificial love is not for the weak at heart. It takes a truly strong woman to love in this way. And when she does love in this way, she unleashes and generates a life-giving power that has the capacity to transform everything around her. For love, in the Hebrew Bible, is not a feeling, it is a force. It is a force that can transform drought into harvest, death into life, barrenness into fruitfulness.[26] There is thus no fear to be had of missing our destiny, of giving up our lives, our dreams, our aspirations, when we choose to love sacrificially. For it is precisely when we love in this way that we find our truest destiny and our most authentic lives.

It is precisely when we love in this way that healing and new beginnings are made possible, and our wildest dreams and deepest aspirations can become manifest.

The Seduction of Boaz

Having stumbled into the promise of love, Ruth must now begin the delicate task of cultivating this love, that it might see the light of day, that it might become a reality. But for her life to change, she herself has to change. For the catalyst for outward change is always inner change. She must leave behind the old Ruth, the calloused and hardworking Ruth, and become soft and available. She must leave behind her role as caretaker, to become bride and beloved. She must interrupt her doing and learn to receive. This is probably harder for Ruth than anything she has ever done. For to open oneself up to receive is much harder than to give. When giving, one is still in control, one is still master of one's own life, no matter how hard that life is. But to open up to another that we might be given unto, is an act of stunning vulnerability. It is an opening up of the heart, an entrusting of one's heart, of one's deepest desires, into the knotted and clumsy hands of another. There is nothing harder for a woman to do than this. Especially if her heart has already been broken once at the hands of another.

And so, the harvest being over, Ruth is told to "bathe, anoint, and dress" herself (3:3) and go down to the harvest festivities and lie down next to Boaz. We have here the three elements of the sacred marriage trope encountered in the story of Inanna. Inanna also, as she began her transition from maiden to queen, was told to bathe, anoint, and dress. These three actions thus mark a pivotal moment in a woman's life, as she transitions from her old self to her new self, from maiden to queen, and in the case of Ruth, from poverty to riches, from barrenness to fruitfulness, from death to life.[27] But there is more. Ruth is also told to "uncover [Boaz's] feet" (3:4). What does this mean? Parallel passages containing the same expression have a clear sexual connotation with "feet" alluding to the "genitals."[28] Ruth is thus asked to uncover Boaz's genitals. The act of "uncovering" furthermore alludes to forbidden sex in other passages.[29] Is Naomi here instructing Ruth to have illicit sex with Boaz, in order to trap him into marriage? Or is she rather instructing Ruth to reveal, to disclose, to uncover Boaz's true feelings for her, that he had so meticulously hidden from her? There is no telling for sure. What is clear is that Naomi is giving Ruth the permission to trespass on something sacred, something that has not yet been offered, something that has not yet organically come to light. Ruth here is given the permission to manifest that which had been carefully hidden; to bring to light, into being, that which was still an aborted and confused reality within Boaz's own heart. She is given the permission to speak his love into being. How can this be? What of the man's agency? Surrendered as she has been to love, Ruth has earned the privilege to do so. And surrendered as she is to a destiny higher than her own narrow agendas, Ruth is neither grasping for, nor desperately clawing at Boaz's heart. She is simply revealing what has been there all along.

And that she does. Let us pay attention to her words: "Spread your wings over your handmaid, for you are a kinsman redeemer" (3:9). Ruth is here echoing Boaz's words to her earlier in the story: "May you have a full recompense from the Lord, the God of Israel under whose wings you have sought refuge" (2:12). It is as though Ruth is saying to Boaz: that which you willed for God to do unto me, do this yourself. Be an embodiment of divine protection for me, give to me that which you most desired I receive from the Most High. Express your divine masculine, enact the highest version of yourself, birth the man you did not know lay hidden in the depths of your being. What Ruth is doing is effectively drawing Boaz's highest self out; she is, by her words and actions, awakening Boaz to all that he could be, to the man he was always meant to be, and the higher calling he was always meant to have. And this is what seduces Boaz. Much more than her having bathed, anointed, and dressed (although this cannot hurt!), what moves his heart is hearing his deepest truth expressed through this woman's words. What slays his heart is seeing all that he could be reflected in her eyes. This is a true lesson in seduction. For a woman's true erotic power lies not in her enticement of man, that is to say, her harping on his weakness, but in her inspiring his strength. What makes a woman truly irresistible, what pulls love out of a man's heart, is what she calls forth from that man.

For a man loves by *loving,* much more than by *being* loved by the woman in his life. It is inasmuch as a woman can inspire a man to become his highest self, that his love for her will be awakened and become consolidated. Rather than lowering her expectations in order to attract a man's love, a woman ought to raise them. For a man's love will be only as strong as her expectations are high. A woman's expectations and desires are thus not mere caprices (although they can be). Rather, when serving love, those expectations and desires emerge as an intrinsic part of her innate wisdom and are essential for a man's love to be awakened and nurtured. At the same time, these expectations cannot become prescriptions. What is profoundly feminine about Ruth is that she makes her desires heard, and then allows for Boaz to fulfill them in his own time and way.[30] Nowhere in the conversation is she making ultimatums or giving timelines to Boaz. Rather she says what she has to say and then takes a step back, trusting that Boaz will come through. Ruth's audacious and courageous request is coupled with a profound attitude of surrender and trust. She knows when to speak, and she knows when to fall into silence. She makes her move courageously, and then is able to relinquish control over the outcome of her move. Therein lies her erotic power. She sets the bar high, but she also gives the man room to maneuver, and time to gather his strength to respond to her desire. As such, she is inspiring rather than nagging. To inspire a man, a woman needs only share her vision for the relationship. Nagging, on the other hand, is meddling with the if, the when, and the how of the man's response, thereby disempowering the man to act on her behalf.

This surrender on Ruth's part is not easy. Especially given her natural proactiveness. Ruth is used to getting things done, to making power moves. Now she must learn to wait. Her mother-in-law has to exhort her to "sit still" (3:18),[31] something that is deeply out of character for Ruth. And yet, this wait must happen if space is to be created for the man's agency to be activated. A man's initiative is directly proportional to a woman's ability to "sit still" and honor his timing and decision-making process. The man will assume his responsibilities, and more, to the extent that he feels the breathing space to do so, a space opened by the woman's "sitting still," from her adopting an attitude of restfulness and trust in his ability to respond to her desire. Thus, a man's proactiveness emerges out of a woman's restfulness. And it is to the degree that a woman is capable of resting in the man, of trusting him, that the man will come through for her. Anything less than this "sitting still" will feel coercive to the man, leading to him either do nothing or act half-heartedly and resentfully out of duty—both options being passion killers and love slayers. For a man to act out of a place of love, in a way that intensifies his love rather than stifles it, he must feel completely free to respond, or not, to her, and to do so in his own time and way.

It is this delicate balance of audacity and surrender that makes Ruth so powerful. And it is to the degree that she shows herself proficient in both arts that Ruth rises to the level of the true *ezer kenedgo. Ezer* because she is not the only one in need of saving, so is Boaz. In a way Ruth, through her audacious request, has saved Boaz from a dead-end life of mere "comfortableness," and called forth out of him the strong redeemer under whose wings she could find the refuge that he always was meant to be. Her courageous vision is what releases the divine masculine in him and raises him up to his highest calling as a man: that of shepherd-king, protector, and life-giver. In a way, Boaz delivers himself by delivering her. Thus, by heeding this woman in the night, by allowing himself to open up to her words, Boaz is able to become all that he was meant to be and to live up to his name, "strong man" (*ish gibor*).[32] Thus by redeeming Ruth from her poverty and miserliness, Boaz redeems himself. But Ruth is also the *kenedgo,* the one able to be both "for" and "against." Ruth, in her actions of "disclosing" Boaz's secret love, and in her courageous request for his redemptive action on her behalf is, undeniably, trespassing onto Boaz's comfort zone. She is asking of him more than he has been willing to give. In asking for more, she is acting "against" the Boaz hereto set in his ways and in his comfortable routines. But Ruth is also "for" Boaz inasmuch as she asks in a way that empowers him to act rather than castrates or disempowers him, and what she is asking for has the effect of raising him up to a higher calling rather than casting him down and breaking his throne as Eve did to Adam. But there is more. As Boaz finds himself awakened and inspired by Ruth's actions and words, his power becomes activated, released, and begins to flow in a profoundly life-giving way, saturating not only Ruth, but the whole world.[33]

The Renewal of the Cosmos

And so "Boaz married Ruth; she became his wife" (4:13). I love the reciprocity here. Typically, the expression for "married" in Hebrew (*laqah*) implies the idea of force, of a taking, and remains the actions of a man towards a woman. Here, however, for the second time in the Hebrew Bible (the first being Rebekah's marriage to Isaac),[34] we have the notion of a woman's response and explicit consent towards the man: "And she became his wife" (4:13). The woman is not, as is typically the case in the Hebrew Bible, the object of the man's initiative. Both here are subjects in this partnership. There is a striking equality and reciprocity in this couple's story that is unheard of in the rest of the Biblical canon. An equality which, nonetheless, constitutes the blueprint of the Creation story, where both partners were called to rule the world together. The story of Ruth and Boaz pours a healing balm upon the story of the first couple. Contrary to the drama that unfolded in Genesis 3, the woman now raises up the man rather than breaks him; and the man, by listening to her, saves the world—including the woman—rather than destroys it.

But it is first and foremost Ruth who finds herself renewed by Boaz's redemptive love. It is interesting that the question "who are you?" (*mi at?)* is asked of Ruth twice. Once by Boaz when he finds her lying next to him (3:9), and the other by Naomi upon Ruth's return home from the threshing floor (3:16). Clearly, her intimate encounter with Boaz has transformed her, has shifted her deep in her identity. It is thus not just status that has shifted for Ruth, but something within herself has opened up, has been revived. She, who up until now had closed herself up to love and to a woman's life, finds herself suddenly allowed to envision such a life. Ruth, by choosing to follow Naomi, had essentially turned a page on her destiny as a woman, wife and mother. And although she was still capable of compassionate and selfless action, her woman's heart, worn out from so many crushed hopes and tragic endings, had shut down. She had become like a "fountain locked," a "sealed up spring" (Song of Songs 4:12). When Boaz takes her as his wife, her heart, for the first time, becomes unsealed, and her womanhood—so long crushed by hardship—is set free. Just as she had awakened the man in him, he now awakens and releases the woman in her.

And so, under Boaz's wings, Ruth begins to blossom, moving from life to death, from barrenness to renewed life: "And he cohabited with her. The Lord let her conceive and she bore a son" (4:13). This is the first time that God is mentioned explicitly. It is also the first time that God intervenes in a woman's conception. In other Biblical stories, God simply "remembers" the woman and "opens the womb." Here, however, God goes a step further and plays an active role in her conceiving. The rabbis of old believed that God needed to intervene because Ruth was too old for conception.[35] Ruth's conception is therefore not only unexpected, but supernatural. From chance encounters we have moved to divine intervention and miracles. It is as though God's presence was being drawn more and more into the story. The chance encounter with Boaz was God's response to Ruth's selfless actions, but the miraculous conception was God's response to Boaz's courageous response to Ruth's desire.[36] God moves to the degree that human beings move. And it is to the degree that the characters of the story love each other selflessly, that God's power becomes activated on their behalf.[37] As such, the selfless love that Ruth and Boaz have for each other has sacramental power—the capacity to attract divine providence and blessing.

But there is more. Beyond Ruth's renewal, Boaz's actions also bring about a cosmic renewal. The period of the Judges, in which our story is set, ended with the expression: "In those days there was no king in Israel, everyone did as he pleased" (Judges 21:25). Our story reverses this and comes full circle by mentioning the genealogy of King David, the first king worthy of Israel. By renewing Ruth, Boaz has in effect renewed his own genealogy with the birth of a son who would eventually become the ancestor of kings. The royal line of Judah had in effect ended with Boaz with no heir in sight, until Ruth arrived in his life. The line of the kings of Israel is thus mended by the birth of the son of Boaz, and the future royal throne is salvaged. Thus, were it not for Ruth's audacious request, the line of the kings of Israel, with its powerful and wise kings such as King David and King Solomon, would never have seen the light of day. Were it not for Ruth the Moabite, Israel would never have become the powerful and renowned kingdom of a King David or King Solomon, never attain the honor of becoming "light onto the nations,"[38] with foreign kings and queens flocking to it from the ends of the world. And so, Israel owes its golden age to a single act of hospitality and of *hesed.* By welcoming Ruth and making her his own, Boaz single-handedly regenerated Israel and propelled it into royal and cosmic history. Thus, Israel found itself renewed by its acceptance and care of a stranger within its midst. The fruitfulness of Israel and its ascension in human history had everything to do with its attitude towards the stranger in its midst. To the degree that Israel showed itself capable of welcoming this stranger, it became renewed, reenergized, and raised up to become a blessing onto the nations.

But beyond the mere revival of Israel, the story of Ruth gives us a glimpse at the revival of the nations as well. Beyond the renewal of

Israel, we can discern the possibility of cosmic renewal. For this love story between Ruth and Boaz can be read as a prefiguration of the reconciliation of Israel with the nations, and the mutual fecundation that can happen at each other's contact. Just like Ruth awakened Boaz to his highest calling and draws out his life-giving power, likewise, the nations of the world, in turning towards Israel–whether as foes or as friends—continuously prevent it from forgetting its sacred election and unique destiny among the nations. And just as Ruth is renewed by Boaz's love, the nations can find themselves renewed through their contact with Israel. So, beyond the renewal of Israel, the book of Ruth really anticipates the renewal of the world, its reconciliation with Israel, as a lion with a lamb, and the arrival of the King-Messiah predicted by the Hebrew prophets:[39]

> A shoot will come up from the stump of Jesse
> From his roots a branch will bear fruit
> The spirit of the Lord will rest on him....
> Righteousness will be his belt
> And faithfulness the sash around his waist
> The wolf will live with the lamb
> The leopard will lie down with the goat
> The calf and the lion and the yearling together;
> And a little child will lead them
> (Is. 11:1–6)

Conclusion

The story of Ruth and Boaz is really a Hebrew version of the Sumerian "sacred marriage" trope. All the elements are there. Like Inanna, we have a woman empowering a man to become king. Boaz, until the coming of Ruth, was nothing but a mere and ordinary landowner. Through her influence, however, he rises to the level of the Sumerian shepherd-king, one who does not live merely to accumulate possessions for himself, but whose destiny finds itself transformed into a protective and life-giving one. And like Dumuzi, we have Boaz giving new life to his woman, opening up her womb, and thereby renewing the world. Their marriage is one of unprecedented equality and reciprocity, a return to the Edenic ideal for the man and the woman, and the key to cosmic harmony. For the world rests on the selfless love between man and woman. And it is to the degree that we, as women, can inspire our men to greatness, and that they, as men, respond to us in love, that the forces of chaos will be held at bay, and the world will be restored. The Messianic era, the restoration of Israel and the redemption of the nations and of the world thus rests, not on the securing of borders or the rebuilding of temples, but on the humble and fragile love bond between a man and a woman.

Chapter 5

Woman Wisdom and the King's Heir

Introduction

Tradition gives King Solomon the authorship of the book of Proverbs, along with the book of Ecclesiastes and the Song of Songs.[1] The book of Proverbs reads like a teaching of a father to a son, but, given its author, and its many allusions to court life, was most likely meant to be a training manual for the king's son, or heir to the throne, in order to prepare him for the difficult task of reigning over Israel. King Solomon was king of Jerusalem in the 10th century BCE; the book of Proverbs can thus be dated to that time. His reign was markedly different from his predecessors.' Unlike his father King David who spent most of his reign in battle against the enemies of Israel, Solomon's reign was one of peace, centered on cultivating political, economic, and intellectual ties with precisely those enemy nations. The book of Proverbs will reflect the cosmopolitanism of its author and his intimate knowledge of Egyptian and Sumerian literature, notably the texts centered around the worship of the goddess.[2] The Biblical text criticizes Solomon's curiosity towards the cult of the goddess as a sign of his having fallen into idolatry, but his writings betray a very different story. Deeply sensitive and open to the divine feminine, King Solomon nonetheless never loses his faith in the God of Israel. His writing is clearly influenced by Egypt and Sumer, and he borrows freely from the literature surrounding the Egyptian goddess Ma'at, and the Sumerian goddess Inanna. But his borrowing is not a form of apostasy, but rather serves to expand, enrich, and transfigure his understanding of God revealing a radically new face of God: The face of a woman. For God, in the book of Proverbs is not male. God in the book of Proverbs is a woman, an outspoken, daring, and brazen woman, who does not hesitate to venture out in the streets of Jerusalem to advertise her goods. She is Woman Wisdom. This identification of God as a woman clearly situates our book in the mother's house canon. Let us take a closer look.

Masculine vs. Feminine

Although the two main conversants in the book of Proverbs are male, the central character is clearly Woman Wisdom. She appears at three junctures of the book (Prov. 1; 3; 8), in rich poetic sections which stand out from the usual proverbial and aphoristic style of the book. Detailed descriptions are given of her origins, of her comings and goings, and of the goods that she promises. The King's son is exhorted to "listen" to her in the same way that he is taught to listen to his father *and* mother, the book of Proverbs being one of the rare books in the Hebrew Bible where the mother is paired with the father in the education of the heir. Woman Wisdom is moreover depicted with traits reminiscent of both the Egyptian goddess Ma'at, and the Sumerian goddess Inanna. These similarities between Woman Wisdom and these Ancient Near Eastern goddesses immediately alert the reader that she is more than just a symbol or a metaphor. She is a deity, she is divine, and the King's son is to relate to her as such. She is not, however, separate from the God of Israel. Indeed, the book of Proverbs makes a considerable effort to identify Woman Wisdom with *God* himself (or should we say, herself). But there is more: Towards the end of the book of Proverbs, Woman Wisdom morphs into the virtuous wife. The wife, or spouse, thus becomes one of the figures of wisdom and of the divine feminine and detains the same authority as Woman Wisdom. She, too, ought to be listened to if it is to go well with the King's heir. The book of Proverbs is thus saturated with feminine figures, from Woman Wisdom, to the Ancient Near Eastern goddesses that birthed her, to the virtuous wife who embodies her.

Vertical vs. Horizontal

Although the "fear of the Lord" is mentioned several times in the book of Proverbs (1:7; 9:10; 14:2; 14:27; 15:33; 24:21), no further mention is made of God. Rather, it is the voices of mother and father which fill the pages of the book of Proverbs. It is as though the "fear of the Lord" was to be experienced through obedience to the father's and mother's teachings. Nowhere in the book of Proverbs do we witness an authoritarian God that one ought to submit to and obey. Rather, the fear of God is parsed, in the book of Proverbs, as the capacity to listen to a voice outside of oneself, as the willingness to move beyond oneself, transcend one's narrow and rigid categories at the contact of an Other.[3] Far from pointing the King's heir to a divine authority before which he must bend his knee and submit, the book of Proverbs labors at refining the heir's conversational skills. The whole book is in fact structured as a conversation between a father and a son, and its key word is *shma,* "listen." Now this is interesting inasmuch as the word *shma* is typically used, in the Pentateuch, to describe Israel's duty to listen to *God:* "Hear oh Israel, the Lord, our God, is one" (Deut. 6:4).[4] Listening in the context of the Hebrew Bible is thus associated with an availability to hear God's voice and obey it. In the book of Proverbs, however, the *shma*'s object becomes the father and the mother. Rather than God, it is the father and the mother who now become the ones that the heir ought to listen to and obey. And it is to the degree that the heir is able to lend his ear to his father and mother, that he will reign successfully and wisely. Wisdom is thus not acquired vertically, through prayer, study or ritual, but horizontally, through difficult and challenging conversations. God again is found "in between" people, his wisdom accessible only as the heir opens up to others.

Law vs. Wisdom

The emphasis in the book of Proverbs on wisdom is also significant, and points to a very different path than that of unquestioned obedience and submission to God which typically characterizes the path of the merely pious man. Contrary to piety, wisdom implies the transgression of norms and boundaries, it implies an exploration of life without external limitations, the courage to make mistakes and to learn from them, a taste for the forbidden and for the off-limits. What defines the father and mother's authority to teach is precisely their life *experience.* They have wisdom because they have *lived,* because they have explored, transgressed, made mistakes, taken wrong turns, and learned. When the king speaks to the heir of the "forbidden woman," or of the dangers of too much wine, both of which drain a king's strength and prevent him from ruling wisely, he is speaking from experience.[5] The path of wisdom, however, although allowing for mistakes and transgressions, also requires the humility to learn, to grow in wisdom through these mistakes. The wise king must be humble enough to realize that he has stumbled too far and for too long and begin to make his way back to what he might have lost of himself in the process, to "return," or repent.[6] Wisdom, contrary to law, requires a certain flexibility—the flexibility to change course at any given moment. It is this flexibility and humility which ultimately saves the wise man from the ever-present dangers and snares inherent to his oft-forbidden explorations.

Holiness vs. Hospitality

In his journey beyond the borders of the permissible, the wise man will have many challenging and life-altering encounters. Far from seeing these encounters as somehow tainting him and weakening his integrity, the wise man will allow himself to dissolve into these encounters, only to emerge from them expanded, broadened, enlarged. Contrary to the holy man, who seeks isolation from the world and purity from the contact with otherness, the wise man hungers for the world and thirsts for contact with otherness.[7] The wise man knows that he cannot find wisdom in separation, only in integration, by opening himself up to otherness. Hospitality to the other constitutes thus the very gateway to wisdom. The wise man knows that he must journey with others on this quest, and that wisdom refuses herself to the solitary seeker. It is together that wisdom is found, not alone. We see evidence of this journey in the pages of the book of Proverbs. Not only is King Solomon journeying among Egyptian and Sumerian sages in his quest for the divine feminine, but he is also journeying with Canaanite sages—the sworn enemies of Israel. The last few proverbs are penned by a number Canaanite sages[8] and offer some of the most beautiful verse on the virtuous wife as the very figure of Woman Wisdom.

Doing vs. Receiving

With Woman Wisdom being the centerpiece of the book of Proverbs, we should expect that she would want to be approached differently than the patriarchal God. Contrary to the father's house God, whose holiness and distance is unnegotiable, Woman Wisdom seems to long for intimacy. We see her setting a table for a banquet, the latter often serving as a prelude to physical intimacy.[9] The God of the father's house seeks obedience, he emphasizes responsibility, disciplined action, and proper ritual. Woman Wisdom, on the other hand, invites her seekers to rest, to receive, to enjoy her goods. She would rather be engaged in conversation than obeyed. When she calls, she expects a retort, no matter how brazen, not blind and silent obedience. The God of the father's house is encountered in the sacred premises of the temple. Woman Wisdom leads her seekers to the intimacy and playfulness of the bedroom. She longs to surrender to her seekers rather than to be surrendered to. She invites rather than coerces; she offers rather than is offered to. In the father's house, the believers offer up to God the best of their harvests. In the mother's house, Woman Wisdom is the one who prepares and sets the table. She serves rather than is served. Woman Wisdom thus gives us a very novel understanding of the God of Israel, one that is shockingly different than what we are used to. But this identification that the author of Proverbs makes between Woman Wisdom and God remains to be seen. Let us then turn to our text.

The Goddess and the King

The first thing the reader notices upon encountering Woman Wisdom is her proximity with the God of Israel. The ode to Woman Wisdom in Proverbs 8 is particularly illuminating and gives a number of descriptions of Woman Wisdom that parallel what we already know of God.[10] The first similarity between the two has to do with the exhortation to listen: "It is Wisdom calling, Understanding raising her voice.... Listen (*sham'u)!*" (Prov. 8:1–6). This parallels the command given in the book of Deuteronomy to listen to God: "Hear (*shma*) O Israel. . ." (Deut. 6:4). Woman Wisdom then goes on to describe her attributes: "Mine are counsel (*ezah*) and resourcefulness (*tushyah*). I am understanding (*binah*) and power (*gvurah*) is mine" (Prov. 8:14). These are almost to the dot the same attributes given to God in the book of Job: "With him are wisdom (*hokhma*) and power (*gvurah*), his are counsel (*ezeh*) and understanding (*tvunah*)" (Job 12:13). It almost seems like our author is quoting the book of Job. We have the same parallelism and almost the same wording. Woman wisdom, just like the God of Israel, is also found only by those who seek her: "Those who love me I love and those who seek me will find me" (Prov. 8:17). We find the same exhortation to seek in the book of Isaiah, this time concerning God: "Seek the Lord while he may be found, call to him while he is near" (Is. 55: 6–9).[11] Likewise, the God of Israel also commands our love: "You shall love the Lord…" (Deut. 6:5). Finally, the temporality of Woman Wisdom is the same as the God of Israel's: "The Lord brought me forth as the first of his works, before (*qedem*) all of his works of old, from eternity (*olam*) I was established, before the origin of the world (*miqedmei erez*)" (Prov. 8:22–23). Here we have three temporal expressions (*qedem, olam, miqedmei erez*), all three belonging to the semantic field of eternity, of a time prior to human temporality. Woman Wisdom and God share the same temporality, that of primordial time or eternity. Clearly, there is a subtle attempt on the part of our author to identify Woman Wisdom with the God of Israel. Like him she must be listened to and obeyed, like him she is found only by seeking, and like him she belongs to the realm of eternity. The question is why Solomon chooses to identify this feminine figure of wisdom with the God of Israel. Perhaps he does so as part of a larger scheme to expand his readers' perspective and understanding of God to include his feminine attributes. Perhaps as a way to remind his readers of the lost and forgotten feminine attributes of this God whose earliest self-definition included both a feminine and a masculine face.[12]

But the plot thickens. In addition to identifying Woman Wisdom with the God of Israel, the author of the book of Proverbs also uses language to describe her that is reminiscent of the Ancient Near Eastern goddesses Ma'at, Asherah, and Inanna.[13] Most of the descriptions, however, (to the exception of one) allude to the Egyptian goddess Ma'at. This is not surprising given the intimate connection that King Solomon enjoyed with Egypt.[14] But more needs to be said about this Egyptian goddess if we are to catch the connections between the two. Ma'at is first and foremost the goddess of cosmic order. She is intimately associated with the moment of creation, having emerged at the origin of time from the Egyptian sun-god Ra and having stood by his side as he spoke the world into being.[15] Ma'at is also the goddess of justice, the principle that serves to protect the cosmic order from devolving back into chaos. In fact, her very name means "straight," alluding to the rigor and integrity of her character. The justice that she embodies can be accessed through her teachings, compiled by the Egyptian scribes into 42 proverbs that the Egyptian needed to keep in order to ensure his afterlife. Finally, Ma'at is intimately connected to the Pharaoh, for only through her will he reign justly and serve his royal purpose as the guardian and protector of the cosmic order.[16] This intimate bond between the goddess Ma'at and the pharaoh is depicted in Egyptian iconography as the King offering up the Ma'at back to the gods, in the place of food and drink.[17] Egyptian iconography also depicts her intimately embracing the pharaoh from behind, protecting him with her wings.[18] Her connection to the pharaoh is further emphasized by her being typically depicted holding the *ankh* (symbol of eternal life) in one hand, and the scepter in the other. She is the one, if possessed by the pharaoh, who detains the key to his life and his authority. To the degree that the pharaoh nurtures this intimate connection with the goddess Ma'at, he will live and rule justly.

The descriptions of Woman Wisdom will parallel those of the goddess Ma'at on all of these points. Like the goddess Ma'at, Woman Wisdom finds herself brought forth from the Creator and standing by his side as he creates the world:[19] "The lord brought me forth[20] as the first of his works. I was appointed from eternity, from the beginning before the world began.[21] There I was beside him as a master craftsman at his side"[22] (Prov. 8:22–31). Just like Ma'at, Woman Wisdom emerges from the Creator and participates in the creating process. The book of Proverbs also associates Woman Wisdom, like Ma'at, with the founding principle of justice: "The proverbs of Solomon, son of David, king of Israel: For learning wisdom (*hokhma*) and discipline; for understanding words of discernment; for acquiring the discipline for success, righteousness, justice, and equity" (Prov. 1:1–3). In this passage Woman Wisdom (*hokhma*) is directly related to righteousness, justice and equity, just like her Egyptian counterpart Ma'at. Finally, her intimate connection to the king is described in almost sexual terms: "She is a tree of life to those who embrace her, those who lay hold of her will be blessed" (Prov. 3:17).[23] And it is to the degree that he cleaves to her, like the pharaoh's of old did to Ma'at, that he will reign justly:[24] "By me kings reign and rulers make laws that are just. By me princes govern and all nobles who rule on earth" (Prov. 8:15–16). Like Ma'at, Woman Wisdom is seen holding "long life in her right hand and honor in the other" (Prov. 3:16), and bestowing those on her beloved should he choose her.

Thus, not content to identify Woman Wisdom with the God of Israel, our author also identifies her with the Egyptian goddess Ma'at. The question of course is, why? Why broaden the comparison of Woman Wisdom beyond the monotheistic God to a pagan goddess? Beyond merely reminding his readers of the feminine attributes of God, the author of our text seems to want to expand the way that the king, and by extension all of us, ought to relate to the God of Israel. The Egyptian goddess Ma'at introduces the notion of intimacy between herself and the pharaoh that is unheard of in the land of Israel. The God of Israel is seen as a father, yes, to the king, but never as beloved of the King. The God of Israel commands, exhorts, disciplines, and teaches, as a father would. But in Egypt (and throughout the whole Ancient Near East) the goddess is embraced, is cleaved to in an intimate and sexual embrace. Might Solomon be anticipating the Hebrew prophets' descriptions of God as the bridegroom and husband of Israel, and the intimate and covenantal relationship between the two? Might he in fact be the first, under the Egyptian influence, to have broadened the Hebrew concept of God to that of beloved, and not just father? Could it be that Solomon glimpsed, in the way the Ancient Near Eastern goddess were related to, the possibility of a deeper bond to his God, a bond defined as beloved to lover, as wife to husband?

Thus, the book of Proverbs teaches us ultimately that the God of Israel is more than a mere father that must be obeyed and feared. The God of Israel also has a feminine heart, a feminine desire to connect more deeply, more intimately with the king. The God of Israel, portrayed as Woman Wisdom, is inviting; She longs to share a meal, a conversation, an embrace with the king. She longs to become the confidante of the king, to become his intimate partner in crime, his spouse, and his protector. Thus, far from succumbing to the lures of the Ancient Near Eastern goddesses, as the Biblical text seems to indicate, King Solomon was in fact hard at work at discerning, in their very features, the feminine face of the God of Israel. King Solomon, in his apparent hunger and thirst for the goddesses of the Ancient Near East, was in fact hungering and thirsting for another representation of God, one that was more feminine, less forbidding, more alluring, seductive, and encompassing. And it is this representation that the Hebrew prophets would later adopt in their descriptions of God and Israel as bridegroom and bride—a radical departure from the authoritarian, paternal God of the Pentateuch.

There is but one condition for intimacy with Woman Wisdom, however: the king must learn to *listen* to her voice. In other words, one of the essential virtues of the king of Israel must be the humility to open up to an authority, a voice that is not his own. The king must recognize that there exists a higher authority than himself, before which he ought to bend the knee. The position of the king of Israel is thus not one of authority and power, but one of sensitivity and surrender to the feminine face of God, to Woman Wisdom. This is why the preferred ride of the kings of old was the humble and gentle donkey, and not the arrogant and fierce horse. Like the donkey, the kings were expected to serve rather than be served, and to remain lowly and humble, ever open to the voice of Woman Wisdom in all its forms. This is why the kings, upon their inauguration, were given the scroll of the law to copy in the privacy of their own home. To remember that their authority was only legitimate to the degree that they were themselves under authority, the authority of the Most-High God. As such, the king of Israel was to resemble the shepherd-king Dumuzi, and shepherd his people, lead them, tend to them rather than exercise force over them. And it is to the degree that the king would remain connected to the feminine and open to the loving embrace of Woman Wisdom, that he would be safe guarded from morphing into a tyrant or a despot, oppressing the people rather than caring for them.

The Wife and the Husband

But the Biblical text does not stop there. The author of our text goes one step further and describes the "virtuous wife"[25] as the very embodiment of Woman Wisdom. In other words, Woman Wisdom is accessible to every man through his wife—on the condition that she be capable. This is undoubtedly one step further than the Egyptian understanding of wisdom. Whereas the goddess Ma'at remains an inaccessible goddess only available to the king, here we have Woman Wisdom drawing shockingly close, and allowing herself to go through the miracle of incarnation. As such, ordinary women can become the earthly manifestation of Woman Wisdom to their husbands, provided of course that these women be virtuous. Let us take a look at what our text says.

The first thing we notice are the number of connections that the author of the book of Proverbs makes between the virtuous wife and Woman Wisdom.[26] Of Woman Wisdom, the author says that she "is more precious than rubies" (Prov. 3:15, 8:11). Likewise, the capable wife's "worth is far beyond that of rubies" (Prov. 31:10). Woman Wisdom rewards her seekers with "a crown of splendor" (Prov. 4:9).[27] The virtuous wife is "a crown to her husband" (Prov. 12:4). Woman Wisdom's wisdom is "from the Lord" (Prov. 2:6)[28] and a "prudent wife is from the Lord" (Prov. 19:14).[29] Here we see a clear intention on the part of the author of the book of Proverbs, to identify Woman Wisdom with the virtuous wife. Thus, a man cannot find wisdom in isolation and needs to rely on a virtuous woman to guide him. And it is to the degree that he, like the king of Israel, shows himself to be humble enough to recognize that he does not have the monopoly on wisdom but, on the contrary, needs to learn to heed another voice than his own, that he will find his way in the world. It is to the degree that he can bend his ear to his wife's counsel, that he will stand tall among the greats of the world. His stature, his success, his mark on the world, all are built on his relationship with a virtuous woman. And to succumb here to cliché: Behind every great man stands a great woman!

The question of course, is what makes for a woman's virtue? The expression used here is the one we encountered in the book of Ruth: *eshet chayil.* We already explored in the preceding chapter on Ruth the meanings of this word. Suffice to say that *eshet chayil* has little to do with the Victorian virtues of modesty, submission, and obedience. The character Ruth is none of these things. She is neither modest (she brazenly seduces Boaz in the night), nor is she obedient (she takes bold initiatives often against other people's wishes). So, what does it mean to be an *eshet chayil?* It means to be like Ruth: strong, loving, and courageous. This is the sign of a "virtuous wife." In this sense, Job's wife, in her defiant exhortation that her husband curse God, is showing strength, love, and courage. We will see in what follows how the Shulamite in the Song of Songs is an *eshet chayil,* and this, again, in spite of her lack of Victorian virtues. Finally, Queen Esther will also fail the Victorian test of modesty and obedience, while nevertheless rising to the level of an *eshet chayil.*

Conclusion

The book of Proverbs, although a teaching of a father to a son, has shown itself to have a powerful feminine flavor. For the teaching of the father hides a deeper teaching: that of Woman Wisdom, the feminine face of God that the son needs to learn to love and connect to intimately. For, beyond the father, it is to Woman Wisdom that the heir to the throne of Israel must learn to relate. The father will not always be there to advise and guide this heir. But Woman Wisdom will remain an ever-present figure in the life of the heir to the throne, ever inviting, ever seducing. He might at times be unfaithful to her, he might at times lose sight of her, as we will see in the next chapter, but she remains ever faithful and true, ever by his side. Moreover, the teachings of Woman Wisdom can be accessed through the connection with a virtuous woman. Thus, in as much as the king remains connected to the feminine, to the good women in his life, he will continue to rule justly and wisely. Woman Wisdom, far from remaining on her goddess throne, has stepped down in a stunning move of incarnation. Thus, ordinary and unassuming women can, with mere words, turn around entire lives and destinies. And likewise, we who follow in her footsteps.

Chapter 6

Ecclesiastes and the Lost Goddess

Introduction

Tradition establishes King Solomon as the author of the book of Ecclesiastes.[1] This book has a very different flavor, however, from the book of Proverbs that we just studied. In the book of Proverbs, we had a king teaching the heir to the throne how to rule justly. This just rule was in turn dependent on the heir's cultivating an intimate connection with the God of Israel. Just like the Egyptian pharaoh needed to remain in tune with the goddess Ma'at and follow her precepts in order to protect the cosmic order, likewise, the king of Israel needed to continuously heed Woman Wisdom—the feminine face of God—and cultivate an intimate relationship with her, receiving her, embracing her, never letting go of her, as one would a beloved spouse. The book of Ecclesiastes opens up on a very different setting. Instead of a king teaching a son, we have a king who seems to have lost his own way, who seems disoriented, with no moral compass. The book opens up on a scene of chaos where the stability of the cosmic order is threatened by a growing uneasiness, a growing awareness of the absurdity of life. As we journey more deeply in the book, we enter a kingdom that seems to be in shambles, a kingdom where justice has no residency. Finally, we see a king entirely consumed with his own achievements and success—hardly a figure of the shepherd-king that he is meant to be. And among the ruins of this lost kingdom, Woman Wisdom is nowhere to be seen. Clearly, in the book of Ecclesiastes, we are in the presence of a king who has lost his Ma'at, who has lost his connection to Woman

Wisdom. At the same time, the book of Ecclesiastes is a book about a king who ultimately finds her again, who ultimately reconnects with his Ma'at, and reconciles with Woman Wisdom. This will entail, however that the king reunite with the dimension of the feminine, with the woman, with the spouse. Thus, although Woman Wisdom seems to elude us in this work by Solomon, she remains there, behind the scenes.

Masculine vs. Feminine

The book of Ecclesiastes, from the outset, does not seem to have much to say about the feminine dimension. We have a king engaged in a monologue about his own life. From the onset, we are struck by the solitary figure that this king represents. There is no mention there of any meaningful relationships, of a counselling wife, or even of children. Instead, we have a list of his own personal achievements and accomplishments. It is as though this king had lost his ability to relate, to converse, to engage with otherness. It is as though he had lost a sense of his priorities, privileging his own solitary achievements over the wealth of relationships. Moreover, Woman Wisdom, who was so prominent in the book of Proverbs, and who had been depicted there as the patron "goddess" of the kings of Israel, is conspicuously absent. And the only time where she might have been mentioned is to identify her as missing: "All this I tested with wisdom. I thought I could fathom it, but it eludes me.... As for what I sought further but did not find, I found only one human being in a thousand, and the one I found among so many was never a woman" (Eccles. 7:23–28). This passage puts the elusiveness of wisdom in parallel with the elusiveness of woman. With the book of Proverbs fresh in our mind, it is clear that the author is here referring to the elusiveness of Woman Wisdom. The king has here clearly lost his connection to Woman Wisdom; he has lost his Ma'at. And yet, this elusive feminine figure eventually resurfaces towards the end of the book of Ecclesiastes,[2] in the figure of the wife and in the exhortation by the king to enjoy her. This resurgence of the lost beloved wife is highly significant and will speak to the lengths that it took for the king to reunite with the lost and forgotten feminine dimension.

Vertical vs. Horizontal

In the book of Ecclesiastes there seems to be a breakdown of both the vertical and the horizontal dimensions, making it a thoroughly godless book, where transcendence is neither accessed vertically nor horizontally. We see first the dissolution of the vertical connection when Ecclesiastes cries out, in the face of rampant injustice, that there is "no comforter" (Eccles. 4:1).[3] The word "comforter" (*menahem*), will become one of the key terms in the prophetic literature and refer solely to God (cf. Lamentations 1:2, 9, 16, 21). What Ecclesiastes is saying here—two millennia before Nietzsche would dare utter the same heresy—is that there is no God. And because there is no God, there is no justice. But the horizontal dimension is also absent in the book of Ecclesiastes. As mentioned before, the king of our story is profoundly alone, much more even than Job who at least had friends and a wife by his side. Our king, however, has no one that he can speak to, no one that he can confide in. There is, in this biblical book, a striking and poignant absence of dialogue. This is highly unusual in as much as biblical literature is profoundly dialogical. From the early dialogues of God and human beings to the dialogues between family members which punctuate the travels of the first Hebrews, to finally, the dialogue face-to-face between Moses and God. In the book of Ecclesiastes, dialogue has broken down, and with it the "in between" where God might still emerge. Yet, we do have one dialogue going on uninterrupted: The dialogue of the king with himself. Now it is tempting to see there no more than an uninterrupted monologue, thereby imprisoning the king more deeply in his solitude. But Egyptian literature has a precedent of this genre which is particularly illuminating: *The Dispute Between a Man and his Ba*.[4] The *ba* in Egypt referred to the part of the human being that survived it when it died. In other words, the *ba* refers to the spiritual aspect of the human and was often depicted in the form of a bird.[5] Thus, although there is a notable absence of human dialogue partners in the book of Ecclesiastes, the king seems to have found a way to connect to his deeper self, his spiritual self, his *ba,* and it is with this deeper self that he seems to be engaging in dialogue with. Moreover, there is a nakedness, a vulnerability in this dialogue that testifies to its authenticity. In this dialogue with his *ba,* king Solomon in effect allows himself to "lose face," to take off his royal mask, and really grapple with the dead-end to which his life-journey seems to have taken him. He courageously faces his confusion, his doubts, his despair. And it is precisely in this poignant unveiling of his naked, destitute soul, that the king will begin to find his way back to his Ma'at, to his long-lost Woman Wisdom.

Law vs. Wisdom

From the first chapters, the book of Ecclesiastes speaks of transgressive behavior. In his explorations, the king will allow himself to be limited by nothing. The tone is set from the beginning: "I, Koheleth, was king in Jerusalem over Israel. I set my mind to study and to probe with wisdom *all* that happens under the sun" (Eccles. 1:12). The word "all" (*qol*) alludes here to the totality of the created realm.[6] Of this created realm, all is now at the disposal of the king, there are no forbidden places, no limits, no sacred boundaries. Everything is to be open and accessible to his explorations. Nothing is proscribed, nothing is off-limits, and everything is up for grabs. We are here in a lawless universe, unmarked by prohibition and limits. And yet, it is precisely in this transgressive behavior that King Solomon will access his wisdom. For it is only upon realizing that his transgressive behavior has reached a dead end, that the king's awareness will be heightened as to his own limitations. And it is precisely at this moment, in the realization of his powerlessness, in the recognition that all his efforts have come to naught, that everything is "futile" (*hevel*), that the king reaches a higher state of awareness, a state of wisdom. For what is meant by wisdom if not the brutal awakening to one's fragility, precarity, in one word, one's humanity. For wisdom remains elusive to those who have it all under control and who seem to know where they are going. Only upon hitting rock bottom, can a man begin to glimpse the presence of his ever-faithful companion: Woman Wisdom. Only upon realizing that he has lost his way can a man begin to heed the voice of his long-lost beloved goddess. Thus, it is at the heart of chaos that the King will find his Ma'at again; it is at the heart of transgression that he will find grace.

Holiness vs. Hospitality

The book of Ecclesiastes, although a deeply Hebrew book, is also surprisingly hospitable to the wisdom of Egypt. As with all the books authored by Solomon, characterized by the ever-present welcoming space for the wisdom of the nations,[7] the book of Ecclesiastes is replete with Egyptian words, concepts, and philosophy.[8] The repeating assertion that "all is futile" (Eccles. 1:2) testifies to the Egyptian influence over this work. Egypt, in contrast to its more religious neighbors, had a whole literature of protest against the gods. As such, the book of Ecclesiastes, with its repeating mantra "Utter futility! Said Koheleth—Utter futility! All is futile" (Eccles. 1:2) is echoing the Egyptian literature of protest.[9] The idea that nothing has meaning, that the reward of the just is the same as that of the unjust, that there is no comforter, all of these are marks of a deep-seated revolt against God and testify to the Egyptian influence over the work. At the same time, and interwoven with the Egyptian thread of despair, we discover, over and over again, a thread of hope. At the heart of the deepest darkness of Ecclesiastes, there opens up, albeit fleetingly, a dimension of light, an allusion to Eden—of a time when chaos had not yet broken into the cosmos, when all was still good (*tov*). In these moments—mere glimpses into the overwhelmingly catastrophic tone of the book—Ecclesiastes seems to reconnect with his long-lost Hebraic heritage and allows himself to draw upon its vivid and rich imagery. The book of Ecclesiastes seems to have been composed as a counterpoint of Egyptian and Hebrew voices, written as a call and response between the two worldviews. Thus, although the book of Ecclesiastes is overwhelmingly a dark and despairing work, it also opens up, albeit fleetingly, on a different reality, a different wavelength, the frequency of hope.

Doing vs. Receiving

Much more than a book of musings, the book of Ecclesiastes is a book bursting at the seams with activity. In it, the king is feverishly at work searching, experimenting, reveling, drinking, building, acquiring, observing, buying, and learning. There is hardly a moment of repose, hardly a moment where he takes a break from his investigations. Tragically, the more the king seems to strive to find the meaning, the wisdom he is looking for, the more it eludes him. The more heated he becomes, the more initiatives he obsessively engages in, the emptier and more meaningless his life becomes. It is only when he hits rock bottom and gives up in despair, that a new dimension opens up before him: A dimension of grace, accessed only in an attitude of rest and receptivity. Only when he begins to make his way away from the quarry does he stumble back into a garden of delights. Only when he puts down his arms in defeat and takes off his armor of achievements and accomplishments, does he find himself cradled by Woman Wisdom herself. But these moments are far and in between, and it takes truly a refined perception to glimpse them in the whirl of activity that animates the book.

The Lost Goddess

From the outset of the book, it is clear that we are dealing with a king who has lost touch with his Ma'at. Recalling the traits of the Egyptian goddess Ma'at from the book of Proverbs, we remember three characteristics: Ma'at is first and foremost the goddess of cosmic order. She was present with the Creator Ra when the world was brought forth and she remains the guarantor of that order.[10] Second, Ma'at (whose name means "straight") is the goddess of justice, and the king is the first responsible for keeping her precepts if his kingdom is to fend off the ever-present threat of invasive chaotic forces. This safeguarding of justice is, moreover, the highest offering the king can make to the gods, and the guarantee of their continuing to look upon him and his kingdom with favor.[11] Finally, Ma'at is more than an abstract principle, she is also to be the beloved of the king, the one who embraces him from the back and protects him.[12] And it is to the degree that the king nurtures his connection with the goddess, who, as we saw in the book of Proverbs, is none other than Woman Wisdom, that he will rule justly.

When we look at the book of Ecclesiastes, however, we realize that on all three points, the king seems to have lost touch with his goddess. The very first verses of the book of Ecclesiastes open upon a scene of cosmic chaos: "Utter futility!—said Koheleth—Utter futility! All is futile!" (Eccles. 1:2). Here the king is not merely saying that his own life is meaningless; he is saying that the whole cosmos is absurd and going nowhere. The created world is no more punctuated by the "good" *(tov)* as narrated in the creation story,[13] it is "meaningless" (*hevel).* Thus, instead of the weighty words of the Almighty flooding darkness with light as we have in the creation story, we have here the despairing words of a man having lost all sense of gravitas, at grips with the "unbearable lightness of being," the futility of the created order. The scene of chaos opens ever wider as we witness the presence of all the elements of creation, but in total disarray. The earth, the wind, the sea, man are all present as in the creation story, but this time their presence is cast as "wearisome" (Eccles. 1:8), as "nothing new" (Eccles. 1:9), as not "enough" (Eccles. 1:8). Whereas the creation story was written symphonically, as a majestic progression from heaven, to sea, to land, climaxing with the creation of the human couple, the opening verses of Ecclesiastes are, on the contrary, suffocating, circular, and stagnant.[14] Finally, the conclusion of this ode to chaos sets itself in stark opposition with the conclusion of the creation story: "And God saw (*yreh*) all that he had made (*asa'*) and found it *very good*" (Gen. 1:31). The words of the king mirror the words of the Creator himself but insolently conclude the opposite: "I observed *(raiti)* all the happenings *(maaseh)* beneath the sun and I found that all is *futile and pursuit of the wind*" (Eccles. 1:14). And then the finishing blow: "A twisted thing that cannot be made straight, a lack that cannot be made good" (Eccles. 1:15). Clearly, this is a king whose kingdom has sunk into chaos, and whose responsibility as guardian of the cosmic order, of the Ma'at, has been tragically neglected.

This neglect of the goddess Ma'at, who was the sole protection against the forces of chaos, has now made the kingdom vulnerable to these forces. And as the cosmos sinks into chaos, the kingdom itself begins to fracture socially and politically, and injustice becomes rampant. Instead of the weighing of the hearts by Ma'at and her decreeing of the fate of the dead based on their just or unjust deeds,[15] we have "the same fate" overtaking both the just and the unjust (Eccles. 9:2), with all, "the righteous and the wicked, the good and the bad, the clean and the unclean, those who offer sacrifices and those who do not," sharing a common destiny (Eccles. 9:2). Instead of the just being ushered into the "field of reeds,"[16] the Egyptian afterlife—a lush environment of trees and rivers in the company of the gods—both the righteous and the wicked return to "dust" (Eccles. 3:20), "know nothing" (Eccles. 9:5), and "have no more recompense" (Eccles. 9:5). Instead of the king acting out his role as protector of the weak and of the destitute,[17] we have the "tears of the oppressed" who have "no comforter"[18] (Eccles. 4:1). In such a broken kingdom, "an upright man is requited according to the conduct of the scoundrel, and sometimes the scoundrel is requited according to the conduct of the upright" (Eccles. 8:14), and "slaves" ride on "horseback" while "nobles" walk "on the ground like slaves" (Eccles. 10:7).

Finally, we have the breakdown of the king himself, his tragic realization that *he* has lost his grip on the kingdom, and that the latter is about to go to one who is not his heir: "Better a poor but wise youth than an old and foolish king who no longer has the sense to heed warnings. For the former can emerge from a dungeon to become king, while the latter, even if born to kingship can become a pauper" (Eccles. 4:13–

15).[19] This realization is made with bitterness and with a poignant admission of a failed life: "So I loathed life.... So too I loathed all the wealth that I was gaining under the sun, for I shall leave it to the man who will succeed me—and who knows whether he will be wise or foolish" (Eccles. 2:18–20). This breakdown in the royal line is the result, by the king's own humble and tragic admission, of his own shortcomings and flaws as a ruler: "If you see the poor oppressed. . .and justice and rights denied, do not be surprised, for one official is eyed by a higher one. . .the king himself profits from the fields" (Eccles. 5:8–9).[20] In other words, the collapse of the kingdom through violence and injustice goes back ultimately to the moral breakdown of the king himself. And it is the king who self-incriminates when he cries out: "Woe to you land whose king was a child and whose princes feast in the morning" (Eccles. 10:16).[21]

Clearly, on all points, we are faced with an old and miserable king who, by his own admission, has lost touch with his Ma'at. But in losing his Ma'at, the king senses that he has lost his own *ba,* his own soul and it is this sense of his own vacuity, of his own emptiness that will propel him into extravagant economic ventures and self-aggrandizing architectural projects. No more able to please the gods with his Ma'at offering, the king now sinks into a narcissistic self-indulgence and self-worship. Unable to partner with the feminine anymore, the king's hereto protective and noble role degenerates into the works of a masculinity gone toxic. Let us turn to these dire times.

The Lost Garden

After the opening chapter where we witnessed the dissolution of the cosmic order into chaos due to the king's having lost his Ma'at, we now witness the king's own moral breakdown. In chapter 2, we have a king striving to fill the void that has been left by his neglect of his royal function as the guardian of Ma'at. Instead of a king intent on protecting the cosmic order, we find a man in the throes of toxic masculinity, engaged in a heated, obsessive, and narcissistic quest for meaning, success, and pleasure. He first begins with the quest for wisdom and knowledge: "I set my mind to study and to probe with wisdom all that happens under the sun.... I said to myself: 'Here I have grown richer and wiser than any that ruled before me over Jerusalem, and my mind has zealously absorbed wisdom and learning.' And so, I set my mind to appraise wisdom and to appraise madness and folly" (Eccles. 1:12–17). He then sets his heart on searching out all possible pleasurable experiences: "Come I will treat you to merriment. Taste mirth!. . .I ventured to tempt my flesh with wine and to grasp folly" (Eccles. 2:1–3). Finally, he turns to grandiose projects and self-aggrandizing ventures: "I multiplied by possessions. I built myself houses and I planted vineyards. I laid out gardens and groves, in which I planted every kind of fruit tree. I constructed pools of water, enough to irrigate a forest shooting up with trees. I bought male and female slaves, and I acquired stewards. I also acquired more cattle, both herds and flocks, than all who were before me in Jerusalem. I further amassed silver and gold and treasures of kings and provinces; and I got myself male and female singers, as well as the luxuries of commoners—coffers and coffers of them. Thus, I gained more wealth than anyone before me in Jerusalem" (Eccles. 2:4–10).

There are a number of connections between this chapter and the creation story. Both passages feature the elements of garden (*gan*), of fruit bearing trees (*etz pri*), of water (*mayim*), wind (*ruah*), and the quest for knowledge (*da'at*).[22] There are two fundamental differences, however: in Ecclesiastes 2, it is not God who is creating (*asa'*) the garden, the fruit bearing trees and the water, but Solomon (*asa'ti*). Thus, in this passage, Solomon, in a way, is trying to replicate Eden on his own, he is trying to build it, to make it happen, to force his way into it himself. The second difference is more problematic. The quest for limitless knowledge and experience that was forbidden in the garden, as embodied by the forbidden tree of knowledge/experience, is now unleashed by Solomon with no limitation: "I withheld from my eyes nothing they asked for, and I denied myself no enjoyment" (Eccles.

2:10). This is the second profound contrast between our passage and the creation story. Whereas in the creation story, a limit was placed on what the human couple could know or experience, whereas in the creation story a sacred boundary was drawn between the human and the divine realms, in Ecclesiastes 2 this limit is dissolved, and this boundary is overstepped. What Solomon is in effect doing here, is reaching for divinity. Like the pharaoh of Egypt, Solomon, in attempting to replicate Eden and in transgressing all limitations, is assuming the throne of a deity. There are profound similarities here between Solomon and Eve. Both yearn for limitlessness, both seek to withhold nothing from their "eyes" (Eccles. 2:10; Gen. 3:6), both usurp a divine prerogative—Solomon creates (*asa'*) and Eve gives (*natan*)—and as such, both reach for divine status. And both, in the end, because of this usurpation and the inability to inhabit their creaturiality, ultimately lose Eden.

Instead of the "good" (*tov*) that Eden represented, Solomon only finds "futility" (*hevel*). It is interesting that this chapter accounts for seven occurrences of "futility" (*hevel*), echoing the seven occurrences of "good" (*tov*) that we find in the Creation story.[23] In his usurping grasp for Eden and for the good (*tov*), Solomon only finds "futility" (*hevel*). Solomon realizes that he cannot force his way into Eden, he cannot reconstruct it for himself, he cannot lay a hold on it. The harder he tries, the more this Eden seems to escape him, to remain out of his reach, to dissolve into nothingness.[24] For this is ultimately the meaning of the word *hevel*. The first occurrence of this word is in Genesis 4, with the naming of the second son of Eve, Abel (*hevel*). In contrast to the first son Cain (*qayin*), whose name comes from the root *qanah*, which means to possess, acquire, grasp, the man Abel (*hevel*) has nothing, he owns nothing and his life is but a breath—he dissipates from the story as quickly as he appeared.[25] Such is the meaning of Abel (*hevel*): mere breath,[26] that which one cannot hold, grasp, possess—fleetingness, temporariness, precariousness. And this is what Solomon is realizing at the end of his exhaustive search, that what he is reaching for he can never possess, never hold on to, never truly grasp. Like a breath (*hevel*) it will always escape him, it will always dissipate in his hands, flow through his fingers. Eden remains a dream, an illusion, a utopia. And it is at this point, when he realizes that this Eden he has striven for all his life will always remain out of his reach, that Solomon breaks down in despair: "And I loathed life. For I was distressed by all that goes on under the sun, because everything is futile and pursuit of wind.... So too, I loathed all the wealth that I was gaining under the sun.... And so, I came to view with despair all the gains I had made under the sun...All his days his thoughts are grief and heartache, and even at night his mind has not respite" (Eccles. 2:17–23).

After a lifetime of searching, of building, of striving, Solomon bitterly realizes that the garden of Eden cannot be found by searching, by seeking, by striving. He painfully recognizes that all his efforts have come to naught, that all his achievements lie in ruin, that he is powerless, utterly powerless, in this world. And it is precisely at this moment that a profound illumination strikes him: "There is no *good* (*tov*) for a man[27] but to eat and drink and find satisfaction in his work" (Eccles. 2:24).[28] After what seemed to be an unending string of *hevels* (Eccles. 2:1; 2:11; 2:15; 2:17; 2:21; 2:23), suddenly, the *good* (*tov*) that characterized the original created world appears. At last, this "good" (*tov*) has revealed itself to the king in the very heart of his despair. At the moment where the king was most helpless, most at loss, most powerless, there emerges before him a profound vision of the Eden he had lost. Such an Eden cannot be grasped at however, it cannot be hoarded. It can only be graced: "There is no good for a man[29] but to eat and drink and find satisfaction in his work. This too I see is *from the hand of God.* For without him, who can eat and find enjoyment? To the man who pleases him, God *gives* (*natan*) wisdom, knowledge, and happiness; but to the sinner, he *gives* (*natan*) the task of gathering and storing up wealth, to hand it over to the one who pleases God" (Eccles. 2:24–26). In contrast to the gathering and storing up of wealth that the king has been doing, Eden can only be "given" (*natan*). Let us remember that the word "give" (*natan*) alludes back to the creation story where God "gives" to man his sustenance (Gen. 1:29). The word *natan* thus alludes back to the origins of the universe, when Eden was given to man by God, when happiness, sustenance, joy were gifts of the creator to a creature who could do nothing but receive it gratefully. This is what Solomon is realizing now: that the garden he was seeking, the joy he was striving for can only be *received*; that the happiness he was grasping for constitutes the inheritance of the humble creature, ever aware of its dependence on the creator, not of the man-god.

Thus, Solomon had to learn that wisdom, happiness, and success can only be received. That it is only in inhabiting his creatureliness, his fragility, his powerlessness that he could become positioned to receive the grace and gifts of the Creator. For Eden is the heritage of the humble and of the meek. And the only way for the king to now make his way back to Eden is to acknowledge his limitations, to accept that he is not a god with limitless power and knowledge over all things. For only then, when he has surrendered his willpower and narrow agendas for himself, can he truly position himself to receive that which can only be bestowed and graced. And as he begins to acknowledge and practice these limits, slowly, slowly but surely, the goddess Ma'at/Woman Wisdom begins to draw near, the forces of chaos begin to dissipate, and the cosmic order begins to become restored.

It is interesting that this vision of Eden, of its gifts (*natan/matat*), and of the good (*tov*) that Solomon has in our passage, occurs seven more times. The second occurrence is in Eccles. 3:12–13 where Solomon also glimpses the truth that there is "no good (*tov*) for men than to be happy and do good (*tov*) while they live. That everyone may eat and drink and see good (*tov*) in all his toil—this is the gift (*matat*) from God."[30] The third occurrence comes a few verses later: "I saw there is no good (*tov*)[31] other than for a man to enjoy his work because that is his lot" (Eccles. 3:22). The fourth comes three chapters later: "Then I realized that it is good (*tov*) and proper for a man to eat and drink and to see good (*tov*) in his toilsome labor under the sun during the few days of life God has given (*natan*) him…this is a gift (*matat*) from

God" (Eccles. 5:17–19). The fifth occurrence differs from the others in that it is written up in the interrogative: "For who knows what is good (*tov*) for a man in life, during the few and meaningless days he passes through like a shadow?" (Eccles. 6:12). But we still have there the common thread of the good (*tov*), of man (*adam*), and the "days of his [fleeting] life" (*yamei hai [hevelo]*), the latter expression being found in the last four occurrences (Eccles. 5; 6; 8; and 9). The sixth occurrence comes a few chapters later: "So I commend the enjoyment of life, because there is no good (*tov*)[32] for a man under the sun than to eat and drink and be glad. . .all the days of the life (*yamei hai*) God has given (*natan*) under the sun" (Eccles. 8:15). The seventh and final occurrence, however, differs from all earlier version in its mention of the wife: "Go and eat your food with gladness, and drink your wine with a good (*tov*)[33] heart, for its now that God favors what you do. Always be clothed in white, and always anoint your head with oil. Enjoy life *with your wife whom you love* all the days of this meaningless life (*yamei chai hevelo*) that God has given (*natan*) you under the sun" (Eccles. 9: 7–9).

King Solomon is given seven visions of Eden, seven reminders of God's gifts and of the fact that Eden can only be received. But it is only in the last vision that those gifts include the wife as beloved. It is as though it took this long for the king to reconnect with the feminine. As the king becomes more and more cognizant of his powerlessness, of his creaturiality, of his dependence on God, the toxic masculinity that inhabited him is slowly and gradually being softened to make room for a more receptive and humble approach to life. And it is at the end of this long journey of detoxification that king Solomon is able to again reconnect to the lost and neglected feminine dimension, to the wife, and by extension, to Woman Wisdom, and to his Ma'at. And as if to reinforce this lesson of humility, of creaturiality, of limitlessness, the author of our passage nails in one last *hevel:* "This too is futile and pursuit of wind" (Eccles. 2:26). In other words, as the king begins to receive, as he begins to be graced with the gifts of the Creator, and as Eden becomes more and more accessible, he must never forget that none of this is truly in his power, in his grasp and in his possession. Never must he relinquish the humility of his beginnings when it was still clear that his life, its success, happiness, and wisdom, was pure giftedness. Never ought he to forget that he built none of this, he deserved none of this, he worked for none of this. Never ought he to forget that, for all his hard work, he has not and never been in control. This profound realization is really the only way to truly relax into life, to stop striving, to stop overthinking and controlling, and humbly wait for God to bless his work and efforts, and to move on his behalf. And it is the only way for him to ultimately open a space in his life for the woman, whether she come in the person of the spouse or of Woman Wisdom.

Conclusion

And so, we have now come full circle. The beginning of our story revealed a king having lost his connection to his goddess, to Ma'at. We saw a world in chaos, a kingdom in disarray, and a broken king still grasping onto the illusion of power. It is only when the king realized the futility of his efforts, the *hevel* of his accomplishments and their inability to bring him rest, joy or happiness, that he began to glimpse the horizon of a new reality—the Eden reality marked by humility, surrender, and receptivity. And it is as the king begins to make his way back to Eden, to the good (*tov*), pushing through the chaos that surrounds him, through the ruins of his kingdom, and through the darkness that inhabits him, that he begins to change, to soften, to reconnect to all that he had lost, from himself to the woman that he had once loved. And it is to the degree that the king stops overreaching, steps down from his ambitions to godlikeness and total control, that room is made in his life, in his heart, in the innermost place, for Woman Wisdom and for the goddess Ma'at. For it is only in the acknowledgement of his limitations, of his despotic and tyrannical grasp on the kingdom, that the king can again offer up the Ma'at to the gods and rule justly.

Chapter 7

At the Feet of The Shulamite

Introduction

Tradition ascribes to King Solomon the authorship of the Song of Songs.[1] The Song of Songs, the third book of the Solomonic trilogy (along with Proverbs and Ecclesiastes), will be very different from its first two books. Proverbs and Ecclesiastes are both set in the king's court, and feature the king's heir being taught how to live a life worthy of his royal position, and how to attain wisdom. The king's heir is taught how to humbly heed a voice other than his own and how to connect intimately to Woman Wisdom, and by extension, to her embodiment in the wife. Thus, although the characters of Proverbs and Ecclesiastes are mostly male, the feminine remains at the center of their quest. Without Woman Wisdom, or her embodiment in the wife, the king cannot achieve the inner balance to rule justly. The books of Proverbs and Ecclesiastes were thus essentially written for a predominantly male audience with the objective of teaching courtly men the importance of cultivating an intimate relationship with the feminine. The Song of Songs, however, has a very different target audience. In the Song of Songs, Woman Wisdom—embodied by the Shulamite—is now the one doing the teaching, and her target audience is the "daughters of Jerusalem."[2] But what is she teaching? She is teaching the arts of love, of how to open the man's heart, how to find favor with the king. For it is in as much as the woman is *loved* that she will influence the king, that she will be able to share her wisdom with him. Thus, before she can fulfill her destiny as the embodiment of Woman Wisdom, a woman must learn to love a man, and to love him well. This is the essence of the Shulamite's teaching. But where we might expect a mature, wizened woman to do this teaching, we encounter, far to the contrary, a young, inexperienced, even reckless young woman. And yet, it is precisely this woman, whose journey we are about to enter, who will teach us the arts of love. For Woman Wisdom is moving, growing, evolving through this young woman as she emerges from reckless to mature lover and it is Woman Wisdom who speaks through her mouth and teaches the daughters of Jerusalem. Let us then turn to the elements of the book that fit with the mother's house genre.[3]

Masculine vs. Feminine

Although we have two lovers in the story, the woman is by far the most important character. She is the one who does most of the speaking; she is also the one who begins the dialogue and who concludes it. Her voice is thus heard as a merism, signaling the centrality of her role in the story. The woman is also the one who initiates the man to love: "Under the apple tree I roused you" (Song 8:5). In other words, she is the one teaching the man, awakening the man to the arts of love. The eroticism of the text reminds us of the sacred marriage stories surrounding the goddess Inanna, and indeed, there are clear parallels between the two texts.[4] The themes of "shepherd-king," of "sister-bride," of "entering the garden," (Song 5:1) the heightened eroticism, the mention of the "mother's house," (Song 8:21) all point to there being an overlap between the two stories.[5] The author of the Song of Songs seems to want his audience to identify the Shulamite—as fragile, reckless, and human as she is—with the great Sumerian goddess Inanna. The question is why? Because what Inanna was to the shepherd-king Dumuzi, the Shulamite will be to the shepherd-king Solomon. Just like Inanna lifts Dumuzi up to his highest royal destiny, we will see the Shulamite deepening the man's capacity for love—from a young, lustful royal, to one whose love is "as fierce as death" (Song 8:6–7). Just as Inanna inaugurated Dumuzi's reign, the Shulamite awakens her king to his highest destiny: which is to simply love. Now this is surprising in as much as we don't expect the highest calling of a king to be love. We would expect, as in the book of Ecclesiastes, for the king to excel in building majestic structures or to fight noble wars. The Song of Songs sees things very differently. Here, the highest destiny of the king is to learn to love a woman. Why? Because only in cleaving to his wife, will he rise to his highest self—one capable of ruling justly, compassionately, wisely and nobly. In the sacred marriage literary context, it is to the degree that the man is capable of receiving the woman, of loving her, that he rises to his royal destiny. Thus, the Shulamite's highest task in our story will be to awaken in her king lasting love. At the same time, her task is to teach the "daughters of Jerusalem" the love secrets of the goddess: How to awaken such a love in their own partners, that they too may reign well.

Vertical vs. Horizontal

The Song of Songs is written entirely as a dialogue between two lovers. God is never mentioned, except once towards the end. This, coupled with the heightened eroticism of the book caused some rabbis to want to excise this book from the canon.[6] The debate was fiery, and finally, one rabbi, Rabbi Akiba, prevailed by comparing the book to the "Holy of Holies" in the temple of Jerusalem.[7] The analogy is very rich and begs interpretation. What could he possibly mean by this? Let us remember that the temple of Jerusalem had several chambers: An outer court for the gentiles, a woman' s court, a man's court, the holy place where the Levites did most of their tasks (sacrifice, ablutions, etc.), and finally, a space that no one could enter, except the high priest, and then, only once a year, to cleanse it. This sacred space, where God's presence was said to reside, was called the Holy of Holies. What Rabbi Akiba is saying, then, is that the Song of Songs, just like the Holy of Holies, constitutes a sacred space where God's very presence is to be found. But how, given that the name of God is not even mentioned? Where then is God to be found in the Song of Songs? God, in the Song of Songs, is to be found "between" the two lovers. As the lovers' love matures, grows, evolves, as the lovers gradually move from their possessive grasp to the offering of their selves to the other, as they move from the self-centered quest for pleasure to sacrificial giving, God's presence begins to suffuse the text. And it is only at the term of a long and painful journey, when the lovers' love has finally been purified in the crucible of suffering, that God's name suddenly emerges, illuminating everything around it: "Place me like a seal over your heart, like a seal on your arm, for love is as strong as death, its jealousy unyielding as the grave, it burns like the flame of the *Lord*" (Song 8: 6).

Law vs. Wisdom

From the onset of the Song of Songs, the lovers break every rule of patriarchy. The first thing one notices is that there is no father. Typically, in patriarchal societies, the marriage was brokered by the men—typically the father of the woman and the future groom, or a relative of his—and only then was the woman asked for her consent.[8] Here, not only is there no father in sight, but the woman seems to be the one making all the moves. She is the one who initiates the relationship, in a language dripping with eroticism and, eventually, is the one also who, not unlike Ruth, proposes marriage.[9] This woman, moreover, breaks all the laws of modesty. Rather than veil herself before her beloved, like Rebekah did when she first saw Isaac, the Shulamite's body is on display in our text, as well as praised by her beloved. The couple also defies the laws of courtship: they prefer to be alone in the countryside rather than in the public eye, they do not respect the boundaries of sexual exploration,[10] and they do not wait for marriage before becoming intimate. She is not a virgin when she meets this man,[11] and neither is he. So, we have a case of a couple making every mistake in the book. What then can we possibly learn from their love affair? And why in the world is such a licentious book in the Hebrew Bible? Perhaps because the point of the story is not so much to teach us virtue as to teach us wisdom. And wisdom only can be acquired through experience, through the messy trials and errors of life. And indeed, both the man and the woman make some fatal mistakes. But they persist, and they grow, and they change. And as they journey together, they begin to understand each other more deeply, they begin to mature as lovers, and they begin to love well. This wisdom of love can be read between the lines of the poetry of the text when, taking a breath from her lovemaking, the Shulamite becomes reflective, and begins to address her sisters, the "daughters of Jerusalem" with what she is learning along the way, with the wisdom she is discovering within herself at the contact of her lover.

Holiness vs. Hospitality

Our text is the very antithesis of holiness (*qadosh*), which, in Hebrew, literally means "separation." In the Song of Songs, the separation between the lovers is constantly being violated, with the woman never wanting to let go of her beloved, and her beloved at times infringing upon her own intimate space and consent. Both trespass on the other's agency. Both overstep their boundaries, go too far, too fast, too soon. It is as though it were a characteristic of love to break down boundaries and fragilize agency. As though there was an inherent violence or violation in the act of love. The author of the text, moreover, does not seem to tire celebrating in poetry this breakdown of the self at the contact with the other. This story is also one of breathtaking hospitality on the part of the woman to her man. In her reception of the man there are no preludes, no rules of engagement, no pre-drawn contracts. She receives him without expectations, without any of the patriarchal protections, without any promises. She is madly in love in every sense of the term. And yet, her reckless hospitality of her beloved is celebrated through the poetic language of the author. Again, what is to be learned from this breakdown of boundaries, from this recklessness on the part of the woman? Perhaps that there can be no growth, no evolution, without being broken open, enlarged, expanded, sometimes pleasurably, sometimes painfully. Love is this process of breaking open of the hereto solitary and self-sufficient self in order to allow for its expansion, its transcendence towards another. The author celebrates this breakdown of boundaries because he senses, precisely in their threat to the integrity and autonomy of the self, the promise of transcendence. In Jewish weddings, the ceremony ends with the shattering of a wine glass. The symbolism is vivid and points to the inevitable and often painful "shattering" that love inevitably produces in the lovers: the shattering of their illusions, of their false selves, of their selfish egos, and of their pride. These "shatterings" are sometimes pleasurable, often painful, but unavoidable if there is ever to be true intimacy and closeness between the lovers.

Doing vs. Receiving

In our story, the woman emerges very quickly as the one making most of the power moves. In fact, for the first four chapters she is the only one taking initiatives. When the man is seen knocking on the woman's door in chapter 5, it is the first time he is making his own move. Clearly, the Shulamite is a very strong and willful woman who knows what she wants and who does not shy away from claiming the object of her desires, sometimes desperately. Tragically, this backfires for her. Rather than attracting the man, she pushes him away. Rather than seducing the man, she repulses him. It is only when she begins to relax into love, when she begins to release her grasp, and go with the flow, that things begin to change for her for the better. In a way, this story is the antidote to the story of Eve. Just like Eve, the Shulamite has deep, unfulfilled desires and just like Eve, she does not hesitate to take hold of what she wants. But like Eve, in grasping for what she wants, the Shulamite ends up losing everything. Unlike Eve, however, the Shulamite will reflect, will meditate, and will ponder on her actions, and begin to study another way: the way of the garden. The way of rest and of receptivity. And it is to the degree that she begins to learn the ways of the garden—to let go, to surrender, and to receive—that the Shulamite will begin to enjoy its abundance and its gifts. And it is to the degree that she enters into this rest, that she will begin to magnetize the man anew.

The Art of Seduction

Today, seduction has everything to do with power, and how to "get" the other to fall for us through certain attitudes and behaviors. We fashion ourselves an identity that they would want to date, we make sure we say what needs to be said and do what needs to be done for them to fall for us. The game of seduction has thus everything to do with hiding one's true self and with controlling the other's agency.[12] The arts of seduction we are about to explore in the Song of Songs reveal a completely different approach. Rather than hiding and controlling, the Shulamite reveals to us the seductive power of vulnerability and of restfulness. As such, her winning over of the man is anything but a power move; rather, it stems from her accepting her limits and releasing her grasp on what she desires. Rather than hide, the Shulamite unveils her heart, her desires for her man, in a deeply feminine way. And rather than try to control and manipulate the man's agency and consent, she rests in the knowledge that the man who truly loves her will come through for her. And it is the combination of these two actions that give her such magnetic power.

The Shulamite's first move is one of stunning vulnerability. She opens the Song with a desire: "Oh give me the kisses of your mouth, for your love is more delightful than wine" (Song 1:1). A few verses later, she expresses the desire to draw closer to him: "Draw me after you, let us run! …Let us delight and rejoice in your love" (Song 1:4). A chapter later, she misses him and longs to see him again: "O my dove, in the cranny of the rocks, hidden by the cliff, let me see your face, let me hear your voice" (Song 2:14). Eventually, she desires to become more intimate with him: "Let my beloved come to his garden and enjoy its luscious fruits!" (Song 4:16). Then she misses him again, wishes that things could be easier, simpler, between them: "If only it could be as with a brother, as if you had nursed at my mother's breast: Then I could kiss you when I meet you in the street and no one would despise me" (Song 8:1). Finally, she expresses the desire for commitment and marriage: "Let me be a seal upon your heart, like the seal upon your hand. For love is as fierce as death, passion is mighty as Sheol" (Song 8:6).

So, the first thing we have is a woman who is attuned to her heart, who knows what she wants. The Shulamite's genius lies in her ability to desire love, even when it is not readily available to her and remain open and available to life, to love, to hope, and to whatever is about to come her way. As such, she is incredibly attractive. Rather than attempting to draw in her lover by setting a low bar, she remains faithful to her own desires no matter how much of a challenge they present to her man. As such, she chooses to inspire her man rather than manipulate him, thereby awakening in him his highest impulses, elevating him, raising him up to a higher destiny rather than catering to his lowest instincts. And therein precisely lies her magnetic power and the power of her seductiveness: Rather than inspiring the downfall of man, rather than causing him to fall in love with her, she invites him to a higher love, a more exigent love, in one word, she challenges him to love her in the way that she longs to be loved. But she also knows that to desire is not enough. For desire can also imprison and become a source of pressure, coercion. And so, coupled with desire, the Shulamite knows that she must also learn the art of restfulness.

The art of restfulness has to do with the Shulamite's ability to wait and to attune herself to the rhythm of love. The Shulamite expresses the art of restfulness twice to the daughters of Jerusalem: "I adjure you, O maidens of Jerusalem, by the gazelles or by hinds of the field: Do not wake or rouse love until it please!" (Song 2:7, 3:5). What does it mean to "not wake love until it pleases"? It means that love needs time to grow, to mature, to awaken. The Shulamite instinctively knows therefore to give her beloved time to awaken to her presence. She realizes that although her own love might be ripe for the picking, her beloved might need more time. She therefore knows to give the man the space to approach her, to court her, to respond to her in his own time and way. As such, and this in spite of the anxiety she continuously harbors, the Shulamite understands the wisdom of remaining restful in the moments of togetherness as well as in the moments of separation without the need to steer, to make an impression, to demand, or to speed things up. Rather, she knows to enjoy the process and find joy in the moments of togetherness as well as in the moments of separation.

At bottom, the Shulamite's erotic power has everything to do with the way that she dwells in the uncertainty of still unanswered desires. For to desire is not to expect. There is a letting-be, a sense of joyful anticipation that follows a genuine desire, even when it still remains unmet. An expectation, however, puts one in a state of nervousness and anxiety if not catered to immediately. But our Shulamite, with all of her neediness, never expects. Her attitude never betrays manipulation, coercion or judgment, rather expressing praise and appreciation when addressing her lover. As such, in spite of often finding herself in a position of longing for more, she continuously chooses the high road of joyful receptivity, trusting that love will eventually find her and continuing to delight in the now. And it is precisely this attitude that makes her so captivating. One could argue that the key to the Shulamite's restfulness lies ultimately in trust: Trust in the love that she has been called to and to its own internal rhythm and exigencies: "Do not "wake or rouse love until it please!" (Song 2:7, 3:5).

In this passage, love is personified as a force or a will which transcends the lovers. The Shulamite here seems to be surrendering to this force, to this will outside of hers, to the experience itself of love. She knows that there is a rhythm of love, that there is an appointed time for love, that there is a story that is being written through her and her lover. And she understands the power of surrendering to love rather than trying to control the narrative. She understands the wisdom of aligning herself to the movement, to the flow of love rather than attempt to impose her own script, expectations and timeline on the experience she has been granted to live. In a powerful moment of insight, the Shulamite compares love to the "very flame of the Lord" (Song 8:6), thereby identifying love to divine agency. Love, as an expression of the divine fire, cannot be controlled, manipulated, forced or coerced. It can only be surrendered to. This is what the Shulamite had to understand: That love cannot be expected, demanded or forced. It is a grace that one can only open up to and make oneself available to.

Thus, the art of seduction entails two simultaneous actions: The attunement of the woman to her own desires, her ability to voice those desires, and the aptness of the woman to adopt an attitude of restfulness when it comes to the relationship's progression in time. At bottom, the seductive woman is a woman who both respects herself and her partner. Such a woman knows to honor her own feelings and desires, while at the same time, honoring the other's timing and agency. The art of seduction is thus a far cry from the contemporary definition of seduction as manipulation and hiding of one's true self. Rather than dishonor the other, by dissimulative and manipulative behavior, the Song of Song's art of seduction remains deeply sensitive to the self's and the other's dignity and honor. Seduction in the Song of Songs is ultimately respect. And it is such a respect, for herself and for the other, that ultimately makes this woman so captivating.

The Secret to Lasting Love

But it is not enough for the woman to know how to seduce her man and invite him into a relationship. Once in a relationship, she must learn to "build" her house, she must learn how to guard the fragile flame of love. She must enter into the "labor of love,"[13] she must engage in the art of "creative fidelity."[14] Labor, creativity, protection, are her new tasks. Too often, however, this labor is neglected; the lovers begin to drift apart in time and the passion they once shared becomes stale. At that moment, the temptation to leave, to give up, to start over with someone else, or to cheat, is almost irresistible. As for the one partner who doesn't want to leave or start over, they'll dutifully try to "make it work," to try to "fix" the relationship. At long last, they will realize that none of their efforts can save the relationship. The lovers will then either part for good or continue to live side by side with no true intimacy, and with the occasional (or regular!) flare of repressed rage and frustration. Either way, the labor of love has not taken place, and the house, rather than being built, has been torn down. Shockingly, the Song grapples with the same problem, and offers a radically different approach to a love gone stale.

Let us take a look at the text. In a subtle passage, a variation of which occurs two more times in the Song, we can decipher, between the lines, the temptation of infidelity: "My beloved is mine and I am his, who browses among the lilies" (Song 2:16). Here, the woman seems completely oblivious to the drama unfolding in the man's heart. While she is proclaiming her faithfulness to the man, the latter seems to be in a very different head space than her: "who browses among the lilies." Those familiar with the Song of Songs know that the lily is a metaphor for the beloved (Song 2:1). This passage, however, mention lilies in the plural, indicating the possibility of there being *other* beloveds, imagined or real. Clearly the man is wrestling with (or succumbing to) the temptation of infidelity. Let us take a look at the second occurrence of the passage: "I am my beloved's and my beloved is mine; he browses among the lilies" (Song 6:3). Here the lilies—i.e. other prospects—endure, but something has changed in the Shulamite's stance. She does not say anymore "my beloved is mine" but rather, "I am my beloved's." We will come back to the significance of this shift. Finally, the last occurrence of the passage reads as follows: "I am my beloved's, and his desire is for me" (Song 7:11). All of a sudden, the lilies are gone. And his desire is for *her,* and her only. The Hebrew word for desire, *teshuqah,* indicates a turning or returning towards the woman, implying a turning away from others.[15] It implies a strong, focused attention on her rather than on others. She is now the only one beloved of the man. Clearly, the love has been salvaged. Once diffuse, the man's desire has come into strong focus; once almost extinguished, the flame of love is going strong again as is evident in the following verses: "For love is as fierce as death; passion is mighty as Sheol; its darts are darts of fire, a blazing flame" (Song 8:6).

The question, of course, is how did she do it? How did she secure this man's commitment, and this in spite of his wandering heart? For it is really she who is pulling the strings here. Let us take a look. The first thing we notice in the text is the subtle shift the woman is making from "my beloved is mine" (Song 2:16) to "I am my beloved's" (Song 7:11; 8:6). Two things are taking place here. First, she is letting go of her possessive grasp. The beloved is no more hers ("My beloved is *mine*"), rather she is his ("*I am* my beloved's). Rather than trying to possess him, she surrenders to him, she is his. As such, she releases him from her possessive grasp, from her desperate need for his love. She releases him from having to be hers, from her own obsessive desire. Rather, she makes herself his, she offers herself to him, rather than grasps on to him. She sets him free.

Interestingly, by setting him free, she simultaneously sets herself free. "I am my beloved's." Here, she moves from her obsession with him, her loss of herself in him, back to herself. She recovers her I. Somewhere, along the way, she had lost herself in him, she had merged with him to the point of not recognizing herself anymore. When the relationship goes stale, two therapeutic questions must be asked: "Am I free?" and "Is the other free?" Have I lost myself in you? Or have I submerged you? Have you lost yourself in me? Have you compromised your integrity, your agency, your dreams for me? Have I for you? The relationship will begin to heal to the degree that each partner reconnects with their lost selves. It might mean asking oneself how they have attempted to control the other, how they have attempted to force them into an ideal, an image of what they wanted them to be. Recovering one's "I" might also mean focusing on oneself, rather than on the relationship. It might mean taking the time and space to heal, to mourn, to emerge, rather than focusing on "fixing" the relationship. Finally, recovering one's "I" might entail a separation. Sometimes the only way to recover one's integrity is to separate from the beloved. Sometimes, the only way the beloved will recognize the depth of their betrayal is when their lover departs from them.

This act of releasing the other from the self's possessive and controlling grasp is not synonymous, however, with giving up on the relationship. At the same time, and in the same movement of letting go, the Shulamite remains steadfast in her love. In other words, while letting go of the man, while releasing him from her expectations, she also chooses to stay the course: "My beloved is mine/I am my beloved's." This she repeats to herself like mantra. Let us be clear, this is an inner shift, not something that she proclaims to the man. *Inwardly*, the woman chooses to stay the course, to get off the fence, to give it her all, to put all the apples in the same basket. In one word, she *commits* to the relationship internally, and this, whether the man is ready or not. This is of course a huge risk, which entails the possibility of time wasted and failure to achieve what she wants. But this is the costly and sacrificial price of overcoming the death throes in which the relationship has fallen. This leap of "faith" (*emounah*)—which in Hebrew means to "remain,"[16] to stay, to not budge—is really the only action powerful enough to conquer death. And so, the woman stays the course, allowing herself to witness what might lie on the other side of her tenacity, what this dark night, this winter might bring. In other words, she enters a place of deep stillness. She stops all strivings, all efforts, all grasping. She makes herself go still. She rests. And it is precisely at that moment that her lover turns back to her.

It is interesting to realize that as long as the woman was trying to make things work, as long as she was grasping at the relationship, "my beloved is mine," the relationship was deteriorating, the lilies were enduring and the man remained caught up in them. It is only when she opened her hand, released her grasp, and entered a season of rest that the man, without any effort on her part, suddenly turned back and made his way to her. Now this is not to say that we have here a universal remedy for infidelity. That the man turned back to the Shulamite does not mean that this will necessarily happen in other situations, even when the betrayed partner has assimilated and applied all of the Shulamite's wisdom. All this teaches us is that, although love cannot be forced, it may be invited back in. The Shulamite's journey shows us that a path to the renewal and rebirth of the relationship is sometimes possible—even in the case of infidelity—should the betrayed partner choose to take it. For love ultimately cannot be worked for, it cannot be earned, it cannot be "resolved" and it cannot be "fixed." Love is a grace that comes when all strivings have ceased. All the woman really did was to stay the course, and remain hopeful and open for what lay beyond the dark night she was traversing, whatever that would end up being. For some women, what lies beyond will be a restored relationship, for others, the grace to know that the relationship has run its course and that a separation is the only loving thing left to do, not just for herself, but also for her lover. The key ultimately lies in allowing rather than managing the love journey. The wait simply attunes us to the inner workings of this love, allowing these to unfold organically and bring the lovers to their destination, wherever that might be.

Conclusion

What is interesting about the Shulamite's teachings is that they are all ultimately about rest. The woman's seductive powers really lay in her ability to rest, to find the stillness to connect to her own desires, and to wait for her lover to respond to her desires (or not!). The secrets to lasting love also entail a form of restfulness, i.e., the ability to stay the course, to not move, to commit oneself, in one word, to remain *still*, while simultaneously setting the other free. This stillness is surprisingly fruitful because ultimately love can only be received as a gift from God. The Song describes love as the very "flame of Yah" (Song 8:6), with Yah being a reference to God's name. Love is thus a grace that comes to those who know to make themselves still, who know to adopt a stance of restfulness. It is not something that the lovers are responsible for, can achieve, make happen, or fix. We can only say "here I am," *hineni*. This stillness that the Shulamite is discovering is, moreover, the antidote for the woman's inherent and dangerous restlessness, inherited from Eve. And in a way, the Song of Songs constitutes a healing text for what occurred in the garden of Eden.[17] We remember that Eve's main problem was precisely her grasping attitude towards life. Although Eve was keenly attuned to her desires, she did not know how to ask for and *receive* these desires from the Creator. And so, she "took" (*laqah)* the object of desire, thereby precipitating the demise of the garden and of everything she hoped for. In relinquishing control, in releasing her grasp, the Shulamite is reversing Eve's actions, insodoing receiving back everything that Eve had lost: love, intimacy, and companionship.

Chapter 8

Esther: From Concubine to Queen

Introduction

Tradition holds Mordechai accountable for the authorship of the book of Esther.[1] Mordechai, as the story goes, was a high-ranking official of the court of the Persian king Ahasuerus, in Babylon, where the Jews had been exiled from Jerusalem decades before. So, Mordechai, unlike most of the authors we have hereto encountered, is not a citizen of the land of Israel; rather, he is a citizen of Babylon, a Jew in exile. As such, his writings will profoundly differ from that of his Israelite predecessors, and the literature that will flow from his pen will constitute a genre in in its own right: the literature of the Diaspora. This Diaspora literature will feature the Jews that stayed behind after the reconstruction of Jerusalem, the Jews that had so well adapted to Babylonian culture they felt no need to return to the land of their ancestors. These are the assimilated Jews, the ones who would remain in Babylon until our present times, the Iranian and Iraqi Jews. The book of Esther thus opens up a window on the intricacies and perplexities of Jewish life in the Diaspora: How to survive as a Jew in a foreign land and, in the case of Esther, as a woman in a male-dominated society. Yet, what is interesting about the character of Esther is that she not only survives in the royal Babylonian court, she ends up thriving there. The story narrates her careful maneuvers in the heavily patriarchal society of Babylon, her inner struggles and anguish, and her eventual stunning rise to unprecedented power and equality with the king of the land. Esther starts out as a humble, unassuming orphan, and ends up taking on the very traits of the goddess of Babylon—Ishtar—the goddess of war and love. Like

Ishtar, Esther ends up mastering both the arts of love and of war. She ends up seducing the king of the land and waging war with her enemies. She emerges out of the darkness of captivity and exile, in all her feminine radiance and power, fiercely defeating the forces of chaos and of darkness, and causing a new dawn to rise in the empire, a time of feasting and of joy. The questions that arise are: How did she do it? And what can we learn as women from Queen Esther's amazing accomplishments? But first, let us turn to the mother's house characteristics of the book of Esther.

Male vs. Female

As mentioned before, the book of Esther is really a story written about women and for women, featuring from the onset the diverging destinies of two women trapped in the oppressive atmosphere of patriarchy: Queen Vashti and Queen Esther. It is easy to ignore Vashti, who very quickly exits the story. But it is impossible to measure Esther's accomplishments without situating them against the backdrop of Vashti's struggles.[2] The two women, although very different, are united in a number of similarities: they are both of royal descent,[3] both of them are successively married to the king of Persia, and both women struggle with protecting their own dignity and personhood in a deeply entrenched and brutal patriarchal setting. Only one of them, however, makes it to the end of the story: Queen Esther. So, the story of Esther is really a story of feminine individuation in a male-dominated society. One wonders, however, how Esther managed not only to survive in such an oppressive context, but to thrive. We long to know this Persian Queen better, to hear her story, and to learn from her. And the book does not disappoint, taking its audience into intimate women's spaces, into Esther's boudoir, so to say, so that we might witness firsthand the making of a queen. The story begins in a harem and ends in a bedchamber. At each stage, we become privy of Esther's discerning and wise actions, and to where such actions, when performed with meticulousness and discipline, can take a woman. For it is in the harem that

Esther is first introduced to the "laws of women," to those practices that open the door into the man's heart and ignite his favor. But it is in the bedchamber that Esther ultimately overcomes her king through courageous and decisive action, thereby sealing her own authority. But what is interesting is that her rise to power in no way weakens the king's authority; rather, Esther's individuation results in the king himself consolidating his own power. As she rises, he rises. So, although the book of Esther's main focus is the female protagonists' journey, the latter exercises a profound influence on her partner's own individuation as a man and as a king. But the reverse is also true. Unlike Vashti, who sought to individuate in opposition to the king, Queen Esther individuates within her relationship with this difficult man that is the king. She individuates relationally and not in isolation. Both partners thus help with the other's rise and individuation as prescribed by the sacred marriage trope. The book of Esther thus belongs, as do the other books we have seen, to the Hebrew corpus of sacred marriage literature.

Vertical vs. Horizontal

The book of Esther is one of the rare books in the Hebrew Bible where God's name is not at all mentioned. For this reason, the presence of the book of Esther in the biblical canon was debated by the rabbis. This eclipse of God, however, is typical of Diaspora literature, where God is not as obviously present and involved as in the land of Israel. This, however, does not make him absent. The rabbis explained this discrete presence of God in their exploration of Esther's name. According to the ancient rabbis, Esther's name might have been built from the Hebrew verb *lehastir* which means "to hide" or "to conceal." Thus, the name of Esther points to the hiding of God's face throughout the story. In the book of Esther, God is not absent, he is merely hiding or concealed. The God of the book of Esther is thus a God who is acting behind the scenes; He is the one pulling the invisible strings of destinies and fates.[4] At the same time, however, this hidden God is not acting alone. His saving power has to be activated by courageous human action and initiative. If Esther had not risen to the task of courageously confronting the king about the fate of her people, God's saving power could not have been released. If Esther had remained neutral, uninvolved, and indifferent to her responsibilities, God's hands would have remained tied, and salvation would not have ensued. And this in spite of Mordechai's threat that salvation would have arisen from "another quarter" (Esther 4:14). In our story, divine favor rests on human initiative, and we are given no hint that salvation would have occurred outside of the scope of Queen Esther's brazen actions and words.

Law vs. Wisdom

In the Diaspora context of the book of Esther, the instinct of survival takes precedence over the meticulous keeping of Jewish law. This obvious disregard for Jewish law by our female protagonist has been a source of horror for a number of Jewish commentators. The translation into Greek of the book of Esther is thus privy to a number of rabbinical edits: When Esther is asked by Mordechai to speak to the king and Esther asks for a fast to take place while she decides on her course of action, the translators of the Greek version of the book of Esther insert a long, pious prayer to God in Esther's mouth, where she asks for forgiveness for having to sleep with the uncircumcised king, and where she reminds God that she has kept kosher all along, thereby giving a religious flavor to Esther's plea.[5] The original Hebrew story, on the other hand, gives little attention to Jewish law, focusing rather on the young woman's survival instincts. And as a survivor, Esther learns to submit, to surrender, and to keep silent. She excels in the art of "going with the flow" rather than in her flawless keeping of the law. Interestingly, it is not only Jewish law that Esther ends up transgressing. She also finds herself having to break Persian law. Submissiveness has limits and can only take our young protagonist so far. For in the end, Esther's surrender and blind submission to Babylonian law turns against her when the genocide of her people is decreed. Rather than continue in her surrendered path, she is forced by this new development to take a stance and break Babylonian law by entering the king's court uninvited, to request an audience. At that point, Esther has to rely on wisdom rather than on blind obedience to the law, and it is through her wisdom, her ability to speak wise, perceptive, and alluring words, that she ends up successfully turning the king's favor back towards herself and her people.[6]

Holiness vs. Hospitality

There is an interesting contrast between the book of Esther and the book of Daniel. Although both take place in the context of Babylonian captivity, and both feature a strong central Hebrew protagonist, their *ethos* is widely divergent. In the book of Daniel, the main character, Daniel, does everything to affirm his Jewish identity in the face of assimilation. He rejects his Babylonian name, asks to be able to keep kosher at the king's table, continues to ostensibly pray three times a day towards Jerusalem. Esther, on the other hand, does everything to hide her Jewish identity and to assimilate. She is known by her Babylonian name Esther, or *Ishtar*. She hides her Jewish identity. She manifests no desire to keep Jewish law, does everything that she is told, and ends up sharing a bed with a pagan king. On the surface, Esther seems to have taken the opposite stance as Daniel. While he carefully cultivates an attitude of holiness, that is to say, of separation, Esther chooses to assimilate without a second thought. At the same time, we can see how there exists in the story of Esther, a subtle form of resistance. This resistance has to do with her hiding her true name, Hadassah. Now this is significant inasmuch as, in the Hebrew context, a person's name marks their identity and destiny. By dissimulating her name, Esther, in a way, is dissimulating her true identity, her true destiny, in a word, her true power. As such, while she is not, like Daniel, taking a public stance for her Jewishness, by hiding her name, Esther is in effect protecting her internality, her inner life, the inner sanctum of her Jewishness. Interestingly, the ancient rabbis see the myrtle (in Hebrew Hadassah) as the symbol of the survival of the righteous living among the wicked.[7]

The myrtle, even among thorns, remains itself, does not become altered. Thus, the myrtle adequately describes Esther's subtle resistance as the refusal to *internally* succumb to Babylonian assimilation. Yet, Esther's internal holiness, or separation, remains only a means to an end, it is only a stage in her individuation. Ultimately, she reaches her full-fledged royal status as Queen only through the courageous and risky act of hospitality of an uncircumcised, impure and unpredictable king. Ultimately, it is through her heroic welcoming of the Other that Esther finds her true self, that she rises to the heights of her true destiny. Holiness is thus not what saves Queen Esther from oblivion and assimilation, as it did for the prophet Daniel. Hospitality is what truly constitutes the redemptive moment of the story.

Doing vs. Receiving

It is interesting to note that Esther is initially neither doing nor receiving. In fact, the young Esther that we encounter at the beginning of the story is completely passive. And, apart from her good looks and her desire to please, Esther does not really leave a strong impression on the reader. Young Esther is content to go with the flow, to do what she is told, and to please the adults in the room. We do not see in her any trace of what she will later become: a powerful seductress and a warrior queen. In fact, the young Esther of our story seems rather bland and insignificant. It is only once she decides to take courageous action that Esther's true nature is revealed. Only when she chooses to take a stance, to risk it all, does she earn her powerful name and destiny as the goddess of love and of war. So, Esther rises to her royal self through action, not submission.[8] She is ultimately a doer, and her sacrificial action is what marks the moment of her individuation into a queen. Yet, at the same time, her courageous action of going to the king uninvited is not what constitutes the redemptive moment of the story. The moment of salvation comes really when she finds the words to awaken the *king's* actions, to awaken in him a response to her desires. It is when she asks the king for help and *receives* that help, that the tide begins to turn for herself and for her people. Ultimately, Esther's genius lies in her ability to awaken the king's generosity towards her, through skillful words and timing. In this, Esther remains a profoundly feminine figure. Rather than take rash and impatient action—as her predecessor Vashti—she chooses to partner with the king and ask for his help against his own edict. And it is to the degree that she is able to move the king's heart in her favor, to bend his ear, and inspire his generosity, that Esther obtains victory for her people. Her whole endeavor is thus not so much a doing than it is an opening up of a space in her marriage for giving and receiving.

The Failed Marriage

The opening scene of the book of Esther is that of a love gone cold between the king and his wife Vashti and the resulting chaos that ensues. It is against this botched covenant between man and woman that Queen Esther's story will unfold, her unprecedented rise, as a woman, and the sacred marriage that she ends up weaving between herself and the king of Persia. But before Esther can arrive on the scene, our story gives us an insight into the makings of a failed marriage, and of what results from this broken union. For Vashti's relationship with the king constitutes the very antithesis of the sacred marriage trope. In the sacred marriage between Inanna and Dumuzi, we witness the rise of a powerful woman or goddess, Inanna, as well as details into her life-giving and empowering union with the shepherd Dumuzi. We remember from the story how it is to the degree that Dumuzi was capable of welcoming Inanna, of loving and pleasing her, that he is able to rise to power and receive the authority to rule from his goddess.[9] As a result of this union, moreover, the whole world is rejuvenated and renewed and the fertile rains are again released onto the soon to be harvested fields. The sacred marriage is thus the guardian of cosmic order, keeping the forces of death, drought, and famine at bay. The story of Vashti and the king, tragically, constitutes the opposite of this on every point.

The first thing we notice about Vashti's relationship with the king is their separateness. There is no dialogue, no interaction, no alliance, no community between the two, rather, they seem to operate in parallel universes—a universe of men and a universe of women. Our text notes that, when the king decides to organize a grand banquet for the high-ranking officials of his kingdom, Vashti chooses to do the same, but for the women: "In addition, queen Vashti gave a banquet for women, in the royal palace of king Ahasuerus" (Esther 1:9). Unlike other Persian court banquets, where women are also present, and notably the queen mother (cf. Dan. 5:10), here, we have a male-only feast hosted by the king, which is then mirrored in a female-only feast hosted by the queen. Our story thereby hints at a deep rift that seems to already have existed between the king and the queen, between the male and female principles, in the kingdom of Persia. There is furthermore no conversation between them. They do not speak to each other. Rather, the king is seen barking orders at his wife, with the queen responding with impudence and brazenness.

But there is more. Instead of the beautiful equilibrium and reciprocity that existed between Inanna and Dumuzi, with each one empowering the other in some way, our story reveals rather the oppressive character of an all-powerful male leaving no room for feminine personhood and agency. This is already evident in the opening lines of the story where the banquet rules of drinking is "no restrictions" (Esther 1:8). In other words, no limits, no boundaries are placed on the male guests' desires, lusts, and impulses. In such a world, the male rules everything, demands everything and obtains everything: "For the king had given orders to every palace steward to comply with each man's wishes" (Esther 1:8). No wonder the queen organized a separate banquet for the women! Such a licentious context where free reign is given to male desire—no restrictions, no boundaries, no limits—is indeed a dangerous place for a woman to be. And in such a world, where nothing limits male desire, there can be no room for a feminine other, for feminine desire, and for feminine agency. The woman in such a world can be nothing more than an object of male gratification, at hand to be ordered around, and discarded when no longer needed. We see this, of course, when the king, already well imbibed, orders for his wife Vashti to be put on display for the other guests in attendance. At no moment does he speak to her directly, leaving open the possibility for her to respond. Rather, he orders his servants to "bring" her (Esther 1:11) into the banquet hall with her royal diadem in order to impress his other guests. Unlike Dumuzi who spent hours wooing Inanna in order to attract her consent, the king here has no concern for Vashti's agency. She is but an object to him, a prop for his own magnificence.

In the court of Ahasuerus, the woman is not an interlocutor. She is not consulted, she is not spoken to, and, more tragically, she is not *heard.* We see this in the gathering of the king's wise *men* (Esther 1: 14). Contrary to Sumer, Egypt, and Ancient Israel, where wisdom is embodied by the woman, here, in Babylon, wisdom has become relegated to the male sphere. The woman is thus completely muted in Babylon. There is in Babylon no goddess of wisdom, nor is there an embodiment of wisdom in the spouse. We are here in a completely patriarchal system with no room for the feminine. In such a context there can be no sacred *marriage,* and therefore, no awakening of the man by the woman, no bestowing on the king of authority, royalty, and reign. And indeed, king Ahasuerus' reign is marked by his lack of authority, and by the chaos of his reign. We see evidence of the king's insecurity in his lavish invitation extended to his officials and courtiers. Our story goes into great detail to describe the lengths that the king went to in order to impress his noblemen: "For no fewer than a hundred and eighty days the king displayed the vast riches of his kingdom and the splendid glory of his majesty" (Esther 1:4). No confident king would need such a display of his power and majesty. This vulgar display of power and authority can only come from one not used to power and wealth. And indeed, we learn from the ancient rabbis that Vashti was the only true royal in the palace; with Ahasuerus having been a mere commoner before marrying into royalty.[10]

But the king is not just insecure, he is also incompetent.[11] What king spends one hundred and eighty days in a state of feasting and drunkenness? The book of Ecclesiastes warned us against such a monarch: "Woe to the land whose king was a servant and whose princes feast in the morning. Blessed is the land whose king is of noble birth and whose princes eat at a proper time—for strength and not for drunkenness" (Eccles. 10:16–17).[12] Such a king is unfit to lead and, indeed, we see this in the way that the king ends up never being able to take a stance without the help of his advisers, and in the manner that the latter in turn end up influencing and manipulating him (cf. Esther 1:13–21; 3:7–14). Such a king does not deserve his subjects' reverence and respect, let alone his wife's: "But Queen Vashti refused to come at the king's command" (Esther 1:12). And so, as a result of this failed sacred marriage, the kingdom is thrown in chaos. This chaos is blamed by the king's advisers on the queen's refusal to obey the king (Esther 1:16–18), but Queen Vashti's refusal can be contextualized in an already pre-existing chaos—that created by a king not having been invested with proper authority to rule, a king devoid of character and self-discipline, and a king incapable of putting a limit on his will to power, in order to allow for the feminine voices of wisdom to inspire and empower his rule. Such a king is incapable of injecting life into his kingdom, he is unable to bring about the cosmic renewal needed for the earth, and his reign to bear fruit. Rather, the story reveals an oppressive climate of stagnation and irrevocability: "Let it be written into the laws of Persia and Media, so that it cannot be abrogated that queen Vashti shall never enter the presence of king Ahasuerus" (Esther 1:19). In such a decree there is no flexibility, no room for deliberation or dialogue, no compromise, no way out. By such a dogmatic decree, all the persons concerned become trapped in a status quo that leaves no room for renewal, rebirth, or progress. We are in a rigid universe where everything is doomed to remain the same. As Ecclesiastes notes: "There is nothing new under the sun" (Eccles. 1:9).

There is, however, one small redemptive detail about the king that our story notes in passing but which will prove fruitful as the story progresses: "Sometime afterward, when the anger of King Ahasuerus subsided, he thought of Vashti and what she had done, and what had been decreed against her" (Esther 2:1). The king misses Vashti. In other words, while impulsive and coarse, the king is not heartless. As the story progresses, we see that the king is capable of a whole range of noble feelings, from regret, gratitude, clemency, generosity, to righteous anger. It is this which saves this king and makes it possible for Queen Esther to eventually create a lasting and fruitful partnership with him. The king is crude and barbaric, but he is also capable of love and of loyalty. And it is on this terrain that Queen Esther will build her marriage, thereby not only empowering herself, but also this king who, we will see, will grow and mature alongside of her own individuation.

Life in the Harem

The scenes that follow the violent abduction of Esther to the palace offer an almost painful contrast. We are given a rare glimpse into the secrecy of a Babylonian harem. There, the women are particularly well taken care of, offered five-star culinary delicacies, given an entourage of maids, special beauty treatments, and expensive gifts of perfumed oils and cosmetics. For these women coming mostly from the working class, used to herding animals in dusty and arid steppes, or laboring in thorn and rock-filled olive groves or dirt-filled fields of grain, this is surely an upgrade. The only work they are given is that of intensive self-care routines in preparation for the king's bed. Over the twelve months of treatment, the women will see their hereto cracked and dry skin and hair recover their suppleness and shine, the callouses on their hands and feet meticulously sanded off, the perennial scent of livestock and dirt on their skin replaced with scented oils and perfumes from the East, and their eyes and lips enhanced by Egyptian cosmetics.

Yet, although the women live in luxury, their sacrifice is unspeakable, for who is to tell who and what these women were torn from:

aging parents, lovers, younger siblings. The twelve-month treatment of these women, although certainly luxurious, also constitutes a washing and scrubbing away of everything which, in their bodies, is reminiscent of their past lives. At the end of the twelve months, gone are all signs of their hardened and weathered bodies, accustomed to hard labor in the steppes or in the fields, gone are the calloused hands that once picked grain, herded sheep, caressed the heads of younger siblings, and lovers' bodies. Gone are the cracked feet that once walked freely and purposefully in the morning dawn to the next village, or to the field. The harem takes away all of this and constitutes an erasure of these women's working bodies, of their past productive lives spent working in the fields, in the home, nurturing others. The individual life of each woman thus finds itself conformed and molded into that of a generic beauty queen whose only purpose from now on will be to serve as a "playmate" to the king. Thus, these women find their agency, their freedom, their loves, and their dreams embalmed by the myrrh and perfumed oils massaged into them. Their bodies are no more a subject, but a mere object, a plaything in the king's playpen.

There is here a form of totalitarianism reminiscent of the book of Daniel whose opening chapter reveals the same suffocating predicament. There too, we find a group of young people that have been forcefully taken captive, yet, upon arriving to the king's court, given special treatment. Like the women in the king's harem, these men are also given special foods, and while their bodies remain untouched, it is now their minds that are conformed and molded to the Chaldean language and worldview. Both Daniel and Esther, however, manage to find favor with the chief Eunuch of the king and are given some breathing room. And both try to protect their identities by preserving their Hebrew names: Daniel does so by modifying the Babylonian name that is given to him, and Esther by hiding her true name. But while Daniel chooses to ostensibly resist the machine of assimilation, Esther chooses to surrender to it. Numb from the trauma of her capture, the young woman seems to have lost all the fight in her, choosing rather submission and scrupulous obedience to the voices of authority that surround her. And so, not only is Esther "taken" (*laqah*), a verb which implies violence and forcefulness (Esther 2:8),[13] but she also bends over backwards to please and win her captors' favor (Esther 2:9). She also submissively goes through the motions of protecting her identity, not as an act of revolt or of refusal to assimilate, but as ordered by Mordechai (Esther 2:10) and, when the moment comes to go unto the king, she does not "ask for anything but what Hegai advised" (Esther 2:15). Her spirit, broken by the forceful separation from the only man she has ever loved, Esther is but the shadow of the beautiful, vibrant, loving, and strong-willed woman she used to be. For to have been named Ishtar, she must have had character and willpower.[14] But these traits have been progressively subdued, if not erased, during the last twelve months of harem life.

Yet, in spite of her resignation, Esther ends up not only winning the hearts of all who saw her, but she also manages to seduce the king of Persia in one night. "Yet" says our text, "yet Esther won the admiration of all who saw her" (Esther 2:15).[15] This is a shocking turning point in our story. Rather than inspiring pity, the wounded young woman ends up turning heads and piercing hearts. The question of course is how? Wherein lies her seductiveness. It cannot be mere beauty, since all of the other women are just as beautiful! It must be something else. Let us turn to the text again: And Esther "did not ask for anything but what Hegai, the king's eunuch, guardian of the women, advised. Yet Esther won the admiration of all who saw her" (Esther 2:15). Our text reads Esther's winning the "admiration" of all in connection with her "not asking for anything but what Hegai...advised." The author of this passage seems surprised that, even though Esther asks for nothing, she ends up obtaining the highest favor of everyone around her. But it can be argued that it is precisely in not asking for more than what is advised that she gains favor. How so? By following Hegai's advice, Esther shows herself to be wise, capable of reading the room, and of listening to others. Let us remember that the seat of wisdom in the Ancient Near East lies in the ears, in the ability to listen to others and to open up to possibilities beyond one's narrow conceptualizations or agendas. Thus, beyond her beauty, Esther shows signs of wisdom, of a rare ability to listen, to align, and to flow with life's designs. And it is precisely this wisdom which sets her apart from the other women. Like so many Biblical women before her, Esther is not only beautiful, she is also wise.

The seductive power of Esther thus does not come from striving. It does not emerge from her hard work beautifying herself, it does not emerge from her scheming or devising strategies to win the king over. Simply put, the woman is most seductive when she is the least trying to be. More importantly, a woman is most attractive when she knows to put another's desire before her own, as she has had to learn over the last twelve months in the harem. And while many would find this to be the sure sign of her disempowerment, I would argue that therein lies precisely her power, her "soft power." For only a woman who shows herself capable of yielding to the man she loves, will in turn be yielded to by her lover. Only the woman capable of surrendering to her lover can in turn be surrendered to. For by yielding and surrendering, the woman wins her man's heart. And now, as the goddess of his heart, she can, in turn, win his favor when the time comes, and when it truly matters. For the woman who knows to yield to her man in the small daily opportunities of their life together, will find that, in the big things, in the things and moments that matter, her man will graciously yield to her. Exactly like King Ahasuerus would himself yield to his Queen, later in the story. But for this turning point to happen, Esther will have to morph from a passive, yielding concubine to a courageous queen, capable of voicing her *own* desires.

The Making of a Queen

There is no turning point without a crisis. Had the edict not been pronounced against the Jews of Persia, Esther would have remained an obscure concubine, with but a momentary rise to fame, only to eventually be discarded and forgotten. For "charm is deceptive and beauty is fleeting" (Prov. 31:30).[16] Eventually the king would have become bored of this woman so intent on pleasing him and of doing what she was told. And Esther would never have risen from meek and docile concubine to the warrior queen she would become. For this transformation to happen, Esther needed to change. And for her to change, tragedy needed to strike. And so, it did.

Having been informed of the king's irrational and vicious decree to destroy all Jewish life in his kingdom, under the influence of his perfidious advisor Haman, Esther is exhorted by Mordechai to plead with the king on behalf of the Jews of Persia. Knowing that going up to the king's throne room unsolicited merits the death penalty, Esther initially refuses. But Mordechai rebukes her sternly saying: "Do not imagine that you, of all the Jews, will escape with your life by being in the king's palace. On the contrary, if you keep silent in this crisis, relief and deliverance will come to the Jews from another quarter, while you and your father's house will perish. And who knows, perhaps you have attained to royal position for just such a crisis" (Esther 4:13–14). There comes a time in a woman's life where she must either evolve or die. A time where she either faces the crisis head on or allows that crisis to annihilate her. There are moments in the journey of love where the pain is so profound that change, transformation, movement becomes inevitable if a woman is to escape the disintegration of her personality. Yet, that change is often perceived as a more dire threat than the status quo. So many women resist change, resist evolution, resist the moment of individuation from concubine to queen, because of their fear of consequences, of what people will say, their fear of how their man will react, their fear of reprisals, of violence, or simply their fear of endangering the already fragile equilibrium of their marriage, and of ultimately losing everything they have worked for, for so long. And so, women too often choose to remain in the status quo, thereby tragically forfeiting the powerful woman they could have evolved into and forsaking the heights to which they could have raised their man. For change cannot occur without moving into the moment of death, and it is this death that Esther chooses to courageously face.

And so, Esther valiantly accepts to step into the crisis, to enter into the storm, and to face the darkness that has suddenly become unleashed in her life. She accepts the fate of her own undoing symbolically, through the ritual gesture of fasting for three days. The act of fasting in the Ancient Near East was performed to symbolize the dissolution and undoing of the self before God. The adept would wear sackcloth—used to bury the dead—and pour ashes over their head—symbolizing the decomposing corpse. Through this act of ritual annihilation before God, the adept hoped to open a space, a path for divine intervention and power. The time span of "three days" also echoes one of the most well-known stories of the goddess Ishtar who, in her desire to conquer the underworld, descends, naked, into it, remaining there as a mutilated corpse for three days.[17] At the end of the three days, she is saved by a god and rises out of the underworld, the Queen of Heaven *and* of Earth. By choosing to fast for three days, Esther is thus following in the footsteps of Ishtar: dying to her old self in order to arise out of the ashes, a victorious Queen. And so, Esther accepts to risk it all, to lose it all, for a new life, for the sake of deliverance, of transformation, and of evolution: "If I am to perish, I shall perish" (Esther 4:16).

Only such a woman can rise to the status of queen, and, like Queen Esther in this moment, "put on royal apparel" (Esther 5:1). This detail in the text marks the powerful transformation that is taking place within Esther as she chooses to take action. Up until now, she was a mere concubine in the mind of the king. Esther's mention that she had not been with the king for thirty days speaks already of the king's growing disinterest in her. Soon she will end up locked up in the harem of concubines, once the king has found a fairer body to share his bed. It is only through her acceptance of the challenge given to her that Esther escapes this fate. But, in order to rise to the task at hand, Esther has to abandon her concubine's garment for that of royal Queen. She has to abandon her passive, submissive, pleasing and "play-it-safe" approach attitude, for decisive, courageous, and daring action. And as she moves into this new dangerous and unknown territory, she shifts inwardly from passivity to activity, from submissiveness to disobedience, silence to confrontation. But the price of her individuation from concubine to queen is heavy: she might lose everything, she might "die." The Hebrew verb that is used to describe her approach of the king is *qarav* (Esther 5:2), the same verb that constitutes the noun *qorban*, "sacrifice." The text is here using Levitical language in order to convey that Queen Esther is offering herself as a sacrifice for her people, she is accepting to die that others might live, she is ready to risk safe for the sake of abundance.

Such is the sign of true royalty: the courage of true passion, of a complete investment of one's self for the sake of deliverance. Yet, too often, we are afraid to give it our all, to invest our whole selves in the relationship, to put all our apples in the same basket for the sake of transformation and evolution. We prefer to remain stunted versions of ourselves, we prefer to survive, or to "get by" in a mediocre, often dire situation rather than courageously pour our hearts into the relationship. Many of us prefer to live as shadows of our true selves rather than risk the pain of continuously keeping our hearts open to the possibility of deliverance and transformation. But what the story of Queen Esther teaches us is that only by pouring her whole self into the relationship, only by risking it all, by exposing her heart to the continuous pain of disappointment and betrayal, can a woman rise to her royal self, and insodoing, elevate everyone around her. What the story of Esther teaches us is that only a woman capable of offering up (*qarav)* her heart, capable of continuously pouring her heart and her love into the broken crucible of her relationship, will in the end experience rebirth, renewal, and resurrection. Such a woman, if she does not give up, will rise from concubine to queen, and as she does, receive a new beginning, a new start, for herself, her man, and her entire home.

The Seduction of Ahasuerus

Because Esther is ready to risk it all, she gains it all back and more: "As soon as the king saw Queen Esther standing in the court, she won his favor" (Esther 5:2). "As soon as" he saw her. This brutal king, whose cruel edict was about to decimate an entire ethnic group, now melts before his young and courageous Queen. One has to recognize the tenderness of the king's feelings towards his Queen. The minute he sees her he rushes her in his presence, without hesitation, without any concern for protocol or courtly procedure. He then graciously asks her what she wants, generously promising her up to half his kingdom. What does she desire? How might he please her? Like the goddess Ishtar who, by accepting to enter the underworld emerges Queen of Heaven and of Earth, Esther, by accepting to risk everything, emerges favored and beloved Queen of a king eager to respond to her desires.

It is interesting to note here that there are two moments in the story when Esther finds favor with the king. The first is when she is brought into his bedchamber and there, surrenders to him without a word. There, she seduces him with her soft and yielding nature, having asked for nothing more than what Hegai suggested. This second moment of favor is, however, radically different. In this second moment, she takes the initiative to come to the king on her own and opens her mouth to speak, not least to ask something of him. At that moment, she who had almost sunk into oblivion, receives the king's favor as well as becomes the recipient of stunning generosity on his part. In this second moment, the king is moved not by her submissiveness, but by her initiative, not by her discretion, but by her brazenness. In this moment, her erotic power lies not in fulfilling the king's fantasies, but in her ability to express to him the desires of her heart. At this moment she is even more vulnerable than when he first welcomed her into his bed. Then, she was vulnerable physically, her body surrendered unto the king. But now, she is even more so. For now, it is her heart that she is surrendering to the king. And it is precisely this vulnerability which deeply and irreversibly moves the king's heart, awakening his desire to please her, to offer his love to her. During her first night with the king, Esther moved the king to take her, to make her his. Now, however, she moves the king to generously give himself to her, to respond to her heart's desires. And it is in this moment that she, for the first time, awakens the king's love. Up until now, her surrendered attitude had done nothing more than kindle the king's desire to have her. But it is in her decisiveness that she awakens his love, that is to say, his desire to give of himself, his eagerness to please her.

What we learn here is that a submissive and pleasing attitude, while it has its charms, can only get a woman so far. There comes a time when she has to rise up into her royal destiny and take action like a Queen. Too often women think that they can kindle a man's love by always cultivating an accommodating, flexible, low-maintenance attitude, never asking anything for themselves. Such an attitude is part of a woman's seductive power, to be sure. But ultimately, the woman, to awaken love in a man's heart, has to learn to inspire not only his desire, but his generosity. And this, she can only do by reconnecting herself to her own desires and gathering the courage to express these to her man in a way that inspires him to act on her behalf. But there is more: By expressing her desire she is, in effect, inspiring her man to rise to a higher version of himself, a version where he is no more taking onto himself but giving of himself. A woman in tune with her own desires and gifted with the capacity to voice those desires will refine her man's affections, purify his love for her and challenge him to rise to his best self. Such a woman is unforgettable, for she elevates her man rather than infantilizes him, she inspires him rather than caters to him. She is the woman that he will fall in love with. But such a woman, while in tune with her own heart, must also know how to speak to a man's heart. For there is a way to speak to a man that will liberate his love, and a way to speak that will shut a man down. And this is where Queen Esther's genius truly lies: She knows exactly when, how, and what to say and it is to her wisdom that we now turn.

Shockingly, the first thing Queen Esther does is associate the king with Haman, inviting them both into her chambers. This is disturbing because, it must be recalled, Haman is precisely the mastermind behind the king's decree to decimate the Jews of Persia. Why would Queen Esther bring such a maleficent presence into her intimate chambers? It is as though Queen Esther understands that the king shares some kind of "soul tie" with Haman. Like the king, Haman is given the highest position in the land and is to be considered by the courtiers as a god, before whom they ought to bend the knee. We know from the book of Daniel that the kings of Babylon often flirted with divinity. In Daniel 3 the king even asks that a statue crafted in his resemblance be worshipped by the entire nation. It is therefore surprising that king Ahasuerus would choose to share his divine status with a courtier. Unless, of course, Haman is seen by the king as an extension of himself, or, perhaps more accurately, as another side of himself. Throughout the story, we see the king succumbing over and over again to the vile and sadistic desires of his courtier. It is as though Haman were some kind of channel for the king's own latent cruelty and barbarity. As though the king's own dark pulsions could at last find expression through Haman's executive powers. Haman is thus nothing more than a channel for the king' own dark, threatening, sadistic, and cruel desires. When Esther invites them both, she is in a way showing that she is willing and capable of welcoming all of the king onto herself: His generous, tender, loyal side, but also his cruel, barbaric, and sadistic side. By inviting the king and his courtier Haman, she is showing a stunning acceptance of the king in all of his complexity. She shows that she loves all of him, his spirit and his flesh, his strength and his weakness, his light and his darkness. And she shows that she can handle all of him, that she is not afraid to gaze into the darkness of his soul and to look at him in the eye.

And so, Queen Esther makes the courageous gesture to invite them both to her chambers for a banquet of meat and wine. And when the right time comes—for Esther also has an exquisite sense of timing—she makes her request known. Let us turn to her exact wording, for it constitutes a tribute to unparalleled feminine genius. Rather than quarrelling with the king, rather than expressing her frustration and disdain for the king's notorious tendency to be manipulated, rather than demanding from him that he meet her expectations for how a king ought to behave, Queen Esther humbles herself and simply asks. "My wish…my request, if your Majesty will do me the favor, if it please your Majesty to grant my wish and accede to my request" (Esther 5:7-8). Six words of supplication are here used by Esther: "wish" (shaal), "request" (baqash) "favor" (matza hen), "if it please" (al hamelech tov), "wish" (shaal) and "request" (baqash). She is neither quarrelsome, nor demanding, nor expecting that the king comply with her desires. Rather, she chooses to honor the king and show him respect by approaching him with humility rather than with haughtiness and entitlement, and this, at the height of his unworthiness and ineptitude. For the king at that moment does not deserve her respect, neither is he worthy of her honor. He has not fulfilled his obligation as king, that is to say, as protector of his people and guardian of order. Far to the contrary, he has flirted with agents of chaos, rewarding them richly, and ultimately, bending to their will. And yet, in spite of this, Esther approaches him with the respect due a king. And not surprisingly, the king, as a result, rises to the occasion.

"Let my life be granted me… from the adversary and enemy" (Esther 7:3-6). It is here that Esther's genius is most evident. Rather than confronting the king as her enemy, as the one at the origin of her plight, she deviates the blame onto Haman, while calling for the king's protection. In other words, rather than portraying the king as her foe, she portrays him as her protector and ally. Rather than focusing on his weakness and on his cruelty, she focuses on his loyalty and love. In other words, she perceives the king as the solution to her problem and not as the source of her problem. She chooses to situate the evil outside of the king and calls for an alliance between her and the king against it. This is sheer genius, for insodoing, she awakens the king's highest instincts, his loving and protective instincts and gets him to fight on her side against the evil which hereto inhabited him. More than genius, this is prophetic insight. For Esther does nothing less than illuminate the king's highest and most noble self. She sees it, she invokes it, and as a result, draws it out on her own behalf. As such, Queen Esther behaves as a prophet, as a seer, gifted with a deep vision and insight about the king's true power and the man that he could become. The Talmud lists Esther among the seven prophetesses of the Hebrew Bible, all of which made use of the same prophetic insight towards the men of their lives: Sarah, Miriam, Deborah, Hanna, Avigail, Hulda and Esther.[18] This specific gift of prophecy is unique to women in the Hebrew Bible and has turned many a man's destiny around. Such a gift or charis is the inheritance of women, although it lies still dormant and unused in most of us. For every woman is a seer, gifted with the ability to see deep within a man's soul and bring forth the hidden strength, nobility and power of the man she loves with her vision and with her words.

Conclusion

In a way, the story of Esther constitutes the reversal of the Babylonian myth of Marduk's defeat of Tiamat. In this story, Marduk, the embodiment of male virility and ordering power, defeats the feminine goddess of chaos and of darkness, Tiamat. From this defeat, the city-state of Babylon is built and its laws are written, the forces of chaos being in this way kept at bay.[19] In our story, it is Esther, the feminine goddess of love and war, who seems to defeat male supremacy and oppression in order to usher in a new era of joy and safety for her own people: The Jews of Babylon. Our story, however, contains many more reversals: Vashti cedes her place for Esther, Haman is hung on the gallows reserved for Mordechai, the Jews escape extermination and have victory over their enemies, instead of the male principle vanquishing the female principle we now have Queen Esther—in Babylonian, Ishtar—defeating the toxic masculine figure of Haman. But the most profound reversal is that of the king. From a tyrannical and unruly ruler, intent on bending the woman's will and agency to his whims—as he did with Vashti—King Ahasuerus now can be seen ushering in an era of unprecedented equality between the masculine and the feminine. For the first time in the ancient world, man and woman rule together in equality. Up until then the king had been signing the decrees of the land. Now, Queen Esther is given the prerogative to sign into law her own decrees (Esther 8:8, 9:32). From a king easily manipulated by corrupt advisors, King Ahasuerus now knows to open his ears to the voice of a woman, to the voice of his Queen. And out of this partnership with his Queen, out of this ability to listen to the woman's voice, wise and life-affirming decisions arise which, rather than throw the kingdom into chaos, deliver and redeem it. Justice at last becomes the law of the land, where the wicked are punished and the vulnerable protected. A sacred marriage has truly taken place between Queen Esther and the King, and the powerful union between the feminine and the masculine again ushers in a season of rebirth and renewal, of "light and gladness, happiness and honor" (Esther 8:16).

Conclusion

Leaving the Mother's House

As I am writing this conclusion, the sun has gone down on a cold winter night in New York City. A dark blue sky with a few shyly peeking stars now cloaks the Jewish neighborhood in which I live. There, Sabbath candles are on display in windows and songs can be heard at festive dinner tables. I've always been intrigued by why *two* Sabbath candles? What is the meaning of this number? The Jewish sages give several reasons for this: the two candles represent the two commandments of the Sabbath, to "remember" and to "keep" the Sabbath.[1] Alternatively, the two candles express the idea that, on the Sabbath, we are given an extra soul. Thus, during the Sabbath hours, we are inhabited by two souls rather than one.[2] But my favorite interpretation, by far, is that of a seventeenth-century Jewish sage, Eliyahu Spira, according to whom the two candles represent husband and wife.[3] According to this sage, the Hebrew word *ner,* which means "light" has the numerical value of 250, giving the two candles the combined numerical value of 500. The Talmud teaches that a man's body is made up of 248 limbs and organs, while a woman's body has 252, amounting to 500 combined organs and limbs. The lighting of two candles thus expresses the union between man and woman, between husband and wife.

But why did the sages choose to usher in the Sabbath bride[4] with this reference to the unity between husband and wife? To answer this, we have to remember what the Sabbath is a celebration of. The first occurrence in the Hebrew Bible of the Sabbath is in the Creation story. There, the Sabbath is blessed as the very pinnacle or crown of Creation, of this seven-day ordering of chaos into cosmos—an ordered, harmonious, and beautiful world where the divine presence can feel at home and welcomed. The Sabbath thus constitutes the crown jewel of Creation, the celebration of a time when this world was everything that it was meant to be, and a powerful projection of what it might still become. But for this new world, this new Creation to be unlocked, the human couple must rise up to its lofty calling of partnering and ruling again together. They must find a way back to each other, they must journey through the ruins and devastation of this world and through the wreckage of their own hearts, back to each other. For the man and the woman, when together, constitute the very foundations of cosmic harmony! They are the two pillars which, when standing together, hold and support this delicate blue orb we call planet earth. This is what the two candles that are lit on Sabbath eve have come to represent to me: the redemptive union between man and woman which holds "everything together"[5] and protects our world from self-destruction.

In a world where the man and the woman are at war and where the forces of chaos are progressively gaining ground, these two candles remind us of a different possibility—that of a truce between the man and the woman, and the resulting healing and repairing of our world (*tikkun olam*). But this truce is long in coming, so deep has the violence been between the two genders. From the violence of patriarchy against women to the distrust of feminism towards men, we seem to be growing further and further apart. Men and women today hesitate more and more to venture out into the treacherous oceans of intimacy, preferring rather the safe shores of solitude or of open-ended relationships/partnerships, with no strings attached.[6] But without the difficult and strenuous labor of love between man and woman, there remains no hope of pushing back the more and more pervasive influx of chaotic forces. And if we do not muster up the strength to journey back towards each other, and the courage to invite each other into the painful recesses of our souls that we might be healed, then then all is lost!

Has not the time come to attempt this journey anew? The women and the men whose stories we have just read pave the way for us. None of these stories feature ideal, picture perfect and enviable relationships. Rather, the relationships between the men and women we have just encountered, are complex, messy, and ambiguous, containing layers of unspeakable pain, betrayal, and sometimes even abuse: Eve has an emotional affair with the serpent, Adam betrays Eve by blaming her for the end of the world, Job curses his wife out, Ruth ends up in an arranged marriage that she did not choose, the Shulamite is cheated on, and Esther is married to a brute. And yet, at the very heart of the pain and of the betrayal, a way is opened for healing, reconciliation, forgiveness, and renewed love. What we learn from these stories is that no relationship is hard enough, broken enough, convoluted enough that love cannot heal and renew it. But a breach must be made for this love. A space must be opened for it. And it is enough for even one partner to single-handedly begin this "work of love." Sometimes it is the woman, because of her unique gift or *charis* for relationship, sometimes it is the man who comes to his senses, like King Solomon.

As we read these stories, we learn not only of love's transformative power, but of *how* to love well. For it is not enough to feel love for one's partner, or to love them in the only way we know how. We have to learn to love them as *they* need to be loved, in a way that will unlock *their* life-giving love. We have to learn their love language, and how to crack them open to receive us. In other words, we cannot merely want to love our partners, we have to learn to *unlock* them. The keys we need have lain dormant, in the Biblical stories that we just read, for millennia. But such keys, to be retrieved, must be seen like the "pearl of great value"[7] that can only be acquired by losing everything we hold dear. The instinct of self-preservation and the fears that guard it, must be exchanged for the reckless love of the Shulamite who knows of no plan B and has no exit plan. Pride and self-sufficiency must be broken open in order to allow for expansion and growth, as was the case for Job. We must learn to lose everything in order to gain it all back, as Eve had to do for Adam's sake. We have to begin to see past our own destinies, towards the destiny of an Other, as Adam did for Eve. Our narrow agendas must be replaced for the broader, more expansive vision of God for our lives, as happened for Ruth. Room must be made for the other's voice to be spoken over our lives, if we are ever to be all that we can be, as King Solomon had to learn. And, finally, courage must be found to confront evil while continuing to stand by and for the evil doer, as Esther masterfully modeled for us.

Such is the high price we must pay to unlock our marriages, heal our broken partnerships, and renew our loves. The "pearl of great value" lies in wait of those gritty men and women capable of laying everything down for its sake: their instinct of self-preservation, their pride, their pipe dreams, their narrow agendas, their self-sufficiency, and their fears. For only in having given up all of these will we be at last ready to *receive* the shocking grace of a second chance at love. Only when we have stopped clawing our *own* way back to Eden, back to love, as King Solomon attempted to, will the door be opened unto us. Only when we have stopped striving, fixing, coercing, manipulating, and nagging our way back to paradise lost, will the keys be surrendered to us. And only by entering the Sabbath rest offered by the Mother's House will we find our way back home. A powerful cherub with a flaming sword guards Eden. Only the humble, the reckless, the broken, and the surrendered are allowed back inside.

BIBLIOGRAPHY

The Admonitions of Ipu-Wer. In *Ancient Near Eastern Texts Relating to the Old Testament*. 3rd edition. Edited by James B. Pritchard. Translated by John A. Wilson. Princeton, NJ: Princeton University Press, 1969.

Alter, Robert. *The Wisdom Books*. New York: W. W. Norton, 2010.

Aristotle. *On the History of Animals*. Translated by Richard Cresswell. Oxford University Press, 1887. https://www.gutenberg.org/files/59058/59058-h/59058-h.htm.

———. *On the Generation of Animals*. Translated by Arthur Platt. https://www.documentacatholicaomnia.eu/03d/-384_-322,_Aristoteles,_12_On_the_Generation_of_Animals,_EN.pdf.

———. *Politics*. Translated by Benjamin Jowett. https://classics.mit.edu/Aristotle/politics.html.

Assman, Jan. *Ma'at, l'Egypte pharaonique et l'idée de justice sociale*. Paris: La maison de vie, 2003.

Baines, John R., and Peter F. Dorman. "Ancient Egyptian Religion." In *Encyclopedia Britannica*; last updated February 3, 2025. https://www.britannica.com/topic/ancient-Egyptian-religion.

Bauks, Michaela. "Sacred Trees in the Garden of Eden and Their Ancient Near Eastern Precursors." *Journal of Ancient Judaism* 3, no. 3 (2021). https://www.academia.edu/19142515/Sacred_Trees_in_the_Garden_of_Eden_and_Their_Near_Eastern_Precursors

Beaulieu, Stéphane. *Eve's Ritual, The Judahite Sacred Marriage Rite*. Ann Arbor, MI: Concordia Publishing House, 2007.

Bechtel, Lyn. "A Feminist Approach to the Book of Job." In *A Feminist Companion to The Bible: Wisdom Literature*. Edited by Athalya Brenner. Sheffield, UK: Sheffield Academic Press, 1995.

Ben Sira. *Sirach*. https://bible.usccb.org/bible/sirach/25.

Bickerman, Elias. *Four Strange Books*. New York: Schocken, 1985.

Bleeker, C. J. "Guilt and Purification in Ancient Egypt." *Numen, International Review for the History of Religions* 13, no. 2 (1966): pp. 81–87. https://doi.org/10.2307/3269416.

Brenner, Athalya. "Looking at Esther through the Looking Glass." In *A Feminist Companion to Ruth and Esther.* Edited by Athalya Brenner. Sheffield, UK: Sheffield Academic Press, 1999.

Bronner, Leila Leah. "Esther Revisited: An Aggadic Approach." In *A Feminist Companion to Ruth and Esther.* Edited by Athalya Brenner. Sheffield, UK: Sheffield Academic Press, 1999.

———. *From Eve to Esther: Rabbinic Reconstructs of Biblical Women.* Louisville, KY: Westminster John Knox Press, 1994.

Buber, Martin. *I and Thou.* Transl. Walter Kaufmann. New York: Touchstone, 1996.

Camp, Claudia. "Woman Wisdom: Bible." *Jewish Women's Archive.* https://jwa.org/encyclopedia/article/woman-wisdom-bible).

Descartes, René. A *Discourse on the Method.* Translated by Ian Maclean. New York: Oxford University Press, 2008.

Dever, William. *Did God Have a Wife.* Grand Rapids, MI: Eerdmans, 2008.

The Dispute Between a Man and his Ba. In *Ancient Egyptian Literature: A Book of Readings.* Vol. 1: *The Old and Middle Kingdoms.* Edited by Miriam Lichtheim. Oakland, CA: University of California Press, 1975.

Doukhan, Abi. *Biblical Portraits of Exile.* New York: Routledge, 2016.

———. "The Woman's Curse: A Redemptive Reading of Genesis 3:16." *Religions* 11, no. 11 (2020). https://www.mdpi.com/2077-1444/11/11/600.

———. *Womanist Wisdom in the Song of Songs: Secrets of an African Princess.* New York: Palgrave, 2019.

Doukhan, Jacques B. "Ecclesiastes." In *SDAIBC.* Vol. 6, *Psalms, Proverbs, Ecclesiastes, Song of Songs*. Nampa, ID: Pacific Press Publishing Association, 2022.

Drewermann, Eugène. *L'évangile des femmes.* Paris: Seuil, 1996.

Eskenazi, Tamara. *The JPS Bible Commentary: Ruth.* Philadelphia, PA: The Jewish Publication Society, 2011.

Fein, Ellen, and Sherrie Schneider. *The Rules: Time-Tested Secrets for Capturing the Heart of Mr. Right.* New York: Grand Central Publishing, 2007.

Fontaine, Carol. "Women in the World of Wisdom." In *A Feminist Companion to the Bible: Wisdom Literature.* Edited by Athalya Brenner. Sheffield, UK: Sheffield Academic Press, 1995.

Gitay, Zefira. "Esther and the Queen's Throne." In *A Feminist Companion to Ruth and Esther.* Edited by Athalya Brenner. Sheffield, UK: Sheffield Academic Press, 1999.

Greene, Robert. *The Art of Seduction: An Indispensable Primer on the Ultimate Form of Power.* London: Profile Books, 2004.

Harding, M. Esther. *Women's Mysteries, Ancient and Modern: A Psychological Interpretation of the Feminine Principle as Portrayed in Myth, Story, and Dreams.* Boulder, CO: Shambhala, 2001.

Irigaray, Luce. *Sharing the World.* New York: Continuum, 2008.

———. *To Be Two.* New York: Routledge, 2001.

King, Martin Luther, Jr. *The Strength to Love.* Boston, MA: Beacon Press, 2019.

Klein, Lillian. "Job and the Womb." In *A Feminist Companion to The Bible: Wisdom Literature.* Edited by Athalya Brenner. Sheffield, UK: Sheffield Academic Press, 1995.

Kramer, Samuel Noah. "Le rite du mariage sacré Dumuzi-Inanna." *Revue de l'histoire des religions* 181, no. 2 (1972), pp. 121-146. https://inanna-blog.wordpress.com/wp-content/uploads/2014/11/kramer_rite-mariage-sacrc3a9.pdf.

———. *The Sacred Marriage Rite: Aspects of Faith Myth, and Ritual in Ancient Sumer.* Bloomington, IN: Indiana University Press, 1969.

Lang, Bernhard. *Wisdom and the Book of Proverbs: An Israelite Goddess Redefined.* Boston, MA: Pilgrim Press, 1986.

Levinas, Emmanuel. "Useless Suffering." In *The Provocation of Levinas: Rethinking the Other.* Edited by Robert Bernasconi and David Wood. Translated by Richard Cohen. New York: Routledge, 1988.

Maimonides, Moses. *Guide for the Perplexed.* gutenberg.org/cache/epub/73584/pg73584-images.html#ch3.22.

Marcel, Gabriel. *Creative Fidelity.* New York: Fordham University Press, 2002.

McKinlay, Judith E. *Gendering Wisdom the Host: Biblical Invitations to Eat and Drink.* Sheffield, UK: Sheffield Academic Press, 1996.

Menu, Bernadette. *Maât, L'ordre juste du monde.* Paris : Michalon Editeur, 2005.

Meyers, Carol. *Rediscovering Eve: Ancient Israelite Women in Context.* New York: Oxford University Press, 2013.

Mitchell, Stephen. "Foreword." In *The World's First Great Love Poem: The Song of Songs.* Edited by Chana Bloch and Ariel Bloch. New York: The Modern Library, 2006.

Neher, André. *Notes sur Qohelet.* Paris: Editions Minuit, 1951.

Niditch, Susan. "Esther: Folkore, Wisdom, Feminism and Authority." In *A Feminist Companion to Ruth and Esther.* Edited by Athalya Brenner. Sheffield, UK: Sheffield Academic Press, 1999.

Nin, Anaïs. *In Favor of the Sensitive Man and Other Essays.* New York: Harcourt and Brace, 1994.

Phipps, William. *Assertive Biblical Women.* Westport, CT: Praeger, 1992.

Pierce, Ashleigh. "Inanna-Ishtar: Recognizing the Personality and Purpose of a Goddess." *Wittenberg History Journal* 44 (Spring 2015), pp. 33-47. https://www.wittenberg.edu/sites/default/files/media/history/2015HistoryJournal.pdf.

Plumley, Martin. "The Cosmology of Ancient Egypt." In *Ancient Cosmologie.* Edited by Carmen Blacker and Michael Loewe. London: Allen & Unwin, 1975.

Schroer, Silvia. "Wise and Counseling Women in Ancient Israel." In *A Feminist Companion to the Bible: Wisdom Literature.* Edited by Athalya Brenner. Sheffield, UK: Sheffield Academic Press, 1995.

Stephany, Timothy. *The Descent of Ishtar: The Sumerian and Akkadian Versions.* Seattle, WA: Create Space, 2015.

Stone, Merlin. *When God Was a Woman.* New York: Doubleday, 2012.

Tao Te Ching. Translated by Stephen Mitchell. New York: Harper Perennial, 2006.

The Teachings of Ptahhotep. Edinburgh, Scotland: Blackwood Press, 2012.

Trible, Phyllis. *God and the Rhetoric of Sexuality.* Minneapolis, MN: Fortress Press, 1986.

———. *Texts of Terror.* Minneapolis, MN: Fortress Press, 2022.

Van Wolde, Ellen. "The Development of Job: Mrs. Job as Catalyst." In *A Feminist Companion to The Bible: Wisdom Literature.* Edited by Athalya Brenner. Sheffield, UK: Sheffield Academic Press, 1995.

Waltke, Bruce, and M. O'Connor. *An Introduction to Biblical Hebrew Syntax.* University Park, PA: Eisenbrauns, 1990.

Walton, John H. *Ancient Near Eastern Thought and the Old Testament.* Ada, MI: Baker Academic, 2018.

———. *The Lost World of Adam and Eve: Genesis 2-3 and the Human Origins Debate.* Lisle, IL: Inter Varsity Press, 2015.

———. *The Lost World of Genesis One: Ancient Cosmology and the Origins Debate.* Lisle, IL: Inter Varsity Press Academic, 2009.

Wolkstein, Diane, and Samuel Noah Kramer. *Inanna, Queen of Heaven and Earth: Her Stories and Hymns from Sumer*. New York: Harper Collins Publishers, 1985.

Zornberg, Avivah Gottlieb. *The Murmuring Deep: Reflections on the Biblical Unconscious.* New York: Knopf Doubleday, 2011.

ENDNOTES

Introduction

[1] My translation. I am using the JPS (Jewish Publication Society) version throughout this book, except when otherwise noted.

[2] I am using here, of course, the Cartesian expression of humankind as "masters and possessors of nature" that René Descartes elaborates in his A *Discourse on the Method*, trans. Ian Maclean (Oxford University Press, 2008), part 6.

[3] Twentieth-century Feminist philosopher Luce Irigaray makes a similar point in her magnificent book *Sharing the World*, where she argues that true civilization can only arise when the other is invited to share in the world of the self. That other could be anyone, the other race, the other ethnicity, the other religion, but most fundamentally, the ultimate, most fundamental other, is the gendered other. Only once the man and the woman have learned to partner up, to work together, to imagine together, to rule together, will the world find again its lost balance and enter the state of true civilization. Once that gendered other is welcomed into the space of the self, all other others will find themselves again seen, heard, welcomed also, and the world will recover its lost harmony: "As long as the other is not recognized and respected as a bridge between nature and culture, a bridge that gender at first is, every attempt to establish a democratic globalization will remain a moral imperative without concrete fulfillment. As long as the universal is not considered as being two, and humanity as being a place of fruitful coexistence between two irreducibly different genders, a culture will never stop imposing its colour and values upon another, including through its morality and religion" (Luce Irigaray, *Sharing the World* [Continuum, 2008], p. 134).

[4] Gen. 1: 28.

[5] Speaking of the "new woman" that is emerging at the beginning of the twentieth century, the famous French erotica writer Anaïs Nin maintains that the weaving together of sex and love will remain the task of women: "Linking eroticism to emotion, to love, to a selection of a certain person, personalizing,

individualizing, that will be the work of women" (Anaïs Nin, *In Favor of the Sensitive Man and Other Essays* [Harcourt and Brace, 1994], p. 8.

[6] The expression "labor of love" is borrowed from the philosophy of Luce Irigaray (Luce Irigaray, *To Be Two* [Routledge, 2001], p. 62).

[7] Cf. Phyllis Trible, *Texts of Terror* (Fortress Press, 2022).

[8] In terms of authorship of the biblical books discussed in this work, we will follow, for the sake of simplicity—and because the question of authorship is somewhat marginal to our discussions—the traditional rabbinical and patristic interpretations. We will introduce each chapter with a short reference to authorship and refer our reader to the rabbinic and patristic interpretations.

[9] William Dever highlights the importance of rediscovering the "Mother's House" as follows: "Carol Meyers (in *Rediscovering Eve*) is right on point, in particular her plea is well taken that if archeologists and biblical scholars pay closer attention to the "Mother's house" they will produce an alternate and better window through which to view Israelite religion.... The home was largely the province of women whose principal concerns were not necessarily those of either the establishment, or of the men who wrote the Bible. Theirs are the religions of hearth and home" (William Dever, *Did God Have a Wife* [Wm. B. Eerdmans, 2008], p. 56). We agree with this assessment but find that the biblical text itself contains traces of this mother's house teaching, notably in the Wisdom literature texts.

[10] NIV.

[11] Martin Buber develops this idea as follows: "Spirit is not in the I but between I and you. It is not like the blood that circulates in you but like the air in which you breathe. Man lives in the spirit when he is able to respond to his You. He is able to do that when he enters into this relation with this whole being. It is solely by virtue of his power to relate that man is able to live in the spirit." Martin Buber, *I and Thou*, trans. Walter Kaufmann (Touchstone, 1996), 89.

[12] Although Ma'at is primordially the goddess of justice, she is also associated with wisdom: "According to the Egyptian religious conception, both man's happiness and his virtue are guaranteed if he lives in harmony with Ma'at. This harmony requires both insight and wisdom. It is jeopardized by foolishness" (C. J. Bleeker, "Guilt and Purification in Ancient Egypt," *Numen, International Review for the History of* Religions 13, no. 2 [1966], pp. 81–87. https://doi.org/10.2307/3269416.

[13] Cf. Genesis 50:20 where Joseph exclaims upon meeting his brothers again: "You meant it for evil, but God meant it for good."

[14] Cf. *The Teachings of Ptahhotep* (5th Dynasty of Egypt, 2375–2350 BCE) where the notion of listening is explicitly connected to wisdom (Blackwood Press, 2012).

[15] There is ample evidence within the Hebrew Bible itself (notably the book of Kings) of the influence of the Inanna/Dumuzi cultic literature (via the Akkadian Tammuz/Ishtar stories and Canaanite Baal/Asherah) on temple worship during the reign of the Kings of Jerusalem. Noah notes that "the prophets themselves did not hesitate to draw some of the symbolism from the cult, and the frequent descriptions in the prophetic writings of the relation between Yahweh and Israel as that of a husband and wife, indicate the existence of a sacred marriage between Yaweh and the goddess Astarte, the Canaanite counterpart of the Mesopotamian Ishtar/Inanna" (Samuel Noah Kramer, *The Sacred Marriage: Aspects of Faith Myth, and Ritual in Ancient Sumer* [Indiana University Press, 1969], p. 90).

Chapter 1

[1] This should not be surprising given that, according to Samuel Kramer "the Sumerian language and literature were basic courses of study in the curriculum of the schools throughout the Ancient Near East" (Samuel Kramer, "The Biblical Song of Songs and the Sumerian Love Songs" *Expedition Magazine* 5/1 (Fall 1962) https://www.penn.museum/sites/expedition/the-biblical-song-of-songs-and-the-sumerian-love-songs/

[2] Two elements will be omitted in the biblical rendition of sacred marriage: sacred prostitution, and the presence of a goddess. In the biblical narrative, the motif of the sacred marriage occurs strictly in the context of monogamous relationship, and between a man and a woman, not a man and a goddess.

[3] There is ample evidence within the Hebrew Bible itself (notably the book of Kings) of the influence of the Inanna/Dumuzi cultic literature (via the Akkadian Tammuz/Ishtar stories and the Canaanite Baal/Asherah stories) on temple worship during the reign of the Kings of Jerusalem. Cf. 1 Kings 18:19; Ezek. 8:14.

[4] Kramer notes that "the prophets themselves did not hesistate to draw some of the symbolism from the cult, and the frequent descriptions in the prophetic writings of the relation between Yahweh and Israel as that of a husband and wife, indicate the existence of a sacred marriage between Yaweh and the goddess Astarte, the Canaanite counterpart of the Mesopotamian Ishtar/Inanna" (Samuel Kramer, *The Sacred Marriage,* p. 90).

[5] Commenting more specifically on the Song of Songs, Kramer observes that: "It is only now when we have more than a dozen Sumerian sacred marriage

songs of celebration and rejoicing that we begin to get a true picture of the parallels between the Biblical book and some of its probably cuneiform forerunners. For it is now evident that the similarities and resemblances between them are not confined to the general stylistic features such as the portrayal of the lover as both shepherd and king, and of the beloved as both bride and sister, or the formal interlacing of soliloquies, colloquies and refrains; they extend to theme, motif, and occasionally even phraseology" (Samuel Kramer, *The Sacred Marriage,* p. 91).

[6] The story of the tower of Babel seems to describe precisely the Sumerian civilization from which the Hebrew nation would emerge through the person of Abraham, shedding light on its potential dangers and pitfalls.

[7] The Biblical narrator of the story of Eve and the tree will borrow many of those motives in his/her construction of the Biblical narrative.

[8] According to Ashleigh Pierce, "one of the most recorded female vocations was that of the bar-wife or innkeeper. In ancient Mesopotamia it was traditional that single women owned all the taverns. Women not only provided beer but also small loans." Such an unattached woman was not necessarily a prostitute, "just a woman separated from the patriachal household. Also, these women were free of the sexual litigations of women within the normal patriarchal status. Ishtar/Inanna was patron goddess of these unmarried women" (Ashleigh Pierce, "Inanna-Ishtar: Recognizing the Personality and Purpose of a Goddess," *Wittenberg History Journal* 44 [Spring 2015], p. 42. https://www.wittenberg.edu/sites/default/files/media/history/2015HistoryJournal.pdf.

[9] I am alluding here of course to the famous book by Merlin Stone, *When God Was a Woman* (New York: Doubleday, 2012).

[10] Diane Wolkstein and Samuel Kramer, *Inanna, Queen of Heaven and Earth: Her Stories and Hymns from Sumer* [New York: Harper Collins Publishers, 1985], pp. 12–27.

[11] The Biblical books of Daniel and of Esther give a deeply humane and nuanced portrait of the kings of Persia, as exhibiting arbitrary and authoritarian tendencies in tension with generous and compassionate actions.

[12] The reverse process might also be true, with the biblical text serving as a source for the Inanna story. As I will show in the next chapter, the narratives in Genesis 1–11 predate the Mosaic authorship by millennia and may well have been a tradition contemporary to the Sumerian civilization.

[13]These are most likely symbols of royalty, although the translations remain unclear.

[14] Merlin Stone discusses this connection between the life-giving power of women and their subsequent deification into goddesses, by primitive societies, as

follows: "The concept of the creator of all human life may have been formulated by the clan's image of the woman who had been their most ancient, their primal ancestor and that image thereby deified and revered as Divine Ancestress" (Merlin Stone, *When God was a Woman,* p. 13).

[15] Cf. John H. Walton, *The Lost World of Adam and Eve: Genesis 2–3 and the Human Origins Debate* (Lisle, IL: Inter Varsity Press, 2015), prop. 14.

[16] Diane Wolkstein narrates that the Anzu-bird "was known to the Sumerians from the story of 'Ninurta Turtle' in which the Anzu-bird unsuccessfully attempts to steal the *me,* the attributes of civilization and knowledge, from Enki, the god of wisdom. The mature Anzu-bird, depicted in Sumerian art with the great wings of an eagle and the face of a lion, craves power and knowledge. … Lilith forms with the Anzu bird and the snake a triad of sexual, lawless creatures who live outside the bounds of the Sumerian community and seek power only for themselves. These are Inanna's suppressed fears and desires … the three creatures embody the primitive, grasping, human aspects Inanna must now recognize and let go of if she is to be deserving of the gifts of 'the throne' and 'the bed'" (Diane Wolkstein and Samuel Kramer, *Inanna Queen of Heaven and Earth*, p. 142).

[17] Lilith does not appear in any other Sumerian texts, but she is mentioned in the Biblical book of Isaiah (chapter 34:14) as well as in Talmudic stories, as a creature characterized by liminality, restlessness and danger (Babylonian Talmud, Tractate *Shabbat* 151b).

[18] Commenting a passage in Isaiah 54, the Talmud makes the following beautiful observation: "Before she is married, a woman is an unfinished vessel, and she makes a covenant only with the person that makes her into a finished vessel. For it says, 'for your husband is your maker, the lord of hosts is his name' (Is. 54:5)." (Babylonian Talmud, Tractate *Sanhedrin* 21a).

[19] The notion of "cutting" as a right of passage into adulthood can be found throughout African and Ancient Near Eastern cultures, from the ritual of male and female circumcision to the brutal deflowering rituals of sacred prostitution common in the Ancient Near East. Herodotus describes the latter as follows: "Babylonian custom… compels every woman of the land once in her life to sit in the temple of love and have intercourse with some stranger … the men pass and make their choice. It matters not what be the sum of money, the woman will never refuse for that were as sin, the money being by this act made sacred. After their intercourse she has made herself holy in the sight of the goddess and goes away; and thereafter there is no bribe however great that will get her … there is a custom like this in some parts of Cyprus" (cf. M. Esther Harding, *Women's*

Mysteries, Ancient and Modern: A Psychological Interpretation of the Feminine Principle as Portrayed in Myth, Story, and Dreams [Shambhala, 2001], p. 159).

[20] Gen. 2:18.

[21] Song of Songs 1:9; 4:4; 8:1.

[22] Babylonian Talmud, Tractate *Yevamoth* 62b, also makes this case: "Any man who does not have a wife is living without happiness, without blessing and without goodness... he is considered without a protective wall, for it says 'woman surrounds her husband' (Jer. 31:21)."

[23] Inasmuch as Ishtar is the Babylonian version of Inanna, her role and purpose are identical to those of Inanna. Like Inanna, she is partnered up with a shepherd-king, Tammuz, whose reign she has inaugurated in a sacred marriage ceremony reminiscent of Inanna and Dumuzi's.

[24] Quoting the Pyramid texts, Bernadette Menu observes : "Le ciel est apaisé, la terre est dans la joie, car ils ont appris que le roi installerait la Maât à la place d'Isfet (Pyramid texts, 1775–1776)." [The sky is satisfied, the earth is joyful, for they have learned that the king instaurerait the Ma'at in the place of the Isfet (Pyramid Texts, 1775–1776). My translation]. » (Bernadette Menu, *Maât, L'ordre juste du monde* [Paris : Editions Micha Lon, 2005], p. 21).

[25] See my commentary of Proverbs 8:15–16 in chapter 5 of this work.

[26] It is as possessor of the *me* that Inanna presents herself right before inaugurating Dumuzi's reign in the above quote. It is by this *me* that she has the authority to do so. In another story, Inanna is depicted as stealing the *me* from the God of wisdom, Enki, and presenting it to the city of Uruk in Sumer. The *me* is then stored in Inanna's holy shrine for the benefit of the people of Uruk (Diane Wolkstein,and Samuel Kramer, *Inanna, Queen of Heaven and Earth,* pp. 26–27).

[27] A number of beautiful Egyptian temple engravings depict the pharaoh offering up the Ma'at back to the gods as a pleasing offering to them, and as a sign of his continuous devotion to, and protection of the Ma'at in his kingdom. One of these is a raised and colored relief of Ramses II making an offering of the goddess Ma'at to the god Amun, inside the temple of Beit el-Wali, Lake Nasser, Aswan, Egypt (c. 1276 BC). Cf. https://www.worldhistory.org/image/5428/the-offering-of-maat

[28] Deut. 17:18.

[29] The *Tao Te Ching* makes a similar point when it describes the ideal ruler/master as showing the ability to remain virile while also "keep[ing] to the female" (*Tao Te Ching*, transl. Stephen Mitchell [New York: Harper Perennial, 2006], verse 28).

[30] Again, the Talmud illustrates this idea beautifully, as follows: "When husband and wife are worthy of it, the Shechinah dwells among them; when they are unworthy, fire consumes them" (Babylonian Talmud, Tractate *Sotah* 17a).

[31] Paul sets this idea in poetry when he writes about the church, but applied here, by us, to the human couple: "And in him you too are being built together to become a dwelling in which God lives by his Spirit" (Eph. 2:22).

Chapter 2

[1] My reading of the book of Genesis and of the Biblical text in general will follow the literary school of exegesis rather than the documentary one. As such, my exegesis of the text will not be so much interested in the historical development of the composition of the text (documentary approach), as it is in the text as it appears to us in its final redacted state (literary approach). My focus in this chapter, and in ensuing chapters, will therefore be the text as it presents itself to us in its finished literary form, and it is this final version of the text that I will explore. How the text came about and who authored will therefore not take up much of my time and I will simply align myself with the Jewish traditional reading of the text on matters of authorship and dating of the text.

[2] M. *Aboth* 1:1.

[3] This is particularly true of our story: "Genesis 2–3 attests to a long mythical tradition in which the personage of Eve developed as a demythologized Asherah figure through deterioration resulting from oral tradition; proof of this can be seen in the fact that both women represent fertility and are associated with the serpent … as well as the tree"

(Stéphane Beaulieu, *Eve's Ritual, The Judahite Sacred Marriage Rite* [Concordia Publishing House, 2007], p. 98). According to Stéphane Beaulieu, the biblical Eve emerges out of the Ashera figure, but the opposite could as well be true. All we can attest to, for sure, is that the two figures share interesting commonalities.

[4] Cf. Gen. 1; 2; 3; and 6. These themes can be found in the Sumerian *Epic of Gilgamesh* and in the stories surrounding the Sumerian goddess Inanna, notably "Inanna and the Huluppu tree," and "The Courtship of Dumuzi and Inanna," compiled in Diane Wolkstein and Samuel Noah Kramer, *Inanna, Queen of Heaven and Earth: Her Stories and Hymns from Sumer* (Harper Collins Publishers, 1985).

[5] John Walton has shown this connection between Sumerian literature and the Hebrew Bible in several of his works, notably his *Ancient Near Eastern Thought and the Old Testament* (Baker Academic, 2018).

[6] One powerful example of this is found in the Hebrew Creation story. As John Walton has shown in his work, the Creation story parallels Ancient Near Eastern/Sumerian/Babylonian temple cosmologies (cf. John Walton, *The Lost World of Genesis One: Ancient Cosmology and the Origins Debate* [Inter Varsity Press], 2009], pp. 77–85). The garden of Eden thus represents the earthly dwelling of God, the temple of God. As such, it should be a place where human beings cultivate the earth in order to bring nourishment to the gods (as is the case in the Sumerian narratives). Rather, in our text, the garden symbolizes God's nourishing of human beings, a complete reversal of the Sumerian perspective.

[7] Gen. 25:12–26.

[8] Genesis 17, occurring after the birth of Ishmael, changes the original blessing "I will make you into a great nation" (Gen. 12:2), into "I will make you a father of many nations" (Gen. 17:4).

[9] The reader must remember that the stories in the book of Genesis predate Moses and, therefore, are set in a very different atmosphere than the remaining four books of the Pentateuch, where Moses leads as the main character.

[10] The divine judgment addressed to Eve is the only one that does not contain the reference to a curse; it is also the only one which does not take the form of a punishment for transgression. Both the snake's and Adam's judgments contain a reference to a curse, the snake is cursed, and the land is cursed, respectively. And both judgments allude to a transgression on the snake's and on the man's part which is cited by God as the cause for the ensuing judgment: To the snake God says: "Because you have done this. . ." (Gen. 3:14), and to Adam: "Because you have listened to your wife. . ." (Gen. 3:17).

[11] Gen. 21.

[12] For a commentary on the centrality of exile in the book of Genesis see Abi Doukhan, *Biblical Portraits of Exile* (Routledge, 2016).

[13] Both the stories of Tamar, Judah's daughter-in-law, and of Abimelech feature characters that prove to have more integrity than the Biblical characters they are interacting with. Upon realizing that Tamar is carrying his child, Judah exclaims that "she is more righteous than I" (Gen. 38:26, NIV). The king of the Philistines, Abimelech, upon realizing that Isaac lied to him about his wife, chastises Isaac for bringing potential guilt upon him, and forbids anyone to touch the couple upon penalty of death (Gen. 26:11).

[14] Gen. 18.

[15] Gen. 18–19.

[16] Cf. Babylonian Talmud, Tractate *Sanhedrin* 107b.

[17] Gen. 12.

[18] According to Samuel Kramer, "the Sumerian thinkers. . .were firmly convinced that man was fashioned of clay and created for one purpose only: to serve the gods by supplying them with food, drink and shelter" (Samuel Noah Kramer, *The Sacred Marriage Rite,* 17).

[19] According to Aristotle, "the male is by nature superior, and the female inferior; and the one rules, and the other is ruled; this principle, of necessity, extends to all mankind." Because the male is more spirited and more connected to the realm of forms (due to his physical make-up) he is naturally more fitted to lead the female who, by virtue of being less spirited and, therefore, less self-controlled and disciplined, actually needs a strong lead in her life (Aristotle, *Politics,* 1.5).

[20] Gen. 2.

[21] Phyllis Trible makes the same point: "Only after surgery does the male identify himself as male. . .their creation is simultaneous not sequential. One does not precede the other even though the timeline of this story introduces the man first." Phyllis Trible, *God and the Rhetoric of* Sexuality (Fortress Press, 1986), 98.

[22] In his *On the Generation of Animals*, Aristotle observes that male animals have a hotter body temperature than female animals. He also observes that female animals tend to be "less spirited than the male. . .softer, more vicious, less simple, more impetuous. . .while the males, on the contrary, are more spirited, wilder, simpler and less cunning." These variations between the male and the female animals are, according to Aristotle, the effect of differences in body temperature. Because the female animals have a lower body temperature they are "less spirited," that is to say, less capable of resisting their impulses or their instincts. As such, the female, although more merciful, is also more prone to negative emotions such as jealousy, rage, and violence. Although she often knows better and is as good as the male at knowing the difference between good and evil, her physical nature makes it difficult if not impossible for her to control her passions and develop the discipline necessary for virtuous behavior (cf. Aristotle, *On the Generation of Animals,* 4.1. [https://www.documentacatholicaomnia.eu/03d/-384_-322,_Aristoteles,_12_On_the_Generation_of_Animals,_EN.pdf]; and *On the History of Animals,* 9.1. [https://www.gutenberg.org/files/59058/59058-h/59058-h.htm]).

[23] The Biblical text exhibits a surprising gender fluidity. We have women serving as judges and army commanders (Deborah), and we have women serving as prophets (Myriam and Anna in the New Testament), all roles typically dominated by males. We have women proposing marriage (Ruth, the Shulamite) and we have women making pivotal decisions for the tribe (Rebekah, Abigail), again typically male-dominated roles.

[24] Because of their physical differences (the woman being less spirited and more grounded/stable than the man, cf. note xxxvii), the woman was more likely, according to Aristotelian reasoning, to love stability and prefer the hearth of the home, whereas the man, propelled by his natural energy, would always want to emerge from the home into the political arena. Thus, women of ancient Greece were typically relegated to roles within the private domain while the males enjoyed positions in the public domain.

[25] My translation.

[26] Buber says this beautifully and ascribes all authentic encounters to grace, outside of all attempts to forcefully make things happen: "The You encounters me by grace—it cannot be found by seeking" (Martin Buber, *I and Thou*, 62).

[27] This is also the observation of William Phipps: "*Eze*r never connotes someone in a servile role. *Ezer* often refers to a superior person and is frequently associated with divine assistance." William Phipps, *Assertive Biblical Women* (Praeger, 1992), 138.

[28] See, for example, Psalm 121:1: "I will lift up my eyes to the hills from whence comes my help (*ezer*)."

[29] Diane Wolkstein and Samuel Noah Kramer, *Inanna, Queen of Heaven and Earth*, 33.

[30] Ibid., 45.

[31] Paul's understanding of the submission of the woman to the man is however polemic and occurs right after the exhortation that the man and the woman submit to each other (Ephesians 5:21). The command for the woman to submit to the man is also directly followed by a command to the man to be unto her as Christ was to the Church, offering up himself in sacrificial love.

[32] See section 2 of my article: "The Woman's Curse: A Redemptive Reading of Genesis 3:16," *Religions* 11, no. 11 (2020). https://www.mdpi.com/2077-1444/11/11/600).

[33] Ibid.

[34] Ibid.

[35] By the time we get to the Babylonian era, the king is identified with the tree, as is evident in Daniel 4.

[36] In Genesis 6, the word *laqah* is used again, this time to describe the forceful, coercive "taking" of the daughters of men by the sons of God. One wonders if therein does not lie the reason for the flood that will destroy the world in the chapters that follow.

[37] The seat of wisdom in Ancient Egypt was the ear. In the teachings of Ptahhotep, an Egyptian sage, we find the following advice: "He who hears is

beloved of God. He whom God hates does not hear." *Teachings of Ptahhotep,* section 37.

[38] "Several scholars have sought to develop the proposed connection between Eve and a goddess. Some have taken the epithet "Mother of the Living" more seriously and have proposed that behind the figure of Eve stands not only a figure associated with serpents, but also that of a "mother-goddess." Beaulieu, *Eve's Ritual, The Judahite Sacred Marriage Rite,* 149. Our story, however, seems rather to undo this tempting identification between Eve and a goddess, by shattering all her illusions of divinity and throwing her back onto her humanity.

[39] "The story is careful to specify that the man is with her (*immah*)." Phyllis Trible, *God and the Rhetoric of* Sexuality, 113.

[40] NIV.

[41] In one of his essays, Levinas sees in pain precisely this opportunity for the hereto self-enclosed self to break open and to cry out and reach out beyond the prison of the self. Cf. Emmanuel Levinas, "Useless Suffering" in *The Provocation of Levinas: Rethinking the Other,* ed. Robert Bernasconi and David Wood, trans. Richard Cohen, (Routledge, 1988.

[42] Carol Meyers has long hinted at the semantic connection between *teshuqah* (desire) and *teshuvah* (returning). She observes that the "Septuagint has 'your turning [or returning] shall be to your husband.'" She then adds, "Virtually all other ancient translations, like the Septuagint and also early Christian and Jewish exegetical traditions understand the text to say turning or returning. Rather than focus on sexual desire, they have the woman (re)turning to the man. They apparently understood the rare *teshuqah* to have a semantic range overlapping with *teshuvah*, with the woman being drawn (as by desire?) to the one to whom she is turning/returning." Carol Meyers, *Rediscovering Eve: Ancient Israelite Women in Context* (Oxford University Press, 2013), 94.

[43] The Talmud puts this vividly: "'A man takes a wife'.... Because the way of a man is to look for a wife, but it is not the way of a woman to look for a husband. You can compare it to a person who lost an article: who goes looking for the lost item? Surely the loser will look for the thing he has lost (Babylonian Talmud, Tractate *Kiddushin* 2b).

[44]Thus, the second century BCE Palestinian sage Ben Sira bitterly laments women's role in bringing death into the world (Ben Sira, *Sirach* 25:24), referring to the incident in the Garden of Eden. https://bible.usccb.org/bible/sirach/25.

[45] According to Michaela Bauks, gardens "represent a sacred and may be imbued with a sacral character.... In the reception of Greek authors like Herodotus, Xenophon and others, Persian kings came to be portrayed as royal gardeners, with the garden—much like Neo-Assyrian temple gardens—imagined as

holy space… thus the Mesopotamian kings were provided with the sovereignty title 'Rural Man' or 'Gardener.' The Assyrian kings cherished plants and animals in their garden from every portion of their expansive realms; the gardens thus served to represent the extraordinary range of their power. The royal task is thus to save the garden…. In Genesis 2, Adam is taken from the ground and is put into the garden to cultivate and preserve it. With this, he too takes on an aspect of the king-symbolism, which is later taken from him when he is banished from the garden." Michaela Bauks, "Sacred Trees in the Garden of Eden and Their Ancient Near Eastern Precursors," *Journal of Ancient Judaism* 3, no. 3 (2021), 280, 295, 296.

[46] My translation.

[47] "For mortal men, the most essential task of earthly life was to ensure that the fabric of the universe was sustained. Ancient cosmogonies were in agreement that obscure force of chaos existed before the world was created and that although through the act of creation they had been cast away to the outer edges of the world, they nevertheless continued to threaten to encroach on the world. The possibility of such catastrophe could only be averted by the actions of gods and men. That order which embraced the notions of an equilibrium of the universe, the harmonious coexistence of all its elements in its essential cohesion for the maintenance of all created forms was summed up in the word *Ma'at.*" J. Martin Plumley, "The Cosmology of Ancient Egypt", in *Ancient Cosmologies,* eds. Carmen Blacker and Michael Loewe (Allen & Unwin, 1975), 36. Cf. John Walton, *The Lost World of Adam and Eve,* 107.

[48] This is a disjunctive *waw* meaning "yet" or "but." Cf. Bruce Waltke and M. O'Connor, *An Introduction to Biblical Hebrew Syntax* (Eisenbrauns, 1990), 39.2.3.

[49] NIV.

[50] Cf. Judg. 8:23; Prov. 22:7; Isa. 19:4.

[51] NIV.

[52] That God is enthroning man by bestowing him the title of worker and keeper of the garden has already been observed by a number of scholars. But only Beaulieu has noted the "old royal dragon killing motive" in Genesis 3:15 where man seems to be given back his royal power over the forces of chaos. Interestingly, Genesis 3:16 is written in parallel with Genesis 3:15, and also contains the royal symbolism of the "hieros gamos motif" (Beaulieu, *Eve's Ritual, The Judahite Sacred Marriage Rite,* 161). Thus, man is given his royal scepter back on two counts in Genesis 3:15–16: through the slaying of the serpent (*he* shall strike at your head), and the sacred marriage to the woman (*he* shall rule over you).

[53] This idea is also found in Chinese philosophy: "Know the male, yet keep to the female," *Tao Te Ching,* verse 28.

[54]This translation is supported by a passage in the book of Proverbs: "Through me kings reign (*malach*) and rulers decree (*haqaq)* just laws. Through me, princes rule (*yasar)*, great men and all the righteous judges" (Prov. 8:15–16). Here, we have not only a precedent of the preposition *b-* being translated as "through" in the Hebrew Bible in general, but a precedent that takes place precisely in the context of royal rule. And although the Proverbs text does not include *mashal* in its list of verbs signifying rulership, we have here verbs otherwise closely associated with it such as *malach* (to reign), *haqaq (*to decree), and *yasar* (to rule). Thus, there exists a definite semantic field of rulership, of royal rule, in which the preposition *b-* is aptly translated as "through." This text in the book of Proverbs thus sheds a revealing new light on Genesis 3:16b, one which lends a powerful plausibility to it being translated as we have proposed: "Her desire for the man and he shall rule *through/by* her" (Gen. 3:16b).

[55] This understanding of the "shepherd-king" is in line with the Sumerian definition of the "shepherd-king" as a protective force rather than a despotic one, as Samuel Kramer observes: "A Sumerian sovereign was no arbitrary despot, no cruel and capricious tyrant; a king such as Shulgi, for example, was fully aware that he was only the vicar and representative of the gods and responsible to them for the well-being and prosperity of the land and its people. The priests and poets constantly reminded him, in their hymns of glorification and celebration, that he was especially selected by the gods, who had transferred to him some of their divine power and understanding, for no other reason than 'to give good guidance to Sumer;' 'to let the people of Sumer and Akkad refresh themselves under his shade;' 'to supply them with abundant food to eat, and sweet water to drink.' He was the divinely guided monarch 'whose kingship brought joy to man,' 'whose shepherdship brought happiness,' who saw to it 'that the people increased and multiplied,' and 'that all lands lived in peace.'" Samuel Noah Kramer, *The Sacred Marriage Rite,* 12–13.

Chapter 3

[1] Babylonian Talmud, Tractate *Baba Batra* 14b.

[2] Job 1–2.

[3] Maimonides comments on the story of Job by saying that although Job was virtuous, he was not yet wise: "It is remarkable in this account that wisdom is not ascribed to Job. The text does not say he was an intelligent, wise, or clever man; but virtues and uprightness, especially in actions, are ascribed to him. If he were wise, he would not have any doubt about the cause of his suffering, as will

be shown later on." (Maimonides, *Guide for the Perplexed,* part 3, section 22). gutenberg.org/cache/epub/73584/pg73584-images.html#ch3.22.

[4] NIV.

[5] Ellen Van Wolde does a beautiful job at showing how Job's wife "undeniably contributes to Job's development.... She forces him to react. And he who has earlier chosen to bless and not sin, from now on does neither of the two. His wife introduces death and awakens doubt in him. Job is no longer sure of anything and begins to ask himself questions. . .thus the woman plays an important part in the development of the story... With her help Job changes from a cocksure believer into an asker of questions." Ellen Van Wolde, "The Development of Job: Mrs. Job as Catalyst," in *A Feminist Companion to The Bible, Wisdom Literature,* ed. Athalya Brenner (Sheffield Academic Press, 1995), 201–205.

[6] Lyn Bechtel also observes this about the storm metaphor: Nature is used to symbolize an essential aspect of God's functioning. A storm is part of the natural order, yet it is not part of the predictable elements of nature. It represents a degree of randomness. It is movement, energy, violence that can bring death. Simultaneously, a storm frequently contains rain which produces fertility and renews life." Lyn Bechtel, "A Feminist Approach to the Book of Job," in *A Feminist Companion to The Bible, Wisdom Literature*, 237.

[7] Lillian Klein observes that the word for "womb" (*rechem* and *beten)* is used twelve times in the book of Job. Cf. Lillian Klein, "Job and the Womb," in *A Feminist Companion to The Bible, Wisdom Literature*, 197.

[8] Gen. 21:12.

[9] Gen. 24–27.

[10] Gen. 29:20–35.

[11] Num. 27:1–11.

Chapter 4

[1] Cf. Babylonian Talmud, Tractate *Baba Batra* 14b.

[2] Cf. Ruth 1:1.

[3] In addition to the many wars waged on the surrounding nations (cf. the well-known stories of Jephthah, Samson, Barak, and Deborah), one story in particular reveals the absolute chaos that existed internally in Israel. That story is the rape and dismemberment of a Levite's concubine (Judg.19:25–28).

[4] This is also the observation of William Phipps. Speaking of the strategic placement of book of Ruth after the book of Judges in the Septuagint, he argues: "The decision by the Septuagint to have it follow the Judges scroll was probably due mainly to the opening phrase, 'in the days when the judges ruled.' The editors may also have wanted to provide moral and religious relief for those who had

completed reading the bloodthirsty Judges' tales" (William Phipps, *Assertive Biblical Women*, p 48).

[5] Tamara Eskenazi makes this point in her commentary, except that her commentary interprets the book as a subversion of the xenophobia prevalent in the time of the return of the exiles during the leadership of Ezra and Nehemiah. This gives the book a much later date (500 BCE), but the subversive intent remains the same: "The book of Ruth exhibits no overt hostility toward foreigners in general and Moabites in particular.... This acceptance is in sharp contrast to the attitudes toward Moabites in Deut. 23:4–9 and Ezra-Nehemiah which condemn Moabites for their past misdeeds (see, e.g., Neh. 13:1–3). According to Hubbard, such acceptance points to an early date for Ruth, before hostility became normative. According to other scholars such as Yair Zakovitch, the Book of Ruth is a deliberate polemic against the policies of Ezra-Nehemiah and is therefore post-exilic." Tamara Eskenazi, *The JPS Bible Commentary: Ruth* (The Jewish Publication Society, 2011), xviii.

[6] Cf. ibid, lvii.

[7] The word *hesed* is used 26 times to describe God in the Psalms, notably in Psalm 136 where the word *hesed,* "mercy" is repeated at every refrain.

[8] It is used twice to describe Ruth in the threshing floor scene (Ruth 3:10).

[9] And it is used twice to describe God (Ruth 1:8; 2:20).

[10] The connection between the epithet *goel* and God pervades the Hebrew Bible, as noted in Eskenazi's commentary: "The subject of redemption is more prominent in Ruth than in any other biblical book. Writing about Ruth, Ostriker observes that in Ruth, the term redemption 'signifies responsibility and accountability...and there is obviously both a practical and a spiritual dimension to the term. The root *gaal* (redeem) occurs twenty-one times in the story, always referring to human beings as redeemers, but no reader would fail to connect the term with the familiar epithet for God, *goel Yisrael,* the redeemer of Israel'" (Tamara Eskenazi, *The JPS Bible Commentary: Ruth*, liii).

[11] Eugen Drewermann make this same point: "C'est bien dire que le lieu essentiel où se rencontre Dieu, c'est l'amour entre humains" [The locus of the encounter with God is the love between humans. My translation] (Eugène Drewermann, *L'évangile des femmes* [Seuil, 1996], 54).

[12] Eskenazi's commentary makes the same observation: "Alicia Ostriker writes: 'God's kindness invoked by human beings, is also enacted by them. To put it another way, the kindness of human beings reveals the kindness of a God.' Or, as Hubbard has it: God 'acts through human agents ... when people act with *hesed,* God is acting in them.' Although other biblical books explicitly enjoin Israel to emulate God (e.g., Lev. 19:2), Ruth seems to say more: it is almost as if

human actions and words bring God into the world. God-centered people prompt God to show up as it were. This bold theological view is made explicit in Pesikta de-Rav Kahan, which daringly represents Boaz's actions as a role model for God. It has God exclaim: 'Boaz comforts! Will I not comfort?!' At the very least, God expects people to do their part in 'repairing the world': 'Boaz did his part, and Ruth did hers, and Naomi did hers; [then] the Holy One said: I too will do mine'" (Tamara Eskenazi, *The JPS Bible Commentary: Ruth,* li–lii).

[13] This is not out of line with Jewish practice, notably that of *shalom bayt,* where it is allowed to blur some of the halakhic lines for the sake of marital peace. This practice has a Biblical foundation: when God tells Sarah she will give birth to a son, she expresses disbelief, saying: "After I am waxed old shall I have pleasure, my husband being old also?" But when God speaks to Abraham, he says: "Why did Sarah laugh and say, 'Will I really have a child, now that I am old?'" (Genesis: 18:12–13). The rabbis comment that God omitted Sarah's mention of Abraham's age out of concern for their *shalom bayit.* Eskenazi makes a similar comment: "There is a consensus that Naomi's instructions to Ruth transgress the accepted norms. But the sages emphasize the purity of the goal and the piety of the protagonists, which render the instructions excusable and even laudable" (Tamara Eskenazi, *The JPS Bible Commentary: Ruth,* lix).

[14] It is therefore not surprising that the book of Ruth is read at Shavuot, the holiday commemorating the giving of the Torah. Eskenazi comments: "The rabbis, who directed that the book be read on Shavuot, already connected Ruth with the giving of the Torah at Sinai. However, Ruth also contrasts the great revelation of Sinai. Instead of the fire and the blaring of the horn at Sinai, the messages of Ruth, like the revelation granted to the prophet Elijah, come as *kol demamah dakkah,* the 'still small voice' or the 'soft murmuring sound' (1 Kings 19:12)" (Tamara Eskenazi, *The JPS Bible Commentary: Ruth,* lxx).

[15] This emphasis, in the book of Ruth, on kindness versus law is also noted by the ancient rabbis: "R. Zeira said: The scroll [of Ruth] tells nothing either of cleanliness or of uncleanliness, neither of prohibition nor permission. For what purpose then was it written: to teach how great is the reward of those who do deeds of kindness (*Ruth Rabbah 2:15*)" (quoted in Tamara Eskenazi, *The JPS Bible Commentary: Ruth,* lvi).

[16] Bronner also points out the similarities between Ruth and Abraham: "In some places the Ruth narrative actually resembles the older narratives. Ruth, like Abraham, left the house of her father and mother and went into a people. . ." Leila Leah Bronner, *From Eve to Esther: Rabbinic Reconstructs of Biblical Women* (Westminster John Knox Press), 1994, 63.

[17] "The etymology of this name, which appears only in this book, is difficult. The Moabite Mesha inscription uses the form *ryt,* 'satiation' (1:12).... In Hebrew, the name may derive from the root *r-w-h,* 'overflowing with moisture,' as in the 'watered garden' in Isa. 58:1" (Tamara Eskenazi, *The JPS Bible Commentary: Ruth,* 7). Cf. also Jer. 31:12 and Isa. 58:11.

[18] "Ruth knowingly declares her commitment to a future that can bear no imaginable fruit." Avivah Gottlieb Zornberg, *The Murmuring Deep: Reflections on the Biblical Unconscious* (Knopf Doubleday Publishing Group, 2011), 358.

[19] My translation.

[20] "As luck would have it, *Va-yikker mikreha.* The root *k-r-h* is uncommon and conveys happenchance, sometimes with the theological implication of divine providence. In Gen. 27:20, Jacob, pretending to be Esau, uses this verb to explain to Isaac why he has come back so soon from the hunt: 'The Lord your God granted me good fortune,' literally, 'made it happen before me.' A close parallel can be found in the prayer of Abraham's servant who is seeking a wife for Isaac. The servant prays to God, 'make it happen before me' *hakreh na'* (Gen. 24:12). In these passages and elsewhere, the reader is expected to detect the hand of God at work" (Tamara Eskenazi, *The JPS Bible Commentary: Ruth,* 30).

[21] We borrow this expression from a poem by Tupac Shakur, "The Rose that Grew from Concrete."

[22] There exists a semantic connection between the word *qorban* (sacrifice) and *leqarev* (to draw near). Both are built from the same root, *qarav.*

[23] My translation.

[24] NIV; NKJV.

[25] "In Biblical narrative about early Israel, the term *gibor hayil* applies mostly to military men such as the chieftain Gideon (Judg. 6:11) or to young David before he becomes king of Israel (1 Sam. 16:18). *Gibor* related to *gebher,* male, usually designates a male hero; *hayil* is related to *hayal,* 'warrior'" (Tamara Eskenazi, *The JPS Bible Commentary: Ruth,* 28).

[26] The notion of love as a force was beautifully developed by Martin Luther King Jr. in his book *The Strength to Love* (Beacon Press, 2019), chapter 17.

[27] "'Bathe, anoint, dress up.' Although this triplet of verbs designates a sequence of common action, it is also an Ancient Near Eastern literary trope that foreshadows a major change in an individual's life" (Tamara Eskenazi, *The JPS Bible Commentary: Ruth,* 51).

[28] Deut. 28:57; Ezek.16:25.

[29] Lev. 20:11–21.

[30]"Boaz seems grateful and flattered by Ruth's request. The open-ended nature of her request, with its room for interpretation, may be integral to his gratitude" (Tamara Eskenazi, *The JPS Bible Commentary: Ruth,* 61).

[31] NKJV.

[32] Ruth 2:1, my translation.

[33]"Israel is regenerated by the woman from Moab.... By becoming Ruth's metaphorical redeemer—by taking her under his wings—Boaz will find his own redemption. . .in soliciting his redemption she has drawn out of him with gentle force, a possibility of larger life" (Avivah Gottlieb Zornberg, *The Murmuring Deep,* 369).

[34] Gen. 24:67.

[35] The Rabbis comment on the miraculous character of Ruth's conception by narrating how God specifically shaped a womb in Ruth (who previously didn't have one) in order for her to be able to conceive (cf. *Ruth Rabbah,* 7:14).

[36] Cf. note 124.

[37] "A man and woman—if they merit, the Shekhinah is between them. If not, fire consumes them" (Babylonian Talmud, Tractate *Sotah,* 17a).

[38] Isa. 42:6.

[39] Isa. 11:1–6.

Chapter 5

[1] Cf. Babylonian Talmud, Tractate *Baba Batra* 15a.

[2] "One of the peculiarities of dealing with Israel's wisdom tradition is the special need to consider the effects of foreign influence on these texts and their worldview because the subject materials so patently demand this methodological awareness. One cannot speak of wisdom without speaking of Egypt or Mesopotamia. . .the sages were comparative thinkers because of their association vertically through time with tradition and horizontally, (across cultures during the same time period) with wisdom contacts in other cultures. They did not perform their intellectual activities in a theological, ethical, literary or practical vacuum. In the midst of Israel's culture which emphasized its theological uniqueness, the sages worked with the connections and similarities of their teachings to those of their neighbors, creating a kind of intellectual ecumenism. They were wise precisely because they honed their thought on the wisdom of the ages and the experiences of the cultures that preceded and surrounded them." Carol Fontaine, "Women in the World of Wisdom," in *A Feminist Companion to the Bible: Wisdom Literature*, ed. Athalya Brenner (Sheffield Academic Press, 1995), 26–27.

[3] The fear of the Lord is set in parallel with the father's/mother's teachings from the onset: "The fear of the Lord is the beginning of knowledge; fools despise

wisdom (*hokhma*) and discipline (*mussar*)//my son, heed the discipline (*mussar*) of your father and do not forsake the instructions (*torah*) of your mother" (Prov. 1:7–8).

[4] NIV.

[5] Cf. Eccles. 2:3; 7:26.

[6] Return and repent are the same word in Hebrew: *teshuva* (to "return" or "to repent").

[7] King Solomon was particularly intent in trying *everything* in his exploration of wisdom: "I, Koheleth, was king in Jerusalem over Israel. I set my mind to study and to probe with wisdom all that happens under the sun" (Eccles. 1:12–13).

[8] Both Agur son of Jakeh of Massa (Prov. 30), and Lemuel king of Massa are from Canaan. The *Encyclopedia Judaica* identifies Massa as a North Arabian tribe, known from Genesis 25:14, one of the Kedemite peoples whose wisdom the Israelites held in high esteem (*Encyclopedia Judaica*, s.v. "Ishmaelites").

[9] Proverbs 9:1–5, 17–18.

[10] "This at first subtle shift from [Woman Wisdom]'s role as speaker for God to more intimate identity with God takes a dramatic turn in Woman Wisdom's self-description in Prov. 8:22–36. [There] Woman Wisdom is present with God before and during the process of creation, as a playful child or a wise architect" (Claudia Camp, "Woman Wisdom: Bible," *Jewish Women's Archive.* https://jwa.org/encyclopedia/article/woman-wisdom-bible).

[11] If one abides by the Solomonic authorship of the book of Proverbs, the book of Isaiah is written later. Nevertheless, the prophet seems to have understood the Solomonic intention to establish Woman Wisdom as a figure of the divine since he chooses to borrow precisely the same expression to describe the relationship with the God of Israel: "Seek the Lord while he may be found, call to him while he is near" (Isa. 55:6–9).

[12] Cf. Gen. 1:27.

[13] "In some of the books of the Hebrew Bible, "wisdom" is personified as a female character...her portrayal often draws comparisons to goddesses outside the Hebrew Bible such as the Egyptian goddesses Ma'at and Isis, the Sumerian Inanna and the Babylonian Ishtar" (Claudia Camp, "Woman Wisdom: Bible," *Jewish Women's Archive.*, https://jwa.org/encyclopedia/article/woman-wisdom-bible).

[14] Solomon's first wife was Egyptian, testifying to there having been close political, economic, and intellectual ties between the Solomonic kingdom and that of Egypt.

[15] "Ma'at was personified as a goddess and the creator's daughter and received a cult of her own" (John R. Baines and Peter F. Dorman, "Ancient Egyptian Religion," in *Encyclopedia Britannica*; last updated February 3, 2025. https://www.britannica.com/topic/ancient-Egyptian-religion).

[16] "The concept of ma'at ("order") was fundamental in Egyptian thought. The king's role was to set Ma'at in place of Isfet ("disorder"). Ma'at was crucial in human life and embraced notions of reciprocity, justice, truth, and moderation. In the cult of other deities, the king's offering of ma'at to a deity encapsulated the relationship between humanity, the king, and the gods; as the representative of humanity, he returned to the gods the order that came from them and of which they were themselves part" (John R. Baines and Peter F. Dorman, *"Ancient Egyptian Religion,"* in *Encyclopedia Britannica*; last updated February 3, 2025. *https://www.britannica.com/topic/ancient-Egyptian*-religion).

[17] https://www.brooklynmuseum.org/opencollection/objects/4171.

[18] "Ancient texts emphasize the loving relationship between the king and goddess, asserting that a king is 'beloved of Hathor, Mistress of Denderah' or that 'the one whom her heart loves has been chosen to occupy the throne.' In iconography the king is often shown with a goddess embracing him from behind or shielding him with two large wings." Bernhard Lang, *Wisdom and the Book of Proverbs: An Israelite Goddess Redefined* (Pilgrim Press, 1986), 61.

[19] "This near-deification of Woman Wisdom in 8:22–36 cannot help but recall certain ancient goddesses, in this case especially Ma'at, the Egyptian goddess of justice, who was also understood both as the child of the creator god and (especially in Egyptian wisdom literature) as the ordering principle of creation. Allusions to Ma'at may also be seen in Woman Wisdom's claim to establish just rule (8:15–16) and in the depiction of her with long life in her right hand and wealth in her left (3:16), for Ma'at also appears with the *ankh*, symbol of life, in one hand and a scepter in the other." Claudia Camp, "Woman Wisdom: Bible" in *Jewish Women's Archive,* https://jwa.org/encyclopedia/article/woman-wisdom-bible.

[20] The Hebrew word *qanini* has a range of meaning, the least of which being "created." In parallel texts, it can mean "to acquire" (Eccles. 2:7, 4:1) or to "conceive" (Gen. 4:1). Claudia Camp makes the same observation: "'The Lord created me.' This translation (Septuagint) is less likely correct than either 'acquired' or 'conceived,' (cf. 'I was brought forth' in vv. 24–25). Similar ambiguity in 8:30 where wisdom is 'master workman' but could also be translated 'darling child.' In either case, wisdom is present with God before and during the process of creation as a playful child or a wise architect." Claudia Camp, "Woman Wisdom:

Bible," in *Jewish Women's Archive*. https://jwa.org/encyclopedia/article/woman-wisdom-bible.

[21] NIV.

[22] NKJV.

[23] NIV translation. McKinlay sees in this passage an identification of Woman Wisdom/Yahweh with the Canaanite goddess Asherah: "Asherah now merged with Yahweh and becomes wisdom of Yahweh personified who is a 'tree of life to those who lay hold of her' (Prov 3.18)." Judith E. McKinlay, *Gendering Wisdom the Host: Biblical Invitations to Eat and Drink* (Sheffield Academic Press, 1996), 36.

[24] "How then can the feminine *hokhma* appear in the role of a woman who counsels rulers. The models of identification in this case originate not only from the history of religion. I do not intend to deny the background influence of the Egyptian Maat on the figure of the counselling wisdom, since Maat evidently appears as a feminine guide or patroness of rulers. The wisdom role undoubtedly incorporates influences of the Ancient Orient, where quite a few goddesses are known to have functioned as patronesses of kings." Silvia Schroer, "Wise and Counseling Women in Ancient Israel," in *A Feminist Companion to the Bible: Wisdom Literature*, ed. Athalya Brenner, (Sheffield Academic Press, 1995), 70.

[25] Prov. 31:10, NKJV.

[26]NIV. What follows is drawn from the work of Claudia Camp and Silvia Schroer. Schroer shows the following connections: "Indeed in Proverbs, various metaphors are employed to compare the wife to the 'wise woman.' Both Wisdom (Prov. 3:15; 8:11; Job 28:18) and the worthy wife (Prov. 31:10) are much more precious than jewels. Wisdom (Prov. 4:8–9) as well as the worthy wife (12:4) are the crown of a wise husband. … 'He who finds a wife … obtains favor from the Lord' (18:22)…. A prudent wife is from the Lord (19:14)" (Silvia Schroer, "Wise and Counselling Women in Ancient Israel," in *A Feminist Companion to the Bible: Wisdom Literature,* ed. Athalya Brenner, Sheffield Academic Press, 1995, 73). Camp makes the following observations: "Reflections of traditional women's roles—especially aspects of the role of wife—may be seen in the characterization of Woman Wisdom in Proverbs 3:13–18; 4:5–9 and 9:1–6. Lest the modern reader think '*only* a wife,' one must note the real, if behind-the-scenes, social power wielded by the wife as manager of an extended and productive family household and as counselor to husband and children (see Proverbs 31:10–31). Just as the husband of this capable wife 'will have no lack of gain' (31:11), so also Woman Wisdom will exalt and honor the man who prizes and embraces her (3:13–18; 4:8). Both bring the trusting husband a 'crown' (4:9, 12:4)" (Claudia Camp, "Woman Wisdom: Bible," in *Jewish Women's Archive*.

[27] NIV.
[28] CEV.
[29] NIV.

Chapter 6

[1] Cf. Babylonian Talmud, Tractate *Shabbat* 30b; Tractate *Baba Batra* 14b–15a.

[2] Eccles. 9:7–9.

[3] NIV.

[4] King Solomon was well acquainted with Egyptian literature and borrowed many linguistic, literary, and philosophical tropes from Egypt. This is already evident in the way that Solomon structures his book as a monologue, or inner dialogue, most likely borrowing from the Egyptian genre of debating with oneself, used in the classical Egyptian wisdom text *The Dispute Between a Man and his Ba*, from the Middle Kingdom (2055–1650 BCE), in *Ancient Egyptian Literature: A Book of Readings,* vol. 1: *The Old and Middle Kingdoms*, ed. Miriam Lichtheim (Berkeley, CA: University of California Press, 1975), 163–169.

[5] According to Assman, the *Ba* signified the spiritual part of the king that outlived the body and that was capable of navigating into the afterlife. This is why it is signified by a bird capable of flying between heaven and earth. In the Ancient Empire, only the king possessed a *Ba* since only the king was capable of transitioning in this way into the afterlife and unify himself with the sun-god. Later however, the *Ba* became democratized, and all men possessed this spiritual entity that enabled their translation into the afterlife. Cf. Jan Assman, *Ma'at, l'Egypte pharaonique et l'idée de justice sociale* (La maison de vie, 2003), 73–75).

[6] "And God saw all (*qol*) that he had made and behold it was very good" (Gen. 1:31).

[7] The books of Solomon (Proverbs, Ecclesiastes, and Song of Songs) all have the common feature of weaving the wisdom of the nations into their work. We already noted in the preceding chapter how the book of Proverbs borrowed from Canaanite wisdom (cf. Chapter 5, note 159). We now see how much Egyptian wisdom made its way into the book of Ecclesiastes. Finally, we will see that the Song of Songs is replete with allusions to Egyptian and Sumerian wisdom (cf. Chapter 7, note 217).

[8] This should not come as a surprise given the depth of King Solomon's political alliance with Egypt. The Biblical text tells us that Solomon relied on Egypt for his constructions, his model of government, and the upkeep of his military force (1 Kings 10:28, 29). He even married an Egyptian princess (1

Kings 11:1) making him, or one of his sons, the potential heir to the throne of Egypt.

[9] The notion "all is futile" echoes the Egyptian literature of despair (1550–1080 BCE) that one finds in works like *The Dispute Between a Man and his Ba;* or *The Admonitions of Ipu-Wer*, trans. John A. Wilson, in *Ancient Near Eastern Texts Relating to the Old Testament*, ed. James B. Pritchard, 3rd ed. (Princeton University Press, 1969), 441–444.

[10] "Ma'at was personified as a goddess and the creator's daughter and received a cult of her own" (John R. Baines and Peter F. Dorman, "Ancient Egyptian Religion", in *Encyclopedia Britannica.* Last updated February 3, 2025. https://www.britannica.com/topic/ancient-Egyptian-religion). In the tomb of Nefethotep we have the following quote: "O Ra, generator of Ma'at," a clear indication that for the Egyptian mindset, Ra was the generator or father of Ma'at. Cf. Jan Assmann, *Ma'at, l'Egypte pharaonique*, 111.

[11] "The concept of Ma'at ('order') was fundamental in Egyptian thought. The king's role was to set Ma'at in place of Isfet ('disorder'). Ma'at was crucial in human life and embraced notions of reciprocity, justice, truth, and moderation. In the cult of other deities, the king's offering of Ma'at to a deity encapsulated the relationship between humanity, the king, and the gods; as the representative of humanity, he returned to the gods the order that came from them and of which they were themselves part" (John R. Baines and Peter F. Dorman, "Ancient Egyptian Religion," in *Encyclopedia Britannica*).

[12] Cf. note 169.

[13] Cf. Gen. 1:10, 12, 18, 21, 25, 31.

[14] This sense of stagnation is highlighted by Solomon's use of the Egyptian expression "under the sun." This expression has the connotation of repetition in the Egyptian language. But, whereas in the Egyptian context, the expression "under the sun" alludes to the repetition of the cyclical ordered world, in the book of Ecclesiastes, it has the connotation of stagnant repetition, where nothing new emerges. Cf. Jacques B. Doukhan, "Ecclesiastes," in *SDAIBC*, vol. 6: *Psalms, Proverbs, Ecclesiastes, Song of Songs* (Pacific Press Publishing Association, 2022), 969–961.

[15] In the Egyptian context, every man, upon dying, saw his heart weighed by the goddess Ma'at against her feather. If the heart was light enough—that is to say, pure enough—the man would be judged worthy of passing into the afterlife. If the heart was too heavy, the man would not be deemed worthy of an afterlife (Jan Assman, *Ma'at, l'Egypte pharaonique*, 84–87).

[16] The Field of Reeds described the lush afterlife of the Egyptian dead having been deemed worthy by Ma'at of an afterlife (cf. https://www.worldhistory.org/Field_of_Reeds/).

[17] According to Assman, the pharaoh's main task was to make sure that all men were treated justly, and that the weak were protected from the strong. She quotes the *Teaching for Merikare* where the king is said to be a conductor "meant to support the spine of the weak man" (Jan Assman, *Ma'at, l'Egypte pharaonique,* 130).

[18] NIV.

[19] The Biblical account of Solomon's life alludes to his eventually losing his grasp on the kingdom, and living to see his reign handed over to his servant Jeroboam (1 Kings 11:11–13; cf. 11:31, 35).

[20] NIV.

[21] NKJV.

[22] The notion of garden is a direct reference to the garden of Eden; the notion of "all kinds of fruit trees" (Eccles. 2:5) points to the expression "every tree whose fruit" (Gen. 1:29). The "water" of the pools (Eccles. 2:6) points to the "waters" of the rivers and the sea in the Creation story (Gen. 1:10, 21). The notion of "wind" (Eccles. 1:14, 2:11) echoes the Creation story's "wind" sweeping over the water (Gen. 1:2); and the quest for "knowledge" (Eccles. 1:16) parallels the tree of "knowledge" of good and evil in the Creation story (Gen. 2:9). Finally, whereas in the Creation story it is God who "makes" (Gen. 1:7, 16, 25, 26; 2:2), now it is Solomon who "makes" (Eccles. 2:4, 5, 6, 8).

[23] Interestingly, *hevel* (futile) is mentioned here 7 times (Eccles. 2:1; 2:11; 2:15; 2:17; 2:21; 2:23; 2:26), operating a contrast with the Creation story's mention of *tov* (good) 7 times (Gen. 1:3; 1:9; 1:12; 1:18; 1:21; 1:25; 1:31).

[24] André Neher also notes this: "Mais *hevel* est une notion tragique. Je suis empoigné par elle avant d'en avoir conscience. Et lorsque je la perçois, le seul jugement que je puisse formuler à son égard, c'est de constater qu'elle me fuit. . .et de même que l'haleine passe devant moi pour se confondre avec l'atmosphère impalpable où elle n'a plus de figure, de même je ne puis que suivre *hevel* du regard et le voir se perdre" [But *hevel* is a tragic concept. I am grasped by it before even being conscious of it. And when I perceive it, the only judgment that I can formulate about it is that it escapes me. . .like an exhalation which appears before me and merges with the atmosphere, where it has no more form. Likewise, I can only watch *hevel* until it loses itself. My translation]. André Neher, *Notes sur Qohelet* (Editions Minuit, 1951), 63.

[25] For a full analysis of this contrast between Abel and Cain, cf. Neher, *Notes sur Qohelet,* pp. 73–91. There, Neher makes the following stark contrast between

the two brothers: "Ainsi Caïn est la permanence, là ou Abel est la chute. Si d'Abel il ne reste rien, de Caïn il reste toujours plus. A la précarité de l'haleine s'oppose la concentration de plus en plus lourde de l'acquit" [Thus Cain represents permanence, where Abel signifies the fall. Of Abel nothing remains, whereas of Cain there is always a surplus. To the precariousness of the breath is opposed the growing heaviness of the acquired. My translation].

[26] Robert Alter, in his masterful new translation of the Hebrew Bible, translates *hevel* as "breath." Cf. Robert Alter, *The Wisdom Books* (W. W. Norton & Company, 2010), 345–389.

[27] My translation.

[28] This whole section on the "good" will be based on the NIV translation unless otherwise specified.

[29] My translation.

[30] My translation.

[31] My translation.

[32] My translation.

[33] My translation.

Chapter 7

[1] Cf. Babylonian Talmud, Tractate *Baba Batra* 15a.

[2] Song of Songs 1:5; 2:7; 3:5; 5:8; 8:4. A more in-depth exploration of the feminine wisdom of the Shulamite can be found in Abi Doukhan, *Womanist Wisdom in the Song of Songs: Secrets of an African Princess* (Palgrave, 2019).

[3] The Song of Songs is the only other book, alongside Ruth, that explicitly speaks of the mother's house.

[4] Kramer argues that "the Song of Songs or at least a good part of it, is a modified and conventionalized form of an ancient Hebrew liturgy celebrating the reunion and marriage of the sun god with the mother goddess which had flourished in Mesopotamia from earliest days. This sacred marriage had been part of a fertility cult which the nomadic Hebrews took over from their urbanized Canaanite neighbors who in turn had borrowed it from the Tammuz-Ishtar cult of the Akkadians, a modified form of the Dumuzi-Inanna cult of the Sumerians" (Samuel Noah Kramer, *The Sacred Marriage Rite,* 89). Cf. 1 Kings 18:19; Ezek. 8:14.

[5] Kramer observes that "it is only now when we have more than a dozen Sumerian sacred marriage songs of celebration and rejoicing that we begin to get a true picture of the parallels between the Biblical book and some of its probably cuneiform forerunners. For it is now evident that the similarities and resemblances between them are not confined to the general stylistic features such as the

portrayal of the lover as both shepherd and king, and of the beloved as both bride and sister, or the formal interlacing of soliloquies, colloquies and refrains; they extend to theme, motif, and occasionally even to phraseology (Samuel Noah Kramer, *The Sacred Marriage Rite,* 91). In another work, Kramer adds to these parallels the notion of "entering the man's/woman's garden" and the "mother's house" present in both works (Samuel Noah Kramer, "Le rite du mariage sacré Dumuzi-Inanna", *Revue de l'histoire des religions* 181, no. 2 [1972], 121–146. https://inannablog.wordpress.com/wp-content/uploads/2014/11/kramer_rite-mariage-sacrc3a9.pdf.)

[6] Stephen Mitchell speaks as such of the unlikeliness of the Song's inclusion in the Biblical canon: "Reading this remarkable translation again after many years, I was struck by the sheer unlikeliness that the Song of Songs should have been included in the biblical canon. After all…this is a poem about the sexual awakening of a young woman (a girl, really) and her young lover. . .the lovers are unmarried. The poem does not mention God—not once. What were the ancient rabbis thinking?" Stephen Mitchell, "Foreword," in *The World's First Great Love Poem: The Song of Songs,* eds. Chana Bloch, and Ariel Bloch (The Modern Library, 2006), xi.

[7] Rabbi Akiba is said to have exclaimed at the council of Jamnia (CE 90): "For in all the world there is nothing to equal the day on which the Song of Songs was given to Israel, for all the writings are Holy, but the Song of Songs is the Holy of Holies" (Mishnah, Tractate *Yadaim* 3:5).

[8] In both the stories of Rebekah and Rachel, marriage is first brokered by the men of the family, and only then is the woman asked for her consent.

[9] The expression "Place me like a seal over your heart, like a seal on your arm" (Song of Sol. 8:6) can be understood as a marriage proposal.

[10] Chana and Ariel Bloch note this also: "For centuries, exegetes have considered their relationship chaste, ignoring that plain sense of the Hebrew. The word *dodim,* which occurs six times in the song. . .is almost always translated as love, though it refers specifically to sexual love. Moreover, the metaphors of feasting suggest fulfillment, particularly when they are in the perfect tense, and the verb 'to come into' or 'to enter' often has patently sexual meaning in Biblical Hebrew" (*The World's First Great Love Poem: The Song of Songs,* eds. Chana Bloch, and Ariel Bloch, 3).

[11] This is subtly alluded to in the verses "Do not look upon me, because I *am* dark, / Because the sun has tanned me. / My mother's sons were angry with me; / They made me the keeper of the vineyards, / *But* my own vineyard I have not kept" (Song of Songs 1:6).

[12] I am thinking here of two classics of seduction: Robert Greene's *The Art of Seduction: An Indispensable Primer on the Ultimate Form of Power* (Profile Books, 2004); and Ellen Fein, and Sherrie Schneider's *The Rules: Time-tested Secrets for Capturing the Heart of Mr. Right* (Grand Central Publishing, 2007) where all sorts of stratagems and techniques are given in order to attract and ensure commitment and love. And while some of the advice is excellent, the premise of both works remains that commitment and love can be somehow magnetized given the right skill and expertise, and thus that love is something that one can *get* or *obtain* through disciplined action rather than *receive* by grace.

[13] Irigaray speaks beautifully of this "labor of love" in her *To Be Two,* where she elaborates on how the flame of desire might be cultivated and protected (Luce Irigaray, *To Be Two*, 62).

[14] Gabriel Marcel coined the expression "creative fidelity," implying that love has everything to do with creativity, with the ability to make something beautiful out of the cards that one has been given (Gabriel Marcel, *Creative Fidelity* [Fordham University Press, 2002]).

[15] Carol Meyers notes that the Hebrew word *teshuqah* (desire) might have had some semantic connections with the Hebrew word *teshuvah* (return) as is evidenced in more ancient translations of the word: "In his commentary on Genesis, Jerome reveals his understanding of the Hebrew as 'turning.' And virtually all other ancient translations, like the Septuagint, and also early Christian and Jewish exegetical traditions understand the text to say turning or returning. Rather than focus on sexual desire, they have the woman (re)turning to the man. They apparently understood the rare *teshuqah* to have a semantic range overlapping with *teshuvah,* with the woman being drawn (as by desire?) to the one to whom she is turning/returning" (Carol Meyers, *Rediscovering Eve*, 94).

[16] The Hebrew word *emunah* (faith) is built from the Hebrew word *emet,* which implies the notion of steadfastness and permanence.

[17] Phyllis Trible notes this also: "Clearly, Genesis 2–3 offers no return to the garden of creation. And yet, as scripture interpreting scripture, it provides my clue for entering another garden of Eros, the Song of Songs. Through expansions, omissions, and reversals, this poetry recovers the love that is bone of bone and flesh of flesh. In other words, the Song of Songs redeems a love story gone awry" (Phyllis Trible, *God and the Rhetoric of Sexuality,* 144).

Chapter 8

[1] Cf. Babylonian Talmud, Tractate *Baba Batra* 15a.

[2] Susan Niditch observes that, for many women, the true heroine is in fact Vashti: "Gender related issues emerge strongly in the book of Esther. Its heroine

is a woman who offers a particular model for success, one with which oppressors would be especially comfortable. Opposition is to be subtle, behind the scenes, and ultimately strengthening for the power structure. A number of modern feminist writers have in fact found their heroine in Vashti, their empathy with her, while regarding Esther as a weak collaborator with tyranny, an antifeminist. For the writer of Esther, however, Vashti's foolishness is the foil for Esther's wisdom, her dismissal justified, and, indeed, from a narrative point of view, the spark that commences the story." Susan Niditch, "Esther: Folkore, Wisdom, Feminism and Authority," in *A Feminist Companion to Ruth and Esther,* ed. Athalya Brenner (Sheffield Academic Press, 1999), 33.

[3] Both Vashti and Esther are of royal descent. Zefira Gitay notes that "The biblical text suggests that Esther has been well prepared for her role in Ahasuerus's court. Her introduction focuses on her genealogy which connects her through Mordecai to Kish, the father of Saul, the first king of Israel (Esth. 2:25; 1 Sam. 9:1–2). Such a kin relationship is significant: it suggests that Esther is a queen by blood (she is related to the royal family)." Zefira Gitay, "Esther and the Queen's Throne," in *A Feminist Companion to Ruth and Esther,* ed. Athalya Brenner (Sheffield Academic Press, 1999), 140. Elias Bickerman observes that, whereas "concubines were selected from all the women of Asia, ...the queen came from a royal family." Elias Bickerman, *Four Strange Books* (Schocken, 1985), 184. As such, it is very likely that Vashti was of royal blood.

[4] The Talmud comments as follows: "From where in the Torah can one find an allusion to the events involving Esther? He replied to them that the verse states: Then My anger shall be kindled against them on that day, and I will forsake them, and I will hide My face from them, and they shall be devoured, and many evils and troubles shall come upon them; so that they will say in that day: Have not these evils come upon us because our God is not among us? And I will hide [*v'histarti*] My face on that day for all the evil which they shall have wrought, in that they are turned to other gods (Deuteronomy 31:17–18)" (Babylonian Talmud, Tractate *Chullin* 139b). Thus, this passage teaches us how to see the 'hidden hand' of God in a series of historical events that ultimately lead to Israel's salvation. In fact, this is usually the explanation given for its name—Esther—which may stem from the Hebrew verb *lehastir*, "to hide."

[5] Cf. Greek Esther 14:1–19. https://www.biblegateway.com/passage/?search=Additions%20to%20Esther%2014&version=WYChttps://www.biblegateway.com/passage/?search=Additions%20to%20Esther%2014&version=WYC.

[6] Esther as a figure of wisdom is observed by Leila Leah Bronner. Commenting on the Talmud's inclusion of Esther among the prophets of Israel, she writes: "Esther's inclusion among the female prophets evokes our curiosity. What

quality was it that prompted this elevated status? Several of the women listed are expressly named as prophets in the bible, and thus pose no problem. Four of those listed namely Sarah, Hannah, Abigail and Esther, bear no such biblical appellation. Why were they included? Probably because all four display qualities of the 'wise woman' type. Sarah and Abigail and women who advise men (Gen. 21:12; 1 Sam. 25).... Esther too, can be viewed as a personification of typical wisdom virtues." Leila Leah Bronner, "Esther Revisited: An Aggadic Approach," in *A Feminist Companion to Ruth and Esther,* ed. Athalya Brenner (Sheffield Academic Press, 1999), 192.

[7] The Talmud comments: "Rabbi Shmuel bar Naḥmani introduced this passage with an introduction from here: 'Instead of the thorn shall the cypress come up, and instead of the nettle shall the myrtle come up; and it shall be to the Lord for a name, for an everlasting sign that shall not be cut off' (Isaiah 55:13). Rabbi Shmuel bar Naḥmani interpreted the verse homiletically as referring to the righteous individuals who superseded the wicked ones in the book of Esther" (Babylonian Talmud, Tractate *Megillah* 10b).

[8] Susan Niditch also notices this important shift in the book of Esther: "Very much like Joseph, Esther is a passive character at the beginning of her story who will become an active character later" (Susan Niditch, "Esther: Folkore, Wisdom, Feminism and Authority," 76).

[9] Cf. Diane Wolkstein and Samuel Noah Kramer, *Inanna: Queen of Heaven and Earth,* 44–45.

[10] In the Talmudic writings, Vashti insults Ahasuerus by calling him "the son of my father's stable master" (Babylonian Talmud, Tractate *Megillah* 12b) thus alluding to the fact that Ahasuerus might have been a mere commoner and herself the true queen.

[11] Athalya Brenner comments: "Ahasuerus is a veritable paradox. Of nearly absolute power (only the Word is above him), he is more passive than active, drinks more than rules, is easily influenced and sensual. A caricature of a king." Athalya Brenner, "Looking at Esther through the Looking Glass," in *A Feminist Companion to Ruth and Esther,* ed. Athalya Brenner (Sheffield Academic Press, 1999), 35.

[12] NIV.

[13] The word *laqah* in the Hebrew Bible can sometimes have a connotation of brutal violence, as is the case in Genesis 6:2 where the "sons of God" take for themselves wives, "of all whoever they chose." No mention is made here of the woman's consent or of any due process. One might even argue that it is this sexual violence against women that gave rise to the flood, for immediately after

this (Gen. 6:5), God sees the greatness of man's wickedness and begins to devise ways to destroy the earth.

[14] According to the Talmud, Esther's name was a variation of Ishtar, or Istahar, the Babylonian queen of love and war: "R. Nehemiah says: Hadassah was her name. Why then was she called Esther? All peoples called her so after Istahar" (Babylonian Talmud, Tractate *Megillah* 13a).

[15] The JPS Bible translates the *wav* as "yet" and not "and" (Esther 2:15).

[16] NIV.

[17] Cf. Timothy Stephany, *The Descent of Ishtar: The Sumerian and Akkadian Versions* (Create Space, 2015).

[18] Esther as one of the seven prophetesses of Israel is attested in the Talmud: "Our rabbis taught: forty-eight prophets and seven prophetesses prophesied to Israel…Seven prophetesses. Who were these? Sarah, Miriam, Deborah, Hannah, Abigail, Hulda, and Esther" (Babylonian Talmud, Tractate Megillah, 14a).

[19] Bickerman points out the story of Esther is set in the Springtime—a time when, according to Babylonian cosmology, a "battle took place annually between Tiamat, the forces of chaos, and Marduk, the divine patron of Babylon, at the New Year festival in the Spring." Elias Bickerman, *Four Strange Books,* 200.

Conclusion

[1] Tur, Orach Chayim 263:1, https://www.sefaria.org/Tur%2C_Orach_Chayim.263.1?lang=bi; Shulchan Arukh, Orach Chayim 263:1, https://www.sefaria.org/Shulchan_Arukh%2C_Orach_Chayim.263.1?lang=bi.

[2] Babylonian Talmud, Tractate *Taanit* 27b.

[3] Eliyah Rabbah on Shulchan Arukh, Orach Chayim 263:2. https://www.sefaria.org/Eliyah_Rabbah_on_Shulchan_Arukh%2C_Orach_Chayim.262.1?lang=bi.

[4] https://www.chabad.org/library/article_cdo/aid/3753326/jewish/Four-Reasons-Shabbat-Is-Compared-to-Bride-and-a-Queen.htm.

[5] I am referring here to Colossians 1:17 where it is the Christ who holds everything together. It has been my argument, however, that the human couple holds a Messianic role, that of ruling the world together and protecting it, i.e. of "holding it together."

[6] Cf. https://www.theguardian.com/lifeandstyle/2023/apr/26/the-rise-of-voluntary-celibacy-most-of-the-sex-ive-had-i-wish-i-hadnt-bothered. See also, https://www.youtube.com/watch?v=KRxhnSkgxtk&t=2051s&ab_channel=TheDiaryOfACEO

[7] Cf. Matt. 13:45–46.

Index